A DISEASE
IN THE
PUBLIC MIND

A Disease

~ *in the* ~

Public Mind

A NEW UNDERSTANDING OF WHY
WE FOUGHT THE CIVIL WAR

Thomas Fleming

DA CAPO PRESS
A Member of the Perseus Books Group
New York

Library of Congress Cataloging-in-Publication Data
Fleming, Thomas J.
  A disease in the public mind : a new understanding of why we fought the Civil War / Thomas Fleming.
    pages cm
  Includes bibliographical references and index.
  ISBN 978-0-306-82126-4 (hardcover)—ISBN 978-0-306-82201-8 (e-book) 1. United States—History—Civil War, 1861–1865—Causes. 2. Slavery—Political aspects—United States—History—19th century. 3. Antislavery movements—United States—History—19th century. 4. Political culture—United States—History—19th century. 5. New England—Relations—Southern States. 6. Southern States—Relations—New England. 7. United States—Politics and government—1815–1861. 8. United States—History—1815–1861—Biography. I. Title.
  E459.F55 2013
  973.7'11—dc23

                                                                2012045309

Published by Da Capo Press
A Member of the Perseus Books Group
www.dacapopress.com

Da Capo Press books are available at special discounts for bulk purchases in the U.S. by corporations, institutions, and other organizations. For more information, please contact the Special Markets Department at the Perseus Books Group, 2300 Chestnut Street, Suite 200, Philadelphia, PA 19103, or call (800) 810-4145, ext. 5000, or e-mail special.markets@perseusbooks.com.

10 9 8 7 6 5 4 3 2 1

To Alice—For Everything.

To see this country happy is so much the wish of my soul, nothing on this side of Elysium can be placed in competition with it.
—GEORGE WASHINGTON

We are truly to be pitied.
—THOMAS JEFFERSON

If you would win a man to your cause, first convince him that you are his sincere friend. Therein is a drop of honey that catches his heart.
—ABRAHAM LINCOLN

CONTENTS

PREFACE

The Civil War freed almost four million Americans from the humiliations and oppressions of slavery. It is undoubtedly one of America's greatest triumphs. As we celebrate the 150th anniversary of this huge event, however, we must also grieve. The Civil War is simultaneously America's greatest tragedy. No other conflict in the nation's 237-year history can compare to the anguish and grief it inflicted on the men and women who were engulfed by it.

For almost a century, the accepted figure for the number of soldiers killed in the war was 618,222. Recently, an historian who has restudied the census records of 1870 and 1880 has concluded that the toll was at least 750,000. There is a strong possibility that the correct number is 850,000. The Southern Confederacy's records vanished with their defeat. Their toll is only an estimate. If we include the wounded men who died prematurely over the next two decades, the toll for both sides may be 1,000,000. This much is certain: more soldiers died in that four-year struggle than the nation lost in all her previous and future wars combined.[1]

What makes these numbers especially horrendous is the fact that America's population in 1861 was about 31 million. In 2012, U.S. population is about 313 million. If a similar conflict demanded the same sacrifice from our young men and women today, the number of dead might total over 10 million. Think for a moment about how many stricken parents, wives, fiancés, and children would be struggling to cope with this tidal wave of grief and loss.

The enormity of the Civil War's tragedy grows even larger when we realize that the United States is the only country in the world that fought such a horrific war to end slavery. Other nations with large slave populations, such as Great Britain, which had 850,000 slaves in its West Indies islands, Cuba, which had almost 1,000,000, and Brazil, which had at least 3,000,000, ended the deplorable institution with relatively little bloodshed. Even Czarist Russia, with its millions of semi-slaves known as serfs, freed them without a war. Why were the Americans, with a government designed to respond to the voice—or voices—of the people, compelled to resort to such awful carnage?[2]

The question becomes even more perplexing when we consider another startling fact. Only 316,632 Southerners owned slaves—a mere 6 percent of the total white population of 5,582,322. These figures become doubly baffling when a further analysis reveals only 46,214 of these masters owned 50 or more slaves, entitling them to the aristocratic-sounding term, "planter." Why did the vast majority of the white population unite behind these slaveholders in this fratricidal war? Why did they sacrifice over 300,000 of their sons to preserve an institution in which they apparently had no personal stake?

I have devoted much of my literary life to writing about the American Revolution. My exploration of our founding years convinced me of the originality and importance of the heritage created by the men and women who won an eight-year struggle against the most powerful nation in the world and created the modern era's first republic. Ironically, this conviction made me even more baffled by the Civil War's eruption little more than a half century after George Washington, Thomas Jefferson, and their compatriots turned the leadership of the new nation over to the next generation.

I never thought I would do more than muse about the Civil War until my good friend, Byron Hollinshead, director of American Historical Publications and former publisher of two distinguished history magazines, asked me to contribute to a book entitled *I Wish I'd Been There*. A gallery of well-known historians was asked to insert themselves into famous events of the past and describe them as if they were on the scene. I became a spectator/actor in John Brown's 1859 raid on Harpers Ferry.

I was mesmerized, not only by the chief protagonist, but by the reactions of prominent contemporaries, ranging from Robert E. Lee to Abraham Lincoln to Ralph Waldo Emerson. Especially fascinating was the statement of the president of the United States in 1859, James Buchanan. Brown's reckless venture was caused, Buchanan said, by "an incurable disease in the public mind." In his final message to Congress in 1860, as Southern states seceded and Civil War loomed, he repeated the assertion.

Buchanan's frequently hostile biographers have all dismissed or ignored these words. They caught my attention because in two of my previous books, I have explored how illusions play a role in history. Was the president talking about this sort of distortion?[3]

Few presidents have lower ratings than Mr. Buchanan in the polls historians take to rank the nation's chief executives as great, near great, mediocre, or failures. On the other hand, not many presidents had more experience in national politics than "Old Buck." He spent almost forty years as a congressman and senator, plus terms as secretary of state and ambassador to Great Britain, before winning the White House.

I soon discovered that President Buchanan did not originate the phrase "public mind." Thomas Jefferson frequently used the term to describe various aspects of the politics of his era. Writing to George Washington in 1792 about the angry disagreements stirred by the new federal government's financial policy, Jefferson warned, "The public mind is no longer confident and serene." Abraham Lincoln was another man who frequently invoked the phrase. In 1861 he accused the South of "debauching the public mind" about the right to secede. A century later, Democratic presidential candidate Adlai Stevenson declared, "Those who corrupt the public mind are just as evil as those who steal from the public purse."[4]

The public mind is intimately linked with public opinion, which one early nineteenth-century commentator called "that inexorable judge of men and manners" in a republic. But the public mind suggests something less fluctuating than opinion—and more complex than an illusion, which can be swiftly dispelled by events. The phrase implies fixed beliefs that are fundamental to the way people participate in the world of their time.[5] A disease in the public mind would seem to be a twisted interpretation of political or economic or spiritual realities that seizes control of thousands and even millions of minds. Americans first experienced one of these episodes in 1692, when the leaders of the Massachusetts Bay Colony became convinced that witches were threatening their society with evil powers. Over two hundred people were arrested and flung into fetid jails. Twenty-one were hanged, one seventy-one-year-old man was "pressed to death" beneath heavy stones, and at least seven died in prison.

No one has described this public frenzy better than the great New England novelist, Nathaniel Hawthorne. "That terrible delusion . . . should teach us, among its other morals, that the influential classes . . . are fully liable to all the passionate error that has ever characterized the maddest mob. Clergymen, judges, statesmen—the wisest, calmest, holiest persons of their day, stood in the inner circle roundabout the gallows, loudest to acclaim the work of blood, latest to confess themselves miserably deceived."[6]

A similar frenzy seized the nation in the closing decades of the nineteenth century, reaching a climax on January 16, 1919, when Congress passed the Eighteenth Amendment, banning the sale and consumption of alcoholic drinks. Prohibition destroyed the liquor industry, the seventh largest business in the United States. Tens of thousands of people lost their jobs. For the next thirteen years, the ban corrupted and tormented Americans from coast to coast.

Rather than discouraging liquor consumption, Prohibition increased it. Taking a drink became a sign of defiance against the arrogant minority who had deprived people of their right to enjoy themselves. The 1920s roared with reckless amorality in all directions, including Wall Street. When everything came crashing down in 1929 and the grey years of the Great Depression began, second thoughts were the order of the day. Large numbers of people pointed to the state of mind inspired by Prohibition as one of the chief reasons for the disaster.

In 1933, a new president, Franklin D. Roosevelt, made the repeal of the Eighteenth Amendment one of his priorities. But the evil effects of the plunge into moral redemption linger to this day, most notably in the influence of organized crime, better known as the Mafia, in many areas of American life. The experience proved that a passionate minority seized by the noble desire to achieve some great moral goal may be abysmally wrong.

Later in the twentieth century, a European disease of the public mind consumed a horrific number of lives. Communism, with its spurious goal of achieving economic equality, killed an estimated 50 million people in Soviet Russia alone and uncounted millions more elsewhere.

In America, an offshoot of this disease, McCarthyism, roiled our politics and morality for most of a decade after World War II. Spawned by Joseph McCarthy, a junior senator from Wisconsin, McCarthyism prompted thousands of Americans to become enraged investigators and persecutors of their fellow Americans, based on the often spurious accusation that they were or once had been Communists or Communist sympathizers. Many saw their legal, literary, film, or other careers ruined. Some people, driven to despair, committed suicide.

A good example was my friend, novelist Howard Fast, who was forced to write under a pseudonym to make a living. I was among several fellow writers who gave him quotes that his publisher used to help sell these secretly written books.

Analyzing these false beliefs gave me additional insights into how a disease in the public mind works its dark will on the world. It is backed by politicians and other prominent leaders, and often by a media apparatus—newspapers, pamphlets, books, magazine articles, and in the twentieth century, television, radio, and film—that reinforces the disease with massive repetition. At least as important are hate-filled verbal denunciations of real or supposed opponents.

On September 11, 2001, the United States awoke from the illusion that an era of peace and reason was dawning after the collapse of Soviet Communism in 1989. Muslim fanatics flew two passenger planes into the twin towers of New York's World Trade Center, and another plane into the Pentagon in Washington, DC, killing themselves and 2,700 Americans. The disease in the public mind that motivated these true believers was a warped version of the Mohammedan faith.

Perhaps President Buchanan's assertion that a disease in the public mind produced John Brown in 1859 and the ensuing Civil War deserves consideration, at the very least. Let us remember it while we visit a bloodstained Harpers Ferry and begin our journey into the history that inflamed John Brown's already unbalanced brain—the United States of America's entanglement with African slavery.

John Brown's Raid

Sunday, October 16, 1859, was a day of clouds and light rain in the rolling farm country of western Maryland. In a dilapidated two-story house rented from a man named Kennedy, twenty-one young men, five of them black, attended a religious service led by fifty-nine-year-old John Brown. Fiercely erect, with glaring blue eyes in a gaunt face largely concealed by a long grey beard, Brown urged them to ask God's blessing on the insurrection they were about to launch with their attack on the federal arsenal in Harpers Ferry, Virginia.

Brown confidently predicted that the arsenal's twenty thousand rifles and millions of rounds of ammunition would equip a conquering army of slaves from Maryland and Virginia and antislavery whites from nearby Pennsylvania. They would all flock to the cause when they heard the electrifying news that weapons of liberation were waiting for them. With Jehovah's help they were certain to achieve their awesome goal: nothing less than freeing the South's four million slaves.

Brown and his followers had spent the summer at the farmhouse, slowly accumulating weapons and ammunition. In their barn they now had 198

Sharps rifles, 200 Maynard revolvers, and 980 menacing pikes. The Sharps rifles were expensive, highly accurate guns, capable of firing 8 to 10 shots a minute. The six-shot Maynard revolvers were reserved for officers in their prospective army. The pikes, two-edged bowie knives attached to six-foot poles, were intended for the freed slaves, whom Brown assumed would have trouble mastering the intricacies of loading and firing a gun.

Some people, then and now, might wince at the idea of encouraging slaves to plunge these grisly weapons into the bodies of white Southerners. But John Brown was a man who did not flinch from shocking acts on behalf of his cause. The Connecticut-born visionary believed that slavery was an abominable crime, punishable by death—a conviction he had already demonstrated more than once. Among his favorite aphorisms was, "Without the shedding of blood there is no remission of sin."[1]

.   .   .

In the hot days of July and August, the volunteers had pondered maps of the southern states that John Brown had drawn on cambric. Each was filled with numbers he had gleaned from the census of 1850, identifying counties where slaves outnumbered whites, sometimes by ratios of six or seven to one. With the blacks he expected to muster and arm in Virginia and Maryland, Brown planned to focus on these counties, triggering a series of slave revolts that would demoralize and slaughter slave owners and their supporters from the Mason-Dixon Line to the Gulf of Mexico.

If white Southerners counterattacked, Brown planned to retreat into the Allegheny Mountains, where he and his followers would establish "maroon" communities, similar to the ones that escaped slaves had created in the mountains of Jamaica and Haiti. The word is derived from the French word *marron*, meaning a domestic animal run wild.[2]

Brown's band of followers was sure that thousands would rally to a banner held aloft by "Captain" John Brown. To them, he was a famous figure. During the guerilla war that had raged in Kansas earlier in the 1850s, some journalists had hailed Brown as a fighter on a par with the heroes of 1776. Five prominent men from Massachusetts had joined a New York millionaire

in giving him the money and encouragement for this immensely more ambitious attack on what they and Brown called "The Slave Power."[3]

. . .

During the afternoon of October 16, Brown had assigned tasks to his troops.
Eighteen would march with him to Harpers Ferry. In their pockets they carried captains' commissions authorizing them to organize the freed slaves
into companies. Brown's son Owen and two other men would stay behind
at the Kennedy Farm, awaiting word to move the guns and pikes to a site
where they could be used by the new recruits.

At eight o'clock, Brown climbed onto a one-horse wagon loaded with
pikes, some hickory-and-pine torches, and a crowbar, and led his men toward Harpers Ferry, nine miles away. In the moonless darkness the raiders
passed undetected through the thinly populated rural countryside.[4]

Along with weapons, Brown brought two documents he considered of
surpassing importance. The first was a "Declaration of Independence by the
Representatives of the Slave Population of the United States of America."
The declaration denounced slaveholders as pirates, thieves, robbers, liber-
tines, woman killers, and barbarians. Politicians who tolerated this inhu-
manity were termed "leeches" unworthy of being called "half civilized men."

At least as important was a lengthier document—a "Provisional Constitution and Ordinances for the People of the United States." The constitution's forty-eight articles began by emphasizing that citizenship and
participation in the government were guaranteed to all persons "of a mature
age" without respect to race or sex. Another article specified that "all persons of good character . . . shall be encouraged to carry arms openly." Other
clauses guaranteed protection to slaveholders who freed their slaves voluntarily and declared that the "commander in chief" (Brown) owned all goods
and wealth confiscated from the enemy. Toward the close, consistency and
order vanished. Brown had written the Constitution in a near frenzy, working day and night.

These documents reveal John Brown's vision of an America in which
blacks and whites would live as equals. It was an extraordinary ideal for a

white American in 1859, when the vast majority of the nation, North and South, regarded blacks as inferior and potentially dangerous. The presence of five black men in his volunteer army, living in intimate proximity with his white soldiers, proved Brown meant what he had written.

The scrawled, almost illegible pages of the declaration and constitution also offer significant clues to John Brown's personality. A psychologist who made a careful study of Brown's life concluded that their extravagant phrases—and frequent confusion—were part of a pattern that coruscated through his career. Again and again, Brown had nurtured grandiose schemes and dreams that invariably ended in disappointment. The psychologist concluded that Brown was a manic-depressive. In his manic phases he was capable of going for days without sleep and producing magnificent plans that were ruinously short on practical details.[5]

Earlier in the summer, some of Brown's followers had not been as confident as their leader that God had sent them to their rendezvous with history. Prominent among the doubters was twenty-one-year-old Oliver Brown, the youngest of the leader's sons. He had abruptly asked how their handful of men could subdue a town the size of Harpers Ferry—some 2,500 people. Oliver was probably wondering why Frederick Douglass, a former Maryland slave who had become an electrifying antislavery orator and writer, had declined to join his friend John Brown in this venture.

Brown had talked with swaggering confidence about how Douglass's presence would inspire thousands of slaves to rally to their cause. After listening to his plan, Douglass not only declined Brown's invitation, he had predicted that the captain and his followers would be captured or killed within hours of their appearance in the streets of Harpers Ferry with guns in their hands.

John Brown had let Douglass depart without reproaches. The discovery that Oliver Brown had equally grave doubts was a far greater shock. How could his own flesh and blood question the fact, as clear to him as morning sunlight, that God had chosen him to strike this blow that would annihilate slavery? After much debate, Oliver—and others who may have shared his doubts—succumbed to Brown's incandescent faith in his destiny and re-mained in the game.

. . .

By the time the marchers reached Harpers Ferry, it was eleven p.m. and most of the town was asleep. Situated at the confluence of the Potomac and Shenandoah Rivers, The Ferry, as everyone called it, was a moderately well-to-do community, thanks to the steady flow of government cash to the workers in the federal armory and a private gun-making company, Hall's Rifle Works, on an island in the Shenandoah River. A bridge across the Po-tomac served the Baltimore & Ohio Railroad as well as foot and wagon traf-fic. Upstream, another bridge enabled travelers to cross to the right bank of the Shenandoah. Anyone who closed these bridges theoretically isolated the town. This fact, plus the arsenal full of guns, was the reason why John Brown had been attracted to the place.

In his manic confidence in his plan, John Brown ignored aspects of The Ferry that suggested it was a good deal less than an ideal place from which to launch an insurrection. Huge cliffs towered over the town. Any military force in control of those heights could make raiders in the streets or buildings of Harpers Ferry extremely uncomfortable. Another problem was the town's proximity to major population centers. It was little more than sixty miles from Baltimore and Washington, DC, with major highways running to both cities. The Baltimore & Ohio Railroad's main line also ran through the town.

These realities made it unlikely that Brown would have much time to spread the word of his insurrection to the eastern parts of Virginia and Maryland, where slaves were numerous, before whites organized serious opposition. Around Harpers Ferry, there were few large farms worked by gangs of field hands. Almost all the area's slaves were house servants.

Brown's first order, as they approached The Ferry, was to cut the telegraph lines. The strangeness—one might even say the folly—of this command would become apparent in the next few hours. On the Baltimore & Ohio bridge, the raiders quickly subdued the night watchman; they stationed two men on this bridge and two more on the Shenandoah bridge. The rest hurried through the silent streets to the redbrick armory, where an unarmed gateman was their only opposition. He refused to surrender his keys, but Brown used his crowbar to break the lock. Inside they quickly took possession of the armory complex while Brown announced in a prophetic voice: "I want to free all the Negroes in this state [Virginia]." If the citizens interfere with me, I must only burn the town and have blood."[6]

Brown personally led another detachment to Hall's Island to occupy the gun factory there. Meanwhile, other members of his tiny army seized blacks and whites on the streets and herded them into the armory. Another five-man detachment headed into the country to Beall-Air, the plantation house of Colonel Lewis W. Washington, a forty-six-year-old great-grandnephew of the first president. Brown wanted him not only for the moral effect of his name, but also for a ceremonial sword the colonel owned, which the father of the country had supposedly received from King Frederick the Great of Prussia.

When balding, black-mustached Colonel Washington opened the door in his nightcap and confronted leveled rifles, he stepped back and said, "Possibly you will have the courtesy to tell me what this means." The leader of the detachment, Aaron Stevens, snarled that they were planning to free all the South's slaves, and taking him prisoner was a first step. As Washington dressed, the raiders found the ceremonial sword and several rifles, which they also appropriated.

Stevens asked if Colonel Washington had a watch. When he said yes, Stevens held out his hand. "I want it."

"You shall not have it, sir." Washington replied.

Stevens demanded all the cash in the house. "I am going to speak to you very plainly," the colonel said. "You told me your purpose was philanthropic. You did not mention it was robbery and rascality."

Colonel Washington was encountering one of the clauses in John Brown's constitution—all the property of slave owners could be appropriated for the cause. Intimidated by the colonel's defiance, Stevens contented himself with escorting the colonel, two white neighbors, and ten of their male slaves back to the arsenal. John Brown gleefully strapped on George Washington's sword, apparently thinking it gave him an aura of supreme command.[7]

.　.　.

The shriek of a train whistle interrupted Brown's playacting. A Baltimore & Ohio express from Wheeling, Virginia, was approaching the bridge. Halted by an impromptu barricade, the engineer and conductor found an agitated man named Higgins standing beside the tracks, blood trickling from a wound in his scalp. He was the bridge's relief night watchman. When Oliver Brown and his partner on the bridge, a black named Dangerfield Newby, tried to seize him, Higgins had slugged Brown and run for it. He got away with a bullet nick in his scalp. The disbelieving trainmen walked toward the bridge and were driven off by several shots. They backed the train out of range and decided to await developments.

Meanwhile, Shepherd Hayward, a free black who worked as a station porter, walked out on the bridge to find out what was wrong with the train. "Halt!" shouted one of the guards on the bridge. The confused Hayward ignored the order and tried to retreat. A bullet thudded into his back and exited under his left nipple. He staggered into the station crying: "I am shot."

It would take Hayward twelve agonizing hours to die. The first victim of John Brown's insurrection was a free black man. There were many ex-slaves like Hayward in The Ferry—no less than 1,251—and only 88 slaves. One of many details that had escaped "Captain" Brown's manic planning was the way slavery was evolving in border states such as Maryland and Virginia.[8]

The shots awoke many people in Harpers Ferry. Men swarmed into the streets, some carrying guns. They dragged the bleeding Hayward into the station and summoned the town doctor to help him. The physician sent a messenger racing to the nearest large town, Charlestown, Virginia, asking for reinforcements.

Soon word of the seizure of the federal armory swirled through the crowd, followed by the fear that a slave revolt was about to explode. There was a general stampede to the heights outside town. Most of The Ferry's blacks fled with the whites. As dawn reddened the eastern sky, church bells began clanging everywhere. It was a long-prearranged signal for the farmers in the surrounding countryside to reach for their guns to repel a slave insurrection.

. . .

In the armory, John Brown did little or nothing in a military way except strap on George Washington's sword. About three a.m. he walked out on the bridge and told the train's conductor it could proceed. Brown knew the train would stop at the next town on the line, Monocacy, Maryland, and telegraph the news of his incursion. This decision made no sense in the light of Brown's previous order to cut the telegraph lines. Apparently, only now had it dawned on him that he needed help in spreading the news of his insurrection. He apparently did not realize that the news would also arouse white opposition throughout Maryland and Virginia.

Around five a.m. Brown sent three men and two freed slaves armed with pikes back to the Kennedy Farm with orders to shift the rifles, revolvers, and remaining pikes to a log schoolhouse on the Maryland side of the Potomac River. This decision also made little sense. There was no sign of an outpouring of support from the area's slaves to use these weapons. Brown compounded this folly by telling his son Owen that everything at Harpers Ferry was going well.

. . .

Rain continued to drool from the dawn-grey sky. When employees of the armory showed up for work, apparently unwarned by the fugitives on the heights, Brown added them to his bag of hostages. He ordered forty-five breakfasts on credit from the town's hotel, the Wager House. Brown ostentatiously refused to eat any of the food, declaring it might be poisoned—but he permitted his sons and the rest of his army to consume it. Aside from evidence of Brown's growing incoherence, the breakfast order revealed that this farseeing military commander had led his men to war without bothering to provide them with a morsel of food.

By now it was also evident that Brown had made no discernible plans to feed the hundreds—perhaps thousands—of slaves he hoped to maintain in his mountain strongholds. He had also wasted the hours of the night without making the slightest attempt to transfer any of the arsenal's twenty thousand rifles beyond the precincts of Harpers Ferry to arm the slaves. Nor had he displayed the slightest interest in spreading the news of his Declaration of Slave Independence and his Constitution for an equal-rights republic.

By this time many of The Ferry's citizens had recognized John Brown as the man who had called himself "Isaac Smith" and had visited the town many times during the summer while plotting his attack. This discovery more or less coincided with the arrival of several hundred armed militia from Charlestown on a Baltimore & Ohio train. They drove the two guards off the B&O bridge, sealing off any hope of Brown escaping into Maryland. Other militiamen cleared the Shenandoah Bridge. That ended the possibility of the raiders escaping southward into the Blue Ridge Mountains.

From the surrounding hillsides, militiamen began firing into the armory yard. One of the first shots killed Dangerfield Newby. A free mulatto, he had joined Brown in the hope of rescuing his wife and children from slavery in Virginia. In his pocket was a letter from his wife: "Oh dear Dangerfield, com this fall without fail, monny or no Monny. I want to see you so much thatt is the one bright hope I see before me."[9]

. . .

With a thunderous roar, a locomotive pulling cars full of armed Baltimore & Ohio employees crashed through the gates into the upper end of the armory, rescuing most of the hostages, who were being held in the watchman's office. Brown managed to get ten of the most important captives, including Colonel Washington, into the brick firehouse, which had stout oak doors. Confined to this single building, the raiders were still armed and dangerous. They fired often and accurately from the half-open door and from loopholes they created in the walls by knocking out bricks.

Fancying himself a general conducting a siege, Brown sent three of his men out the door under a flag of truce to see if he could negotiate a withdrawal from the town with his hostages. He promised to free them when he was at a safe distance. The militiamen ignored the flags of truce and seized the first man to emerge, William Thompson. They riddled the next man, William Stevens, and mortally wounded the third negotiator, Brown's twenty-four-year-old son, Watson, who crawled back into the engine house to die.

More bullets sang through the open door, mortally wounding Oliver Brown and Stewart Taylor, a Canadian who had been seduced by Brown's faith in his destiny. Another raider tried to escape by swimming the Potomac. He was hit by numerous bullets as he crawled up on a small island in the river and soon died there.[10]

·   ·   ·

Perhaps the most distressed man in Harpers Ferry was the mayor, Fontaine Beckham. He had been the local agent for the Baltimore & Ohio Railroad for twenty-five years. Shepherd Hayward had worked for him. When the porter died around four p.m., the agitated Beckham began venturing out on the railroad tracks to get a better view of the firefight raging between the militia and the raiders in the engine house. He took cover behind a water tank and peered toward the embattled Brown and his dwindling followers. Apparently he was hoping for a sign that the raiders might be ready to surrender.

Crouched in the engine house's open door, Edwin Coppoc spotted Beckham and said, "If he keeps on peeking, I'm going to shoot." He thought Beckham was a sniper with a gun. The hostages begged him not to fire. "They'll shoot in here and kill us all!" shrieked one man. Coppoc ignored them and fired. His first shot missed, but a second bullet killed Beckham instantly. It was another ironic death. Beckham was well known for his friendliness to blacks. In his will he left money to help an ex-slave named Isaac Gilbert purchase the freedom of his wife and three children.

Enraged by Beckham's death, some militiamen took the captured Thompson out on the Baltimore & Ohio bridge and riddled him. They threw the body into the Potomac and used it for target practice. By this time, many of these infuriated opponents of John Brown were drunk. The Ferry's three taverns had done a brisk business all day. There were now more than six hundred Virginia and Maryland militia in the town. Their officers found it impossible to control them.

With only five men left in his army, including himself, John Brown permitted a militia officer to approach the building under a flag of truce and ask him to surrender. Brown refused, still insisting he had a right to negotiate a withdrawal with his hostages. The stalemate continued as night fell, punctuated by desultory firing from both sides.[11]

·   ·   ·

Around ten o'clock another train steamed into The Ferry. Aboard were ninety marines, led by handsome, dark-haired Lieutenant Colonel Robert E. Lee of the U.S. Army. With him as an impromptu aide was a young army lieutenant, J. E. B. Stuart, who had been a cadet when Lee was superintendent of the U.S. Military Academy at West Point in the early 1850s. Colonel Lee was now commander of a cavalry regiment stationed in Texas.

One of the nation's most famous soldiers, thanks to his heroics in the Mexican War, Lee happened to be home on leave. He resided in Arlington, a handsome house across the Potomac River from the capital. His wife, Mary, had inherited the estate from her father, George Washington Parke Custis, the first president's step-grandson.

Colonel Lee had orders to end John Brown's raid as soon as possible. It was already creating shock waves of panic throughout Maryland and Virginia, with rumors of Brown's numbers mounting from several dozen to several hundred to several thousand.[12]

·   ·   ·

Inside the firehouse, Watson and Oliver Brown were dying in awful pain. Oliver asked his father to kill him to end his agony. "You'll get over it," Brown snarled. When Oliver's cries continued, Brown snapped: "If you must die, die like a man." When the boy's sobs and moans finally ceased, Brown called, "Oliver!" There was no answer. "I guess he's dead," Brown said, without a trace of emotion in his voice.

While his sons died, Brown made speeches to his hostages. "Gentlemen," he said, "if you knew of my past history, you would not blame me for being here. I went to Kansas a peaceable man and the proslavery people hunted me down like a wolf." This was neither the first nor the last of John Brown's many lies.

One of the hostages asked Brown if he was aware that he had committed treason by attacking a federal arsenal. "Certainly," Brown said.

Two of the raiders, a brother of the dead Thompson and a young man named Anderson from Indiana, exclaimed in shock at Brown's admission. They announced that they would fight no more. They had joined Brown to free slaves, not commit treason. It was a sad glimpse of the simplicity of Brown's followers.[13]

.   .   .

Meanwhile, Colonel Lee was conferring with the leaders of the militia. The colonel was inclined to storm the firehouse immediately. The locals demurred. A shootout in the dark seemed likely to prove fatal to some of the hostages. Lee agreed to wait until dawn.

Soon after daybreak, Lee ordered Marine Lieutenant Israel Green to pick twelve good men and storm the place, relying on the bayonet to lower the chances of killing any of the hostages. The signal to attack would come from Lieutenant Stuart, who was ordered to give Brown one more chance to surrender peacefully.

Stuart approached the firehouse door carrying a flag of truce; Brown opened it a cautious crack and pointed a rifle at the lieutenant's head. In spite of Brown's beard, Stuart recognized him as "Old Brown of Osawatomie," the Kansas guerilla. Stuart had served in a regiment of federal cavalry sent to pacify Kansas during the confused fighting between proslavery and antislavery settlers. Once, the cavalrymen had captured Brown, but they had lacked a warrant to arrest him and had let him go.

Stuart did his utmost to persuade Brown to surrender, pointing out that his situation was hopeless. He was outnumbered a hundred to one. When Brown tried to negotiate with him, Stuart tried in vain to make it clear that he had no power to change Colonel Lee's terms. Somewhere behind Brown a deep voice called, "Never mind us, fire!" It was Colonel Lewis Washington. Outside, Colonel Lee recognized his voice. "That old revolutionary blood does tell," he remarked to no one in particular.[14]

Lieutenant Stuart stepped away from the door and waved his hat—the signal for the marines to attack. While two thousand spectators cheered, three marines with sledgehammers assailed the thick oak door. It remained amazingly intact. Finally, other marines seized a heavy ladder and used it as a battering ram. The door splintered and a chunk fell inward. The marines, led by Lieutenant Green, clambered through the gap. Rifles barked, bullets whined. One marine was killed instantly; another went down wounded. These casualties disinclined the rest of the marines to show anyone much mercy. Young Thompson and Anderson, who had been so shocked to learn they had committed treason, died from multiple bayonet thrusts before they could explain that they had quit fighting.

Lieutenant Green headed for John Brown, who was trying to reload his rifle. Green thrust his small dress sword into Brown's midriff—and was dismayed to see it bend almost double when it collided with the buckle on the strap of George Washington's sword. The infuriated Green beat Brown over the head with the hilt of the dress sword, knocking him unconscious.

In less than sixty seconds the fight was over, the hostages freed. Only one man surrendered successfully—Edward Coppoc, the killer of Mayor Beckham. One of Brown's black volunteers, Shields Green, who was a fugitive slave from South Carolina, tried to mingle with the captured Harpers Ferry slaves, but they showed no desire to protect him. He was seized by rough hands and made a prisoner.[15]

·   ·   ·

On the other side of the Potomac, Maryland militiamen raced to the schoolhouse, which Owen Brown and his men had invaded with their guns and pikes, sending the teacher and panicked children fleeing into the countryside. By the time the militiamen arrived, this remnant of Brown's insurrectionary army had fled, leaving the weapons behind. The hundreds of pikes were an especially chilling sight to the militiamen. They shuddered at the havoc these weapons might have wrought in the hands of rebelling slaves.

Back in the firehouse, Brown was bleeding profusely from wounds to the head. They were all superficial; while they were being dressed, he regained consciousness. Marines carried him into the armory paymaster's office, where he lay on a pallet while dozens of curious Ferry townsfolk ogled him.

In the afternoon Virginia's governor, Henry A. Wise, and several other politicians, including Senator James M. Mason of Virginia and Congressman Clement Vallandigham of Ohio, arrived to question him. Reporters mingled with these visitors. Colonel Lee asked Brown if he wished the newsmen excluded. Brown said he wanted them to stay. He was eager to "make himself and his motives clearly understood."

Brown swiftly demonstrated his goal was obfuscation, not clarity. He did his utmost to conceal the identity of his northern backers. He also tried to muddle the scope of his insurrection. He told Senator Mason, "We came to free the slaves, and only that."

Congressman Vallandigham asked him if he had been hoping for a general rising of the slaves. "No sir," Brown lied. "I expected to gather them up from time to time, and set them free."

A reporter closed the interview by asking Brown if he had anything further to say. Brown paused for a moment, then replied: "I have nothing to say, only that I claim to be carrying out a measure I believe perfectly justifiable, and not to act the part of an incendiary or ruffian, but to aid those suffering great wrong. I wish to say, furthermore, that you had better—all of you people of the South—prepare yourselves for a settlement of this question . . . sooner than you are prepared for it. You may dispose of me very easily—I am nearly disposed of now; but this question is still to be settled—this Negro question, I mean, the end of that is not yet."

While Brown was talking, Lieutenant Stuart led a marine detachment to the Kennedy Farm, where they seized Brown's maps of the South and his correspondence with his wealthy northern backers—proof of the huge slave insurrection he hoped to create and lead. But finding this evidence and convincing the American people that John Brown was ready to commit mass murder in pursuit of his blood-drenched dream turned out to be two very different things.[16]

CHAPTER 1

Slavery Comes to America

Long before the first slaves arrived in the English colony of Virginia in 1619, slavery was a thriving institution in the New World. Hundreds of thousands of black men and women were already toiling on the farms and plantations and in the mines of the Spanish and Portuguese empires in Mexico and South America and on the offshore islands we call the West Indies.

Few people criticized or objected to slavery; it was one of the world's oldest social institutions, with roots in ancient Babylon, Greece, and Rome. Greece, the proud forerunner of rule by democracy, found no contradiction in insisting that slavery was essential to a thriving republic. The Roman republic and later the empire had tens of thousands of slaves within its borders.

The Hebrew Bible described Abraham and other early leaders of the Jews as slave owners. In the book of Leviticus, Jehovah told Moses that Jews were forbidden to enslave their brethren, but they were free to buy slaves "from nations around you." Another biblical passage had a huge influence on associating slavery with black people: Noah's curse on his son Ham for the sin of seeing his father naked while he was sleeping. (This seemingly harmless act may be a metaphor for a sexual assault.) Noah condemned Ham's descendants to be "the lowest of slaves." Among the offspring of Ham was Kush, the supposed progenitor of the blacks who populated Africa.[1]

The later religion of Islam forbade Muslims from enslaving fellow Muslims. But there was no barrier to enslaving "infidels." More than a million Christians, captured in wars and conquests, suffered this fate. The Muslims also transported thousands of Africans from nations and tribes that lived south of the Sahara Desert for heavy labor in their Mediterranean empire. Over the centuries, these luckless people acquired a derogatory reputation. One Muslim writer described them as "the least intelligent and least discerning of mankind."[2]

This early racism was communicated to white Christians in Spain and Portugal, where there was a Muslim presence for several centuries. Black slaves were numerous in both countries. The Roman Catholic Church found little or no fault with slavery. In 1488, King Ferdinand of Spain gave Pope Innocent VIII a hundred slaves as a gift. The prelate distributed them to various cardinals and Roman nobles. This tolerance was by no means limited to Spain, Portugal, and Italy. The great English humanist Thomas More thought slavery was the proper condition for those convicted of crimes, and he included it in his vision of the perfect republic, *Utopia*.[3]

. . .

By the early 1600s, in the capital cities of Lima and Mexico City, half the population was enslaved Africans. France also participated in the imperial game, founding colonies in the West Indies and in what is now modern Louisiana that were heavily dependent on enslaved Africans. When Great Britain entered the competition for colonies, her powerful fleet soon won domination of the world's seas. The British too turned to Africa, where a veritable industry had developed, dedicated to capturing slaves in the interior and selling them on the seacoast. Over the centuries, the price per slave rose over 1,000 percent.

Between 1501 and the 1880s, when the last two South American states, Brazil and Cuba, abolished slavery, an estimated 12.5 million black men and women were purchased in Africa and resold in America. By far the greatest percentage of this staggering number labored to produce the New World's most profitable product: sugar—a rare luxury in Europe before Columbus. To grow and harvest it required unremitting, exhausting toil in a climate that was thick with diseases such as malaria and yellow fever.[4]

For almost four centuries, Brazil and the West Indies consumed (the word is chosen deliberately) 89 percent of all the slaves shipped to the New World. The Spanish mainland colonies imported only 4.4 percent. About 5.6 percent of this involuntary migration came to Britain's North American colonies.

These colonies were soon heavily involved in the slave-based sugar empire. Tons of molasses from the West Indies travelled to New England, where it was used in hundreds of distilleries to make rum. The same ships sold much-needed grain and other farm products to the overpopulated islands. Some colonies, such as Rhode Island and Massachusetts, participated in transporting slaves from Africa. By 1750, there were a half million slaves in the American colonies. Most of these bondsmen were in the South, but some northern colonies had substantial numbers.

At least 14 percent of New York's population was slaves; for New Jersey the figure was 12 percent, and for Massachusetts 8 percent. Like the rest of the New World's settlers, few Americans criticized the institution. "The great majority," John Jay of New York wrote in 1788, accepted slavery as a matter of course. "Very few . . . even doubted the propriety and rectitude of it."

This attitude was reinforced by the knowledge that slavery was hugely profitable. "The Negroe-trade . . . may justly be termed an inexhaustible fund of wealth and naval power to this nation," wrote one complacent English economist.[5]

·　·　·

There were a few exceptions to this unanimity. In 1688, four Germantown, Pennsylvania, Quakers sent a vehement protest against slavery to their local Monthly Meeting. They declared that purchasing a slave was no different from buying stolen goods. The local Meeting forwarded it to Philadelphia's Quaker elders, who had authority of sorts over all the Quakers in America. The Philadelphia elders deposited it in their files and ignored it. Another century would pass before anyone else heard of it.

In 1700, Samuel Sewall, a Massachusetts judge who was deeply troubled by his role in the 1692 witch trials, freed a black man named Adam. The slave was able to prove that his master, John Saffin, had promised him freedom if he worked hard for seven years. Saffin reneged on the promise, claiming the slave had often been disobedient and defiant. The ex-master objected to Sewall's verdict and the judge responded in a pamphlet, *The Selling of Joseph*, that condemned the injustice of enslaving any human being, black or white. "It is most certain that all men, as they are sons of Adam . . . have an equal right unto liberty and all other outward comforts of life," Sewall wrote.

John Saffin responded in turn with a crude poem that made him one of the first Americans to argue that racial inferiority justified slavery.

THE NEGROES CHARACTER
Cowardly and cruel are these blacks innate
Prone to revenge, imp of inveterate hate
He that exasperates them, soon espies
Mischief and Murder in their very eyes
Libidinous, deceitful, false and Rude
The spume issue of ingratitude
The premises consider'd, all may tell
How near good Joseph they are parallel.[6]

Four decades passed before another American spoke out against slavery—and made a difference in the way many people perceived it.

·   ·   ·

John Woolman was a twenty-two-year-old clerk in a dry goods store in Mount Holly, New Jersey. One day in 1742, he looked up from his desk, where he was adding up the day's receipts, when his employer said, "John, I've sold Nancy to this gentleman. Draw up a bill of sale for her."

His employer and the man beside him were both Quakers—the same faith into which John Woolman had been born. Quakers believed they should try to live as if every man and woman were a priest, with a direct relationship—and responsibility—to Jesus Christ and his teachings. Reading the Bible and meditating on the sacred words often brought a message from God—"a new light"—into their lives.

John Woolman got out a fresh sheet of paper and his quill pen. But something seemed to paralyze his arm. He could not write a word. What was happening to him? Why was a voice in his soul telling him that selling Nancy was *wrong*?

Nancy was a black slave who worked in his employer's house. Woolman did not know her well. In 1742, thousands of American Quakers owned slaves. Neither Woolman nor anyone else knew about the Germantown Quakers of 1688.

Suddenly John Woolman heard himself saying, "I believe slave-keeping to be a practice inconsistent with the Christian religion."

Both the buyer and the seller told Woolman this was a "light" that had not yet reached them. Would he please write the bill of sale? With great reluctance, John Woolman completed the document. By evening, Nancy was gone from Mount Holly. For the next few weeks John Woolman remained deeply troubled. In his journal he reproached himself for not asking to be excused from writing the bill of sale "as a thing against my conscience."[7]

Born on a farm in the Rancocas River valley in western New Jersey, John Woolman was a happy child who responded to the beauty of nature and a growing sense of God's presence in his soul. By the time he began working in Mount Holly, he had decided to devote himself to preaching God's word as it was revealed to him.

A few months later, when another Quaker asked Woolman to draw up a bill of sale for a slave, he refused. This man confessed that keeping a slave disturbed his conscience too. The men parted with "good will," Woolman noted in his journal.[8]

Slavery continued to trouble John Woolman. One day a close friend said he was drawn by the Spirit to make a journey to Maryland, Virginia, and the Carolinas to preach. He asked Woolman to join him. Woolman found the journey very upsetting. In the southern colonies, tens of thousands of slaves toiled on large plantations. New Jersey had only about ten thousand slaves. Most worked on relatively small farms, where the owner usually labored beside them.

Whenever Woolman and his friend stayed with southerners who "lived in ease on the hard labor of their slaves," Woolman found it difficult to accept the food and drink he was offered. Again and again he felt compelled to "have conversation with them in private concerning it." When he revealed his growing conviction that slavery was a sin, many of his hosts politely told him to mind his own business. A few became angry.

Woolman confided to his journal his fear that slavery was casting "a gloom over the land" with consequences that would be "grievous" to future generations. Most colonists—including most Quakers—continued to ignore him. In 1750, Britain's Parliament officially sanctioned the slave trade. The city of Liverpool, which was making millions of pounds from the business, commissioned an artist to portray a black slave as part of their official seal.

John Woolman kept trying to stir consciences. He wrote a pamphlet, *Some Considerations on the Keeping of Negroes,* and a fellow Quaker read it to the Philadelphia Meeting. It was an earnest argument against slavery as an injustice and a violation of the principles of the Christian religion.

With marriage and children, Woolman's responsibilities grew. He worked as a tailor, investing his profits in an orchard. But he spent part of every year traveling to preach against slavery. "What shall we do when God riseth up?" he asked at the Philadelphia Yearly Meeting of Friends.

In Rhode Island, Woolman discovered that Thomas Hazard, son of one of the richest men in the colony, had become so troubled by the question Woolman was raising that he had freed all his slaves. His father, who owned far more slaves, was outraged and threatened to disinherit him. In 1758, when Woolman again addressed the Philadelphia Yearly Meeting, the Quakers appointed a committee to begin working to abolish slavery in the colonies.

The committee decided to visit Newport, Rhode Island, and John Woolman was invited to join them. It was an agonizing experience. Rhode Island's ships and seamen brought thousands of slaves from Africa each year. The sight of the pens and chains aboard the slave ships made Woolman physically ill. In his journal he told of feeling like the biblical prophet Habakkuk when he saw people do things of which Jehovah disapproved. "My lips quivered . . . and I trembled in myself."[9]

Woolman petitioned the Rhode Island legislature to abolish the slave trade. The Newport Quakers, spurred by Thomas Hazard, expressed a cautious "unity" with the idea. The legislature ignored the petition. But Thomas Hazard vowed to devote the rest of his life to fighting for the abolition of slavery.

Back home in New Jersey, Woolman continued the struggle. To bear witness, he stopped using sugar when he realized it was produced by slaves in the West Indies. He called blacks his brothers and sisters, and reminded people that God was indifferent to the color of a person's skin. When he realized most of the clothes worn by colonists were dyed with indigo produced by slaves, he wore only undyed garments. This meant he wore white all year.

In 1772 John Woolman went to England, hoping to enlist English Quakers in a campaign to outlaw the slave trade in the entire British empire. He appeared at the London Yearly Meeting of Ministers and Elders, the most respected body in Quakerdom. More than a few members were rich, and many of them were distinguished scientists and thinkers.

These sophisticated Londoners goggled at John Woolman. "His dress was as follows," one wrote. "A white hat, a coarse raw linen shirt, his coat, waistcoat and breeches of white coarse woolen cloth, with yarn stockings." He presented to the Meeting his introduction from his brethren in New Jersey. It was read aloud. According to one account of the ensuing scene, Dr. John Fothergill, a noted physician, rose to suggest in an icy voice that Woolman's "service"—the concern that had brought him across the ocean—was accepted without any need for him to speak, and he should go home as soon as possible.

Any other man might have slunk out the door, but John Woolman—firmly, calmly, without a hint of anger or reproof in his voice—rose and began explaining why he had come to England. When he finished, there was a long embarrassed silence. Dr. Fothergill broke it by rising and asking John Woolman to forgive him.[10]

This was the beginning of a series of heartfelt welcomes that Woolman received from English Quakers as he trudged north from London through the summery countryside to the town of York. There he spoke again on the evils of the slave trade. But toward the close of his speech, his normally smooth sentences became confused. By that night he was complaining of dizziness and weakness. The following day, everyone realized John Woolman had smallpox.

His English hosts nursed him tenderly, but the disease, one of the worst killers of the time, was inexorable. About 2:00 a.m. a week later, Woolman awoke and asked for a pen. On a piece of paper he wrote: "I believe my being here is in the wisdom of Christ." A few hours later he was dead.

In the eyes of the world, John Woolman died an eccentric failure. But within fourteen years his friend Thomas Hazard would persuade the Rhode Island legislature to prohibit the importation of slaves. Anthony Benezet, inspired by Woolman's pamphlet to the Philadelphia Meeting, founded a school for black children and wrote a series of blazing denunciations of slavery and the slave trade. In the decades after his death, Woolman's journal was reprinted dozens of times, reaching tens of thousands of readers.

. . .

Thus far we have not paid much attention to the black men and women who were the victims of this oppressive global system. How did they respond to the cruelties of what was soon called "the Middle Passage" across the Atlantic from Africa? For weeks, they were chained in a ship's hold with about as much space as a corpse had in a coffin. Since profit was the purpose of the voyage, they were fed only enough to maintain life. No one bothered to dispose of the feces and urine from their bodies, creating a stench below decks that few passengers or crew members could inhale for more than a few minutes.

It should surprise no one to learn that the captives found these conditions unendurable. Not a few slaves committed suicide by jumping overboard during the few minutes each day that they were permitted to come up on deck. Others found ways to break their chains and launched shipboard insurrections, sometimes using weapons smuggled to them by female slaves, who were allowed more freedom aboard the ship. Occasionally the rebels succeeded in capturing the ship and returning to Africa. Most of the revolts were suppressed with murderous fury.

About 10 percent of the slave ships experienced insurrections. One English captain, writing in 1700, told how he searched every corner of his ship each day, looking for pieces of wood or metal that could be used as weapons, and occasionally discovering a concealed knife. He insisted such vigilance was the only way to head off sudden death.[11]

A good example of the slaves' resourcefulness was a near eruption on a ship captained by twenty-five-year-old John Newton in 1751. A slave who was brought up on deck because he had oozing ulcers on his body managed to steal a marlin spike and pass it through the deck grating to the slaves below. In an hour, twenty slaves had broken their chains and loosened the bulkhead doors of the hold. Captain Newton thanked God (he was deeply religious) that he had a full crew aboard. His sailors were able to smash the uprising in a few violent minutes.

As time passed, many slave ships bought insurrection insurance. But this practice led to another abuse. Some captains, fearful that sick slaves would communicate their illness to others on the ship, threw the diseased Negroes overboard and claimed payment for them from the insurance company. There were few limits to the cruelties that slave ship captains felt they could perpetrate without fear of retribution.[12]

.   .   .

In America, recently arrived slaves were often rebellious, especially when they encountered slaves from the West Indies, where brutal treatment made revolts frequent. In 1712, two slaves from the islands led a revolt in New York that began by setting a building on fire. They killed nine white men who were trying to extinguish the blaze. The insurrection was quickly suppressed.

More formidable was a rebellion in South Carolina in 1739. By this time the colony had been importing slaves so rapidly that in some districts blacks outnumbered whites by large majorities. In the West Indies, the ratio was often 10 to 1. But each West Indian island maintained at least one regiment of British troops to keep order. There were no professional soldiers in South Carolina. This may have emboldened a group of slaves from the African kingdom of Kongo to launch a revolt.

Their leader was a slave named Jemmy, who could read and write. Around him he gathered about twenty other slaves, all from Kongo. They were Catholics, like most of Kongo, thanks to centuries of contact with Portuguese traders. Lately the country had been racked by a civil war, which had led to the capture and enslavement of Jemmy and his friends.

Sunday, September 9, was the day after a Catholic feast day celebrating the birth of the Virgin Mary. With the hope of divine blessing, Jemmy and his followers marched on a store on the Stono River, southwest of Charleston, chanting "Liberty!" They killed the owners of the store and seized enough weapons and ammunition to make them a formidable force. Their destination was Spanish Florida, where they expected to receive a warm welcome from fellow Catholics, who were on the brink of a war with the British and Americans.

Hoping to gather recruits and find more weapons, the rebels burned a half dozen plantations and killed at least twenty whites who tried to resist them. By this time the South Carolina government had mustered about a hundred well-armed men on horseback. They overtook the slaves on the Edisto River, where a fierce fire fight erupted. It ended in the rout of the rebels, but not before they had killed twenty whites. A handful of Jemmy's men retreated about thirty miles, where they were overtaken by a group of Chickasaw and Catawba Indians, hired by the South Carolinians. Also in this final fight were some loyal slaves, who were apparently eager to destroy the rebel remnant.[13]

In a gruesome aftermath, the South Carolinians executed most of the Kongo army's survivors. A few were sold to buyers in the West Indies. The heads of many rebels were mounted on stakes along roads around Charleston as warnings to other slaves who might be considering a revolt. The shaken South Carolinians passed a Negro Act, which required a ratio of at least one white to every ten blacks on a plantation—a dictum soon ignored.

The law also prohibited blacks from growing their own food, learning to read, or earning money in their spare time. Another clause made it difficult to free a slave. The goal was to create a system with a minimum of freedom. Only in this claustrophobic world would South Carolinians feel safe.

Over the next two years, slave uprisings elsewhere in South Carolina and Georgia did little to enlarge this sense of theoretic security. Even more sensational was a revolt in New York City in 1741. About 20 percent of the city's population were slaves, stirring uneasiness among the whites. The conspiracy was led by a slave who was urged on by a Catholic priest, a refugee from persecution in Protestant-controlled England.

The plan was similar to the 1712 uprising—to start a series of fires that would devastate the city, then kill the whites as they struggled to extinguish them. But the scale and ambitions of these conspirators were larger. Two Spanish-speaking slaves assured the rebels they would receive help from Spain and France, who were at war with England.

The conspirators met at a tavern frequented by blacks and poor whites; it was run by a man in sympathy with the rebels. In a few weeks, no less than thirteen fires erupted. The most unnerving blaze destroyed the royal governor's house and much of Fort George, the city's principal defense against an attack from the sea.

A woman who lived at the tavern offered to identify the conspirators to escape punishment for a recent arrest for theft. In a series of trials, seventeen blacks were convicted and hanged, thirteen blacks were burned at the stake, and four whites, including the suspected priest, were hanged. Another seventy suspected blacks were deported to the West Indies. The story, reported in newspapers from Boston to Savannah, sent new shock waves of fear and anxiety about black uprisings up and down the thousand-mile Atlantic coastline.[14]

.   .   .

As the thirteen North American colonies became more prosperous and sophisticated, fears of political oppression began to absorb the public mind. In the early 1760s, rebellious James Otis of Massachusetts disputed the British Parliament's claim to the right to tax the Americans. "Taxation without representation is tyranny," he declared, words that the Catholic Irish, ruled as a conquered nation by the Protestant English, had been using in vain for several decades. Men in other colonies took the same stance, as the British, with an arrogance that seemed to come naturally to them, inflicted more taxes.

Benjamin Rush, an outspoken Philadelphia doctor, condemned the "servitude" Parliament inflicted on Americans. Even a moderate Virginia planter like George Washington began to see a transatlantic hand in his pocket whenever Parliament was in the mood. It was imperative for the Americans to resist this incipient tyranny, Washington said, before they were reduced to "the most abject state of slavery that ever was designed for mankind."[15]

This political slavery was defined by a New Englander as "being wholly under the power and control of another as to our actions and properties." The words were obviously inspired by African slavery as practiced in both the North and South. James Otis, in one of his assaults on the British, made the comparison explicit. Was it right, he asked, to enslave a man because he was black? "Will short curled hair like wool . . . help the argument? Can any logical inference in favor of slavery be drawn from a flat nose, a long or short face?" Slavery made no more sense, Otis argued, than the British claim that Parliament had power over colonists living three thousand miles away who, in the course of the previous 150 years, had tamed a wilderness and created free societies.[16]

Parliament, encouraged by the headstrong young king, George III, ignored these explosive words. The New Englanders were soon led by Boston's Samuel Adams, who would later confess that independence had been the "first wish of [his] heart" for a long time. They united the colonies with resentful letters and broadsides circulated by Committees of Correspondence. Newspapers became "political engines" that preached rebellious ideas in fiery prose. Next, boycotts of British products shook the merchant class of the Mother Country and demonstrated a growing American unity of purpose.

In December 1773, Sam Adams's followers dumped thousands of pounds of British East India Company tea, worth a half million modern dollars, into Boston Harbor to protest a three-pence-per-pound royal tax. The British responded by sending four regiments to close the port of Boston, instantly alienating the rest of the colonies. Soon a "continental" congress met in Philadelphia, with delegates from every colony except Georgia.

Britain ignored the congress's respectful pleas to King George, asking him to resolve the crisis. In Massachusetts an embryo army of "minute men," sworn to fight on sixty seconds notice, began drilling in the countryside outside Boston. When the second Continental Congress met in the spring of 1775, George Washington, a delegate from Virginia, wore the military uniform of a colonel of his colony's militia. It was a bold prediction that war was imminent.

On April 19, 1775, gunfire between redcoats and Americans in Lexington, Massachusetts, triggered a running battle that left over a hundred men dead on both sides. To unite the colonies, Sam Adams and his second cousin John, who had displayed considerable ability as a legislative leader, proposed George Washington as commander in chief of an American army.

In the South, some people were uneasily aware that they had "Domestick enemies" to worry about, as well as the British army. Would the British use the slaves' smoldering anger and hunger for freedom to undo the rebellious whites? South Carolina was riddled by fear of this all too real possibility as the Revolution gathered momentum. In Virginia, a farseeing if jittery young rebel, James Madison, started worrying about it as early as 1774.[17]

Little more than a year later, the hotheaded royal governor of Virginia, Lord Dunmore, called on the colony's slaves to desert their masters and rally to his standard with a promise of freedom. An alarmed George Washington wrote from Massachusetts that if Dunmore "is not crushed before Spring, he will become the most dangerous man in America. His strength will increase like a snowball rolling downhill."

Only about 300 of Virginia's 200,000 slaves responded to Dunmore, who formed them into a "Loyal Ethiopian Regiment." The governor's experiment came to an end at the December 9, 1775, Battle of Great Bridge. White Virginians and a sprinkling of free blacks routed Dunmore's recruits and a company of British regulars. Parliament hastily disowned the governor's scheme, which had turned numerous loyal slave-owners into rebels.[18]

.   .   .

Six months later, John Adams, whose speeches in the divided Continental Congress had made some listeners call him "the Atlas of Independence," exulted when the delegates voted to declare America independent. Adams asked a thirty-three-year-old Virginia delegate, Thomas Jefferson, to prepare a written declaration explaining America's decision to become a new country. Few people realized that a major critic of slavery was stepping onto the world's stage.

CHAPTER 2

Slavery's Great Foe—
and Unintended Friend

In his early days as a lawyer, Thomas Jefferson revealed an almost instinctive dislike of slavery. At the age of twenty-one, he had inherited 5,000 fertile acres and 52 slaves, making him a member of Virginia's ruling class. But slavery offended his sense of justice in a deep and intensely personal way. In one of his first law cases, Jefferson had maintained that a mulatto grandson of a white woman and a black slave should be considered a free man. His argument, which the astonished judge dismissed out of hand, declared slavery a violation of every person's natural right to freedom.[1]

Jefferson had been reluctant to accept the task of writing a declaration of independence. Back in Virginia, delegates were conferring on a constitution for the state. Jefferson wanted to be there to argue for the gradual abolition of slavery. He had even drafted his own version of a constitution, with an explicit provision for such a measure. At the same time, he did not underestimate the importance of the document he was asked to create. The rhythms of the Declaration's opening paragraph throb with a deeper timbre than anything else Jefferson ever wrote:

When in the course of human events it becomes necessary for one people to dissolve the political bands which have connected them to another, and to assume among the powers of the earth a separate and equal station to which the laws of nature and of nature's god entitle them, a decent respect for the opinions of mankind requires that they should declare the reasons that impel them to this separation.

We hold these truths to be self-evident, that all men are created equal; that they are endowed by their creator with certain unalienable rights; that among these are life, liberty and the pursuit of happiness.

Thomas Jefferson did not know—nor did anyone else who read these words in or out of the Continental Congress—that he had delivered a deathblow to American slavery. It would take another eight and a half decades to make this an historical fact. In the rest of the first draft of the Declaration, he made his detestation of slavery visible to every member of the Continental Congress.

After the opening paragraphs of fundamental principles, Jefferson began a ferocious indictment of King George III for his "repeated injuries and usurpations" aimed at establishing "absolute tyranny over these states." Like the toll of a funereal bell, the accusations poured out:

He has refused his assent to laws the most wholesome and necessary for the public good . . .

He has made judges dependent on his will alone, for the tenure of their offices and the amount and payment of their salaries . . .

He is at this time transporting large armies of foreign mercenaries to compleat the works of death, desolation & tyranny already begun.

Then came words that virtually exploded on the page:

He has waged cruel war against human nature itself, violating the most sacred rights of life & liberty in the persons of a distant people, who never offended him, captivating and carrying them into slavery in another hemisphere, or to incur miserable death in their transportation thither, this piratical warfare, the opprobrium of infidel powers, is the warfare of the Christian king of Great Britain, determined to keep open the market where MEN could be bought & sold, he has prostituted his negative for suppressing every legislative attempt to prohibit or to restrain this execrable commerce and that this assemblage of horrors might want no fact of distinguished dye, he is now exciting these very people to rise in arms among us and to purchase that liberty of which he has denied them, by murdering the people upon whom he also obtruded them; thus paying off former crimes committed against the liberties of one people, with crimes which he urges them to commit against the lives of another.

To this detonation of detestation, Jefferson added a searing indictment of the British people for doing nothing to prevent or soften King George's abuses. Then came sonorous closing paragraphs, declaring "these united colonies are and of right ought to be free and independent states, that they are absolved from all allegiance to the British crown and that all political connection between them and the state of Great Britain is and ought to be totally dissolved."[2]

Jefferson submitted this draft of the declaration to the Continental Congress. To his dismay, the delegates felt free to eliminate major passages. One of the first to go was the denunciation of slavery. In his old age, Jefferson claimed that delegates from South Carolina and Georgia objected to it, and some northern states that had participated in the slave trade "felt a little tender" on the subject. But tender feelings were hardly a main point. Congress was aware that Americans north and south had been involved with slavery for over a century, and had profited immensely from it.[3] There was a well-grounded fear that the British would be quick to point this out if Jefferson's denunciation were included in the final version. Already, the King's ministers had hired the most famous writer of the era, Samuel Johnson, to compose an anti-American pamphlet in which he sneered: "How is it we hear the greatest yelps for liberty among the drivers of Negroes?"[4]

.   .   .

In Massachusetts, General George Washington was startled by how many blacks were in the impromptu army that was besieging the British regiments in Boston. Most of the blacks were free men like Salem Poor of Framingham, who had distinguished himself by his bravery and marksmanship at the battle of Bunker Hill in June 1775. Poor had volunteered to fight for his country when he heard about the bloodshed at Lexington.

In the Continental Congress, Edward Rutledge of South Carolina demanded a vote to bar blacks from the army. In a debate that foreshadowed future disagreements between North and South, Congress rejected the proposal. At first, Washington agreed with Rutledge. He issued an order forbidding the enlistment of "any stroller, Negro or vagabond."

Later in 1775 the general began to change his mind. None of the white New Englanders objected to having blacks in their ranks. More important, a dismaying number of whites were refusing to reenlist for the coming year. On December 30, 1775, Washington revised his previous enlistment order: "As the General is informed that numbers of Free Negroes are desirous of enlisting, he gives leave to recruiting officers to entertain them."[5]

.   .   .

Around this time, Washington invited a black slave named Phillis Wheatley to visit him in his Cambridge headquarters. Wheatley had arrived in Boston aboard a slave ship in 1761 at the age of seven. Bought by a tailor to be a personal servant for his wife, the child had soon displayed evidence of amazing intelligence. She learned to read and write almost immediately, and was soon mastering Latin. She began writing poetry at the age of fourteen, and in 1773 she published a book of poems in London.

Six months after Washington took command of the Continental army, he found a poetic tribute to him on his desk from this young African woman. In cadences that obviously reflected wide reading in the best English poetry of the period, Phillis Wheatley asked the goddess Columbia to bless General Washington's struggle for his nation's freedom. The last stanza was a climactic plea:

> *Proceed, great chief, with virtue on thy side*
> *Thy ev'ry action let the Goddess guide*
> *A crown, a mansion, and a throne that shine*
> *With gold unfading, Washington! be thine.*

Washington wrote a letter to "Miss Phillis" thanking her for this "polite notice" of him. He added that it was striking proof of "her great poetical talents." He would have arranged to have the poem published, but he feared he would incur "the imputation of vanity." Whereupon he invited the young woman to visit him, if she should ever come to Cambridge. "I shall be happy to see a person so favored by the muses."[6]

It requires a moment's pause to realize the uniqueness of this exchange between a slave woman and a prominent Virginia slave owner. It took place in early 1776, at a time when few if any Virginians would have done such a thing. Some historians have suggested that it was Phillis Wheatley who changed Washington's mind about enlisting free blacks. But it is equally likely that Washington's mind had already begun to change after talking to some of the free blacks whom he had originally barred from reenlisting. Several had come to headquarters to protest their exclusion and reiterated their desire to fight for America's liberty. A group of officers had written a testimonial, urging Salem Poor's reenlistment.

The war lasted another seven often harrowing years. More and more black men joined the Continental army, as the enthusiasm of 1775 and 1776 faded and the grim reality of British determination became apparent. Washington took the lead in telling the Continental Congress that "patriotism" would not a win "a long and bloody war." Again and again, he insisted, "We must take men as they are, not as we wish them to be."

The general made no objection when numerous people hired blacks as substitutes to escape the draft that was imposed by state governments to fill their annual quotas for the Continental army. By 1781, one in every seven soldiers in the American army was black.

. . .

During these years, Washington developed a deep friendship with a young French volunteer, the Marquis de Lafayette. Thanks largely to his family's prominence in the court of the French king, Congress had appointed him a major general. The idealistic nobleman spent large amounts of his own fortune to improve the lot of the often hungry and ragged regulars at Valley Forge and elsewhere. He also displayed courage on the battlefield. When he was wounded at the Battle of the Brandywine in 1777, General Washington told an army doctor to care for him "as if he were my own son."

Lafayette soon began talking with Washington about his detestation of slavery. The general must have been more than a little shocked when the young Frenchman exclaimed during one conversation: "I would never have drawn my sword in the cause of America, if I could have conceived thereby I was founding a land of slavery." These conversations may have played a part in Washington agreeing to another large step in black participation in the Revolution.[7]

. . .

Blacks from New England had continued to enlist in large numbers. Of forty-four hundred free blacks in Massachusetts, five hundred volunteered. In Connecticut the number was close to three hundred. As the American army's ordeal at Valley Forge thinned its ranks, General James Varnum of Rhode Island came to Washington with a new proposal: Why not enlist an entire regiment of black soldiers?

Tiny Rhode Island was having difficulties filling the quotas for its two Continental regiments. The legislature passed a law, declaring that henceforth "every able-bodied Negro, Mulatto or Indian Man slave" would be welcome in these regiments. The state agreed to pay the slaves' owners four hundred dollars per man. Washington told the delighted Varnum that the idea had his approval. Over the next few months, between 225 and

250 blacks became members of Rhode Island's Second Continental regiment. The achievement—stark proof of how quickly blacks identified with Thomas Jefferson's declaration of universal equality—is even more remarkable when we factor in the violent objections of a great many Rhode Island whites.

The protestors tried to persuade blacks not to volunteer. They told the would-be soldiers that the whites would only use them as "breastworks" to stop enemy bullets. (Virginians had said the same thing to persuade slaves not to join Lord Dunmore's Ethiopian regiment.) These exchanges reveal that American slavery did not impose the total control that the political definition implied. Slaves frequently made up their own minds, no matter what their masters said.

Rhode Island's black regiment served in the Continental army for the rest of the war. Its soldiers fought well on a number of battlefields. In 1780, they survived a cruel ambush in Westchester County that cost them almost fifty officers and men. The regiment's success encouraged several officers to urge the creation of similar units in other New England states. But Massachusetts rejected the idea, after a brief debate.

Late in the war, Connecticut recruited a single company of black soldiers using the Rhode Island policy of paying owners to free their slaves. But the idea remained controversial. Rhode Island whites eventually forced the legislature to repeal the 1778 law, claiming it disturbed relationships between masters and slaves.[8]

· · ·

In 1781, Thomas Jefferson responded to a French diplomat who had sent queries to leading men in all the states, asking them to give him a better understanding of their history, traditions, and geography. Jefferson's response, which he completed in 1783, became *Notes on the State of Virginia*, the only book he ever wrote. It contained superb descriptions of Virginia's western scenery and thorough discussions of the state's agriculture and politics. It also included trenchant comments on slavery, which were to become influential in contradictory ways.

Jefferson insisted he was writing as a scientist, trying to report objectively on everything he had seen and studied in Virginia. But in his comments on slavery, it was apparent that his feelings were deeply involved. He began by saying he thought that the Revolution had improved the condition of slaves in Virginia. Masters had grown less harsh and slaves had found pride and hope in the participation of free blacks and slave volunteers in the war's great events. But slavery remained a cruel and destructive enterprise, which undermined the morals of both masters and victims.

"The whole commerce between master and slave is a perpetual exercise in the most boisterous passions, the most unremitting despotism on the one part and the most degrading submission on the other." Jefferson declared the effect of slavery on the white man was as ruinous as it was on the Negro. "The man must be a prodigy who can retain his manners and morals in such circumstances. Our children see this and learn to imitate it, for man is an imitative animal. With the morals of the people, their industry is also destroyed. For in a warm climate, no man will labor for himself that can make another labor for him."

Ultimately, Jefferson feared that slavery might undermine the whole American enterprise. "Can the liberties of a nation be thought secure when we have removed their only firm basis, the conviction in the minds of the people that their liberties are the gift of God? That they are not to be violated but by his wrath? Indeed I tremble for my country when I reflect that God is just, that his justice cannot sleep forever."

Jefferson spelled out the fearful future he dreaded: "Considering numbers, nature and natural means only, a revolution of the wheel of fortune, an exchange of situation, is among possible events . . . The Almighty has no attribute which can take side with us in such a contest." He was saying a revolt among the slaves was all too possible, with the outcome quite possibly in their favor.

Jefferson went on to give an estimate of the black race's abilities "as a subject of natural history." He emphasized he was only speaking from his observations of black slaves, and he admitted in advance it was a subject of "great tenderness." He did not want to "degrade a whole race of men from the rank in the scale of beings which their creator may perhaps have given them."

Alas, with baffling obtuseness, Jefferson proceeded to do the very thing he deplored. "I advance it as a suspicion only, that the blacks, whether originally a distinct race, or made distinct by time and circumstances, are inferior to the whites in the endowments of both mind and body . . . This unfortunate difference in color and perhaps in faculty, is a powerful obstacle to the emancipation of these people."

Jefferson doubted that the freed blacks could live peacefully in the same country with their former masters. "Deep rooted prejudices entertained by the whites, ten thousand recollections by the blacks of the injuries they have sustained, new provocations, the real distinctions which nature has made, will divide us into parties and produce convulsions, and probably never end but in the extermination of one or the other race." Ultimately, Jefferson concluded, freed blacks would have to be resettled in a foreign country to avoid inevitable bloodshed.

Another obstacle to white–black relations, Jefferson continued, was the Negroes' "immoveable veil of black" which tended to "eternal monotony" from an aesthetic point of view. Blacks had "several engaging if somewhat childlike qualities," but they had little ability for reflection or forethought. In reason they were "much inferior" to the whites and in imagination "dull, tasteless and anomalous." While sexually more ardent than whites, their affections were "neither tender nor lasting."

When he penned these lines, Jefferson thought he was writing for only a single individual, or a group of individuals in the French government. After he became American ambassador to France in 1784, he showed *Notes on Virginia* to several friends in Paris, and they persuaded him to publish the book in a limited edition of one hundred copies. From there it was an all-too-predictable step to an edition published in London in 1787. Authors had no copyright protection in the eighteenth century. American editions soon followed and *Notes* became one of the most quoted and debated books ever written. For many whites, especially in the South, Jefferson's words elevated their already negative opinion of blacks to the level of confirmed truth.[9]

CHAPTER 3

The First Emancipation Proclamation

Rhode Island's black regiment inspired a much more difficult challenge—recruiting black soldiers in the American South. The attempt became interwoven with the tragic personal story of one of the American Revolution's most appealing (and most forgotten) younger leaders, Colonel John Laurens.

Almost theatrically handsome, the twenty-seven-year-old Laurens had a rare combination of gifts that made him one of General Washington's favorite aides. He repeatedly proved himself a fearless soldier, and he mingled his courage with a passionate idealism. For him, the Revolution was a crusade to transform the world. He wanted to see Thomas Jefferson's opening words in the Declaration of Independence become a reality shared by all Americans. Even before Congress signed the Declaration, Laurens told a friend: "I think we Americans, at least in the Southern colonies, cannot contend with *a good grace* for liberty until we have enfranchised our slaves."[1]

In 1778, during the winter at Valley Forge, Laurens had been present when General James Varnum persuaded Washington to agree to raise a black Rhode Island regiment. The young colonel decided the idea could and should be applied to his home state of South Carolina. He discussed the idea with General Washington and with his father, Henry Laurens, who was president of the Continental Congress at the time. Ironically, the senior Laurens was also the wealthiest slave trader in South Carolina. Both men told the young colonel that they agreed with him in principle, but they doubted that any southern legislator would approve arming slaves. The fear of an insurrection haunted too many people, especially in South Carolina, where blacks outnumbered whites in many counties.

John Laurens temporarily shelved his plan. But he revived it when the British shifted the war to the South in 1779 and conquered Georgia. He persuaded his father to back him; Washington, although dubious, also gave him permission to make the attempt.[2] Laurens's fellow aide and closest friend, Colonel Alexander Hamilton, wrote a letter to John Jay, the new president of Congress, urging him to press for a resolution supporting the plan.

Hamilton dismissed the idea that slaves lacked the intelligence to be good soldiers. "The contempt we have been taught to entertain for the blacks makes us fancy many things that are founded neither in reason nor experience." He blamed white reluctance to part with "property of so valuable a kind" for the readiness to believe the "impracticability" of emancipation. "Their natural faculties are probably as good as ours," he insisted. Hamilton had grown up in the West Indies, surrounded by blacks, and was speaking from years of personal observations. He assured President Jay that freeing the black recruits would "secure their fidelity [and] animate their courage." It would also have "a good influence" on those who remained slaves.[3]

On March 29, 1779, Congress voted to urge South Carolina and Georgia to raise "three thousand able-bodied Negroes" who would be commanded by Colonel Laurens and other white officers. Congress would pay one thousand dollars to the owner of each slave who met the "able-bodied" requirement. All blacks who served for the duration of the war would be freed, and receive a fifty dollar bonus.

Several members of Congress were stunned by the audacity of this resolution. "If the plan were carried into effect," delegate William Whipple of

New Hampshire said, "it will . . . lay the foundation for the abolition of slavery in America." Based partly on those words, some historians have called the resolution "a first emancipation proclamation."[4]

.   .   .

Colonel Laurens rushed to Charleston with the proposal and arrived to find that the British army in Georgia was marching into South Carolina. He told Governor John Rutledge about Congress's resolution, arguing that the invasion made the black brigade even more important. The governor and his privy council rejected the idea without even a polite discussion.

The southern American army retreated behind breastworks around Charleston and the British called on them to surrender. Terrified that the enemy would free the state's slaves, Governor Rutledge offered to give up the city without a fight if the British agreed to accept South Carolina's neutrality for the rest of the war. Rutledge asked Colonel Laurens to carry this message to the British.[5]

Laurens refused to do any such thing and told the governor that he considered the offer a disgrace. When two other men delivered the message, the British general said it was beyond his authority to make such an agreement and reiterated his demand for surrender. With no other alternative, the South Carolinians dared him to attack. The British retreated to Georgia.

John Laurens resubmitted his proposal, this time in writing. Governor Rutledge and his councilors turned it down without even a hint of politeness. One angry councilor wrote to Congressman Samuel Adams, "We are much disgusted . . . at Congress recommending us to arm our slaves. It was received with great resentment as a very impolitic and dangerous step."

Laurens, who had been slightly wounded in the fighting that preceded the British retreat, persuaded Benjamin Lincoln, the Massachusetts general whom Washington had sent to defend Charleston, to urge recruiting the blacks. Once more the governor turned the idea down. Laurens won election to the state legislature and introduced the proposal there. It was overwhelmingly rejected. Henry Laurens wrote to his son, urging him to forget his "black air castle."[6]

. . .

A few months later, almost half the British army in America arrived by ship from New York and besieged Charleston. In the spring of 1780 the king's men forced General Lincoln and his army to surrender. John Laurens became a prisoner of war. The legislature disbanded and Governor Rutledge fled the state. Rebels under leaders such as Francis Marion, "the Swamp Fox," continued to resist royal rule, and South Carolina was engulfed by a savage guerilla war, during which thousands of slaves fled to British protection.

By 1781, the War for Independence seemed on the brink of collapse in the South and the North was not in much better shape. General Washington had persuaded the British to exchange Laurens for a captured British officer, and he had rejoined the commander in chief's staff. Washington sent him to Paris to plead for an emergency loan of twenty-five million livres—about two hundred million modern dollars. The bilingual Laurens got almost half the money, plus tons of desperately needed uniforms and weapons from the French, although they were on the brink of national bankruptcy.[7]

Buoyed by this aid, a revived Continental Army combined with a French expeditionary force and a French fleet to trap the British southern field army in the tobacco port of Yorktown, Virginia. Colonels Laurens and Hamilton led a climactic assault that captured two key redoubts, forcing the British to surrender.

The war was by no means over. The British still had twenty-five thousand men on American soil. Well-armed garrisons occupied New York, Savannah, and Charleston, and from these enclaves launched savage attacks on the independence men. Colonel Laurens decided that his black brigade was the answer to this problem, and again persuaded General Washington to let him try to make it a reality.

. . .

A new southern commander, General Nathanael Greene, had driven the British from the interior of South Carolina, but his army was too weak to assault fortified Charleston. Greene was from Rhode Island, and he warmly backed Laurens's idea. John Rutledge, still South Carolina's governor, told

Laurens he would let the next legislature, scheduled to be chosen in December 1781, make the decision. Laurens promptly declared himself a candidate and was easily reelected.

Colonel Laurens introduced his proposal for the black regiments with a new clause that he hoped would take his opponents by surprise. Governor Rutledge was urging confiscation of the lands and slaves of hundreds of loyalists who had joined the British in the previous two years of guerilla conflict. Why not raise the black regiments from the thousands of slaves the state was about to seize from these loyalists?

For a while it looked as if the colonel were mustering strong support from other South Carolinians inside and outside the legislature. Governor Rutledge described the debate as a "hard battle" which at times made him "very much alarmed." Colonel Laurens's proposal was put to a vote. A pleased Governor Rutledge was soon reporting: "About 12 or 15 were for it & about 100 against it—I now hope it will rest for ever & a day."[8]

In a bitter letter to General Washington, Laurens attributed his defeat to "the howlings of a triple-headed monster in which prejudice, avarice & pusillanimity were united." Washington's reply attempted to console the young idealist with the observations of an older man who had discarded any and all illusions about human nature. In many ways, it is one of the most important letters Washington ever wrote. It cast a piercing light on the later years of the American Revolution—and the future years of the American nation.

> The spirit of freedom which at the commencement of this contest would have gladly sacrificed every thing to the attainment of its object has long since subsided and every selfish passion has taken its place. It is not the public but the private interest which influences the generality of mankind nor can the Americans any longer boast of an exception.[9]

Laurens's friend Hamilton was equally disappointed by the colonel's defeat. In his letters he had revealed how much he admired his South Carolina brother-in-arms. "You know the low opinion I entertain of mankind," he wrote, revealing the psychic wounds he had suffered from his parents' broken marriage and his penniless West Indian youth. "You s[hould] not have taken advantage of my sensibility to st[eal] into my affections without my consent."

In mid-August 1782, Hamilton excitedly informed Laurens that the governor of New York had appointed him to Congress. The embryo politician begged Laurens to join him. "Quit your sword, my friend, put on the toga, come to Congress . . . We have fought side by side to make America free. Let us hand in hand struggle to make her happy."[10]

Laurens remained committed to his dream of black battalions. General Greene offered him command of the army's light infantry. The colonel would be responsible for repelling British forays into the countryside. Hoping some local military glory would give him the prestige he needed to win support for his plan, the glum idealist accepted the offer.

Laurens was soon telling Greene that "the present is an idle insipid time." The general grew worried about the colonel's gloomy state of mind. The light infantry scored a few minor victories against enemy detachments who ventured beyond Charleston's fortifications. But they were not the sort of triumphs that won much attention. Greene decided to put Laurens in charge of intelligence, and he soon had a network of effective spies inside British-held Charleston.

In late August, General Greene told Laurens of a plan to ambush some three hundred British regulars who were foraging on the rice plantations along the Combahee River in the South Carolina low country. The light infantry was going to hit the British at daybreak, drive them into their boats, and then bombard them with a howitzer from a bluff at the river's mouth as they straggled back to Charleston. It had all the attributes of a sensational victory. Laurens volunteered to join the expedition and asked to command the fifty men assigned to defend the howitzer, which the British were likely to attack by land.

At dawn, the Americans surged across the river to assail the redcoats— and found nothing but stripped houses and cold campfires. Loyalist spies had warned them of the attack. The foragers had boarded their ships not long after midnight and headed down the river toward the sea.

The chagrinned attackers realized that the enemy knew about the plan to bombard them from the bluff. They would probably order some men ashore to make sure the howitzer was not in position to do them any damage. The Americans sent a horseman pounding down the road to warn Laurens, and followed him with 150 light infantrymen and dragoons.

When Laurens arrived at the neck of land leading to the bluff, 150 British infantrymen were deployed in the underbrush along the road. They started shooting the moment the Americans appeared, dragging their howitzer. Laurens fell back and considered his options. He did not know reinforcements were on the road; the news would probably have made no difference to this deeply depressed soldier, who still hoped fresh military glory would help him sell his proposal to free and arm the slaves.

Laurens ordered a bayonet charge and put himself at the head of his fifty-man column. The 150 British opened fire at point-blank range. There was a huge crash and a billow of musket smoke into the dawn sky. When the acrid fog cleared, Colonel John Laurens was lying on his back with a bullet in his heart. A badly wounded captain and several enlisted men lay near him. The rest of the Americans fled, abandoning their howitzer.

The reinforcements arrived not long after the disaster. An assault cost them a dozen men; they decided the enemy position was too strong and allowed the British to withdraw to their ships, taking the howitzer with them. The Americans retreated to a nearby plantation and reported to General Greene that Colonel John Laurens's body would be buried there "with every mark of distinction due to his rank and merit."[11]

Americans of all ranks recognized that they had suffered a fateful wound. "Our country has lost its most promising character," John Adams wrote to Henry Laurens. George Washington reported the news to Lafayette, a sharer in Laurens's dream of abolishing slavery. "Poor Laurens is no more," he wrote. "He fell in a trifling skirmish in South Carolina." Alexander Hamilton was by far the most grief-stricken. "I feel the deepest affliction . . . at the loss of our dear and [inesti]mable friend Laurens," he wrote to General Greene. "His career of virtue is at an end. How strangely are human affairs conducted. . . . The world will feel the loss of a man who has left few like him behind, and America of a citizen whose heart realized that patriotism of which others only talk."[12]

They were also mourning the death of the first emancipation proclamation.

CHAPTER 4

One Head Turning
into Thirteen

For a long time, historians praised the founding generation for their stance on slavery. Washington, Jefferson, Franklin, Adams, Hamilton, and Madison all spoke out against it in various ways. Even men like John Rutledge made no attempt to defend the institution. They called it a necessary evil, temporarily needed for their prosperity. The founders were credited with making large strides toward slavery's eventual extinction.

In the second half of the twentieth century, a new generation of historians, influenced by the civil rights movement, took a very different point of view. They noted ruefully that the Revolution had ended in the creation of a slave-holding republic. Few American slave owners, including the principal founders, applied the Declaration of Independence to their own slaves—or anyone else's. Thomas Jefferson took a particularly bad beating for his authorship of the Declaration of Independence and his numerous statements condemning slavery, while he ran up overwhelming debts living like a lord in his hilltop mansion, leaving him financially incapable of freeing his bondsmen. When it came to slavery, these disenchanted scholars proclaimed, the founders were all talk and no action.

More recently, historians have begun to see that this viewpoint is as untenable as the idea that the founders did virtually everything but induce slavery's death throes. It dishonors men like John Laurens, who gave his life for his vision of a South without slaves. George Washington's decision to enlist black soldiers created a legacy that coalesced with the opening words of Jefferson's Declaration to persuade many northern states to begin eliminating slavery. Historian Christopher L. Brown may have put it best when he said, "The American Revolution presents the first example of slaveholders themselves not just questioning slavery's morality but considering doing something to end the system. It is a defining moment in the world history of slavery."[1]

.   .   .

There were limits to how far the Revolutionary generation was able to go. As the war inched to a close in two precarious years of negotiation and sporadic violence after the victory at Yorktown, General Washington began warning people that the so-called United States of America was exhibiting grave tendencies to disunion. "I see one head turning into thirteen," he told several correspondents. States bickered over borders and declined to pay foreign debts they had incurred independently of Congress. The Continental Congress's first constitution, the Articles of Confederation, was a formula for political paralysis.[2]

The bankrupt Congress had no power to tax, and unanimous agreement was required when something resembling a tax, such as a levy on imports, was proposed. A demoralizing inflation reduced the nation's paper money to a wry joke—the phrase "not worth a continental" (dollar) became synonymous with futility. Congress ignored General Washington's warning that they were causing him "perpetual embitterment" and welched on their promise to pay his officers a pension. They sent the Continental Army's enlisted men home without the sizeable amounts of back pay owed to every soldier.

By the time a final treaty of peace was ratified in 1783, Congress was so unpopular that many people were pleading with General Washington to take charge of running the country. Instead, in a solemn ceremony in Annapolis, Maryland, where Congress was sitting, the general handed the current president his commission as commander in chief and went home to Mount Vernon. When George III heard the news, the stunned monarch stuttered that Washington had become "the gr-greatest man in the world."[3]

It was undoubtedly an important moment in American history. But it was only a prelude to making the United States a respectable nation. Congress remained powerless and bankrupt. The states continued to quarrel; some began charging import duties to nearby neighbors; and they refused to accept each other's paper money, which several printed with a recklessness they had learned from that model of how not to run a country, Congress. Former Colonel Alexander Hamilton advised Governor George Clinton of New York to invite Continental Army veterans to settle in the state, where they might be useful in the event of a civil war.[4]

· · ·

The death of Thomas Jefferson's beloved wife, Martha, in 1782 drove him to the brink of suicide. Worried friends persuaded him to escape the gloom that shrouded Monticello and accept an appointment to Congress. The legislature was a pathetic ghost of its 1776 glory. Frequently there were not enough members present for a quorum. Jefferson soon became involved in one of Congress's few responsibilities, forging a policy for the territory between the Mississippi River and the Appalachian Mountains that the British had ceded in the treaty of peace.

In 1784, Congress named Jefferson head of a committee with orders to work out a plan of government for this swath of the continent. Jefferson proposed that the land be divided into new states that would have freely elected governments and would be accepted as equals by the thirteen states of the original union. Then came a proposal that was totally original. Slavery would be banned in all these lands after 1800. Virginia had ignored Jefferson's pleas to begin a gradual emancipation program, but his detestation of the institution remained intense.

The proposal triggered a violent debate in Congress. All but one Southern delegate deserted Jefferson. Most New England and Middle States delegates responded with enthusiasm, creating a majority of the delegates present. But the creaky Articles of Confederation required a majority of the states. The final vote was a tie, with the New Jersey delegation unable to agree. One of their delegates, who favored the proposal, was too ill to attend the session.[5]

There were other problems with Jefferson's ordinance, notably the identical size of the states he proposed, with little attention to natural boundaries. Not until 1786 did Congress take up the problem again. This time, Jefferson's young friend, James Monroe, was head of the committee to work out a solution. But Monroe became distracted by a new threat: secession. Southern settlers in the future states of Kentucky and Tennessee were angry about Congress's inability to prevent Spain from interfering with American commerce on the Mississippi River. They threatened to turn to some other power for help. "Great Britain stands ready with open arms to receive and support us," they warned.

The New England states, reacting to Spain's offer to open key ports to their ships if the Americans let the Spanish retain control of the Mississippi, scoffed at the western pioneers' agitation. A Boston newspaper declared, "The States of New England, closely confederated, can have nothing to fear." Dismissing Congress as "a useless and expensive establishment," the paper urged the withdrawal of their delegates and the creation of "a new nation . . . of New England." They should leave the rest of the continent "to pursue their own imbecile and disjointed plans."[6]

This was not the first, nor would it be the last glimpse of New England's assumption of moral and political superiority. Around the turn of the seventeenth century, the Reverend Cotton Mather had sent a book he had written on the perfection of New England's version of Protestantism to Mexico City. He was sure the ignorant Spanish Catholics would be converted by his arguments. Mather was unaware that Mexico City already had dozens of bookstores and its citizens were publishing—and reading—thousands of books.[7]

By the time an agreement on the new western states was reached in 1787, James Monroe had left Congress. But Jefferson's idea of a ban on slavery in the new states was still alive. The delegates decided to drop the southwestern territories from the proposal. This persuaded many Southern delegates to approve a ban in new states north of the Ohio River. The Northwest Ordinance, as this descendant of Jefferson's brainchild was soon called, would have an important impact on the future of slavery in America. But it was only a poor imitation of Jefferson's original proposal, which aimed at banning slavery from *all* the new states that he foresaw that America's westward surging pioneers would create.

.   .   .

Meanwhile, at Mount Vernon, George Washington was deeply involved in conversations with fellow Virginian James Madison about creating a stronger central government. As a congressman in the closing years of the Revolution, Madison had won General Washington's respect by backing a strong American union. But the Articles of Confederation repeatedly frustrated him (as well as Washington). It began to dawn on both men that a new constitution was necessary if America was going to survive as a truly united nation.[8]

The scholarly Madison, who had been studying the history of governments for a decade, soon contacted Alexander Hamilton and others discontented with the Articles of Confederation. In 1786, everyone was galvanized when a revolt against local taxes led by a bankrupt former Continental Army officer, Daniel Shays, roiled western Massachusetts and spilled into the western sections of other states. Congress, without an army or money to raise one, could only watch helplessly. Some people asked Washington to use his influence to calm the situation. "Influence is no government," he scathingly replied.[9]

With Washington presiding, fifty-five delegates met in Philadelphia in the late spring of 1787. Only eight had signed the Declaration of Independence, but thirty had served in the Continental Army, which made them especially aware of the flaws of the Articles of Confederation. For three months they debated and discussed and sometimes argued violently about a new constitution. Behind the scenes, at dinner meetings after the days' sessions, Washington pressed the case for a strong president with powers equal to Congress. He saw the lack of this office as the near-fatal flaw of the Articles of Confederation.

The presidency proved to be a very explosive issue. A great many people feared the office could become a dictatorship. Occasionally, when they met as a committee of the whole, where everyone spoke freely off the record, Washington was able to express his opinions. (As chairman, he could not participate in the floor debates.) There, he urged investing the president with the power to veto acts of Congress even if the lawmakers unanimously disagreed with him. Not a few delegates were troubled by this idea.[10]

There were ferocious conflicts on other issues. Small states were fearful that the large states would dominate the government. Eventually, the delegates reached compromises on the disputed points. They agreed to let Congress override a presidential veto if the lawmakers could muster a two-thirds vote. Small states and large states were reconciled by giving each state two spokesmen in the Senate, while the House of Representatives would be chosen on the basis of population.

At this point the South interposed a serious objection. Their large number of black slaves put them at a disadvantage, unless they too could be counted as part of their populations. More than a few northern delegates objected to this idea. Finally, the convention agreed to give Southern states the right to count three-fifths of their slaves in estimating the number of delegates they could send to the House of Representatives.

This compromise triggered acid remarks from some northern delegates. Elbridge Gerry of Massachusetts asked if northerners should have the right to count their horses and cattle as voters. New York's Gouverneur Morris demanded that "free" be inserted before the name of any citizen counted as a voter. He declared he was ready to pay taxes to liberate every Negro in America rather than countenance slavery in the Constitution. The motion was voted down ten to one.

Charles Cotesworth Pinckney of South Carolina warned that if the South did not receive some "security" for the right to own slaves, he would not support the new Constitution. The convention responded by proposing a clause that forbade Congress to ban or even to tax the importation of slaves. This stirred a negative response, even from some Southerners. George Mason of Virginia noted that the people settling the new lands in the Southwest were already calling for slaves. There was a real danger that they would "fill the country" with a surge of Africans. He sarcastically noted that not a few New Englanders were supporting this new demand because their ships made huge profits in the "evil traffic."

The men of the Deep South rose to answer Mason's assault. Pinckney reminded the delegates that slaves were "property" and the South had a right to expect all its property to be "as sacredly preserved and protected to them as that of land or any other kind of property in the Eastern States." John Rutledge spoke with even more precision. "Religion and humanity" had nothing to do with this issue, he declared. "The true question at present is whether the Southern states shall or shall not be parties to the Union." North Carolina made it clear that her delegates felt the same way.[11]

There it was, the specter of disunion that Washington and Madison had feared and went to Philadelphia hoping to dispel. A hastily concocted committee came up with another compromise. The slave trade would be permitted until 1808—an additional twenty years. At that time Congress would have the authority to ban or continue it. Madison and Mason fought this extension. But Connecticut's Oliver Ellsworth rose to voice the opinion of most delegates. They were in Philadelphia to make political, not ethical decisions. The nation's paramount need was political union.[12]

Was this a catastrophic moral failure, as more than a few people in future generations would claim? That is an exercise in the most tempting of all historical fallacies, hindsight. A majority of the delegates had expressed their abhorrence of slavery. Even the intransigent spokesmen for the Deep South made no attempt to defend it on moral grounds. Everyone wished—or hoped—that slavery would somehow come to a peaceful end, even though the practical details of emancipation remained obscure.

.   .   .

The chief creators of the Constitution were proud of the way they had defeated the primary threat that had brought them to Philadelphia—disunion. Few were more pleased with the outcome than George Washington. "No member of the convention" signed the final version of the Constitution "with more cordiality than he did," Madison reported. "Nor [was] more anxious for its ratification . . . he never wavered in giving it his sanction and support."[13]

It might be worth pausing at this point to ask why Washington and his contemporaries saw the union as so crucial to America's future. Their experience in the Revolution and the postwar years is the answer. They were all too aware of how often Britain had tried to lure various states and individuals to abandon the revolution with guarantees of extravagant rewards. The example of South Carolina's 1779 readiness to defect into neutrality to keep an invading British army at bay was a stark reminder of how easily a state could be seduced by a combination of fear and self-interest. It was all too obvious that the collapse of the union would turn America into another Europe, with states making and unmaking alliances and fighting ruinous wars with neighboring states in pursuit of more power and wealth.

.   .   .

That word, "wealth," requires another pause to discuss an invention that began transforming southern agriculture and southern thinking about slavery, virtually from the moment it appeared: Eli Whitney's cotton gin. Born in Connecticut, Whitney was one of those geniuses who saw better ways to make or improve everything from farm machinery to muskets. The big problem with raising cotton was the need to separate the fibers from their seeds, a job that required hours of painstaking labor. Whitney's gin combined a wire screen and small wire hooks to pull the cotton through, while brushes removed the lint to prevent jams. The gin multiplied the productivity—and profits—of raising cotton fifty times above the previous wearisome reliance on human hands.

This intrusion of such a totally unexpected invention (during Washington's first term as president) is perhaps the best reply to those who claim the founders failed to do enough to eliminate slavery. In 1790, there were only six slave states. The number steadily rose with the enormous profits from raising cotton. With the rise came an ever-growing need for more slaves to plant and pick the cotton. The arrival of "King Cotton" is a prime example of the way unexpected events and ideas intrude on a people and a nation, rendering assumptions about the future obsolete.[14]

. . .

For George Washington, slavery remained a troubling question, even while he took on the task of making his vision of a strong president into a working reality. An important reason why slavery remained in the forefront of his thoughts was the influence of the Marquis de Lafayette. By the time the war ended, the Marquis was calling Washington his "adopted father" and unburdening his mind to him on all sorts of subjects. Nothing troubled him more than slavery. Lafayette was especially upset to discover Americans had returned to the slave trade after the war ended. How could any American "perpetrate" such a thing "under our dear flag of liberty, the stars and stripes?" he asked.

As early as 1786, the year before the Constitutional Convention, Washington wrote to a friend, John Francis Mercer, that he hoped "never to possess another slave by purchase." Among his first wishes was to see a plan adopted by the Virginia legislature "by which slavery . . . can be abolished by slow sure & imperceptible degrees." He voiced a similar sentiment to Robert Morris, America's leading financier, in that same year. "There is not a man living who wishes more sincerely than I do to see a plan adopted for the abolition of it [slavery]."[15]

These words are evidence of how far George Washington had traveled from the complacent slave owner of the 1760s, enjoying the wealth and the dozens of slaves that widowed Martha Custis had brought to their 1759 marriage. The master of Mount Vernon was a tough taskmaster, who appraised his slaves' work with a critical eye. He had no illusions that the plantation's blacks enjoyed their bondage and were eager to work hard for him. "There are few Negroes who will work unless there is a constant eye on them," he told Martha during his presidency.

Washington did not flinch from having disobedient or recalcitrant slaves whipped. But he also told his overseers that he wanted "to feed & cloath them well, & be careful of them in sickness." Washington's account books record a steady flow of payments to both black and white doctors for ailing slaves. He clearly disagreed with the British West Indian attitude of treating slaves as easily replaced parts of the plantation business, giving them minimum care or consideration as human beings.

Washington also recognized the validity of slave marriage, which had no legal standing in Virginia. As he grew older, he became very sensitive on this point. He refused to break up marriages by selling the husband or wife. "To disperse families I have an utter aversion," he told one correspondent. He also tried to vary his slaves' diet by giving them permission to hunt and fish and tend gardens. Some Mount Vernon slaves owned boats and guns. One recalled that Washington often asked his permission to use his boat for a row on the Potomac, and always made a point of returning it exactly where the slave had left it.[16]

The Master of Mount Vernon was also ready to recognize talent and leadership among his blacks. He appointed several slaves as overseers of his outlying farms, and rewarded them if they did a good job. He remarked that one appointee, Davy, "carries on his business as well as the white overseers." To improve his dinner table, Davy received extra livestock, such as three hogs when they were slaughtered each year, and he enjoyed larger and more comfortable quarters than his fellow slaves. When it came to talent and willingness to work, Washington was remarkably free of race prejudice. Advertising for a good bricklayer, he told one man he did not care whether the artisan came from "Asia, Africa, or Europe."[17]

CHAPTER 5

The Forgotten Emancipator

No matter how much he grew in his appreciation and understanding of blacks as human beings, George Washington remained aware that slavery could not be eliminated without endangering the still-fragile American union. As president, he devoted most of his time and energy to establishing the new office as a key factor in this political enterprise. The nation swarmed with people hostile to a strong executive, and they soon found a leader in Thomas Jefferson, who had been in Paris as America's ambassador when the new national charter was created. Although Jefferson had agreed to serve as Washington's secretary of state, he had deep reservations about the wisdom of the new Constitution. He would have preferred simply to update the Articles of Confederation.

When President Washington declared America neutral in the war that erupted between England and Revolutionary France in 1793, Jefferson formed a pro-French political party. His followers were soon attacking the president savagely in newspapers and pamphlets. Pro-French mobs surged through the streets of Philadelphia to demonstrate in front of Washington's residence. In a letter to a European friend, Jefferson described the president as a "Samson who had allowed himself to be shorn by the harlot, England." One Jeffersonian journalist, James Thomson Callender, offered a toast at a public dinner "to the speedy death of President Washington."[1]

.   .   .

In the midst of this foreign policy turmoil, over the Allegheny Mountains came an even starker threat to disunion—the upheaval in western Pennsylvania that many people called "The Whiskey Rebellion." The name was in some respects a misnomer. The western counties had long had a surly relationship to the distant state and federal governments in Philadelphia. When Washington's secretary of the treasury, Alexander Hamilton, imposed a tax on the whiskey western farmers distilled from their grain, surliness rapidly became hostility.

Rabble-rousers denounced the "eastern aristocrats," and federal agents who tried to collect the taxes became targets for threats and harassment. From Canada, the British watched this development with considerable interest. They had hopes of confining their former colonies to the eastern seaboard, and they were arming and arousing the Indian tribes in the Ohio River Valley to launch a war of terror and murder against the Americans entering these fertile lands. A secession of the western counties of Pennsylvania, and perhaps of Virginia and North Carolina, fit neatly into this nasty plan. Some sort of satellite nation could be fabricated from these malcontents, financed by British pounds sterling.

President Washington soon saw the whiskey rebels as a menace to the Union. He summoned fifteen thousand militia from Virginia, Maryland, and Pennsylvania and put one of his best soldiers in command of it—Henry "Light Horse Harry" Lee, a brilliant cavalry leader during the Revolution. When this well-armed host descended on the whiskey rebels, their bravado vanished. In a few days they were pleading for mercy. The president pardoned them all, satisfied that he had made a very large point: the federal union was *perpetual* and its laws were to be obeyed by everyone in the nation.

Jefferson and his followers pointed to the lack of resistance and claimed that Washington had made a political mountain out of this local molehill.

President Washington let them talk. He was content to have set an example to which other presidents could turn. It fit nicely into the central purpose of his presidency—to create an office that had the power to deal with crises without waiting for an indecisive Congress to make up its collective mind.[2]

Unfortunately, this foreign and domestic turmoil convinced Washington that it would be a grave mistake to bring an issue as divisive as emancipation before the public. Recently, historians have found evidence that the president was seriously considering it. In 1794, he discussed with his confidential secretary, Tobias Lear, the possibility of selling his western lands to enable him to "liberate a certain species of property which I possess, very repugnantly to my own feelings." But he reluctantly abandoned this idea, which might well have given slavery a mortal wound, if not a deathblow.[3]

. . .

In 1796, the final year of his second term, Washington found himself bombarded with pleas to run for president again. Shrewd politician that he was, he saw this would play into the hands of the Jeffersonians, who would orate about him becoming "president for life." He was also a very tired man. But he remained deeply concerned about the future of this nation to which he had devoted forty-five years of his life. He decided to issue a statement explaining why he chose not to seek a third term—and also advising the American people on the course he hoped they would pursue to reach that elusive goal proclaimed in the Declaration of Independence—happiness.

The result was a document instantly christened "The Farewell Address" and printed in virtually every newspaper in the nation. It contained a great deal of good advice, based on Washington's experience as a general and president. He urged everyone to avoid "passionate attachments" to foreign nations. He praised "morality and religion" as the "great pillars of human happiness." But at the head of his list of concerns was the issue that remained central to his vision of America's future—the federal union.

"The unity of government which constitutes you one people . . . is a main Pillar . . . of your real independence, the support of your tranquility at home; your peace abroad; of your safety; of your prosperity; of that very liberty which you so highly prize." It must be guarded with "jealous anxiety" to shatter "any attempt to alienate any portion of our country from the rest, or to enfeeble the sacred ties which now link together the various parts." Washington admitted that the South, the North, the East, and the West might have special interests or strengths. But they must be first of all *American* "by an indissoluble community of interest as *one* nation."[4]

None of the other large topics Washington touched on came close to inspiring the emotional intensity he poured into the passages exhorting Americans to preserve this bedrock foundation of his hopes for America— and his vision of a nation united by "fraternal affection."

.   .   .

Two years after Washington left the presidency, Thomas Jefferson challenged this principle of the primacy of the Union. President John Adams and the Federalist Party majority in Congress, enraged by the abuse Adams was receiving from the Jeffersonian press for his refusal to alter the policy of neutrality in the ongoing war between Great Britain and France, passed two laws that have become known as the Alien and Sedition Acts. One gave the federal government the power to deport any alien whom it deemed dangerous to the security of the republic. The second empowered the government to prosecute anyone who libeled the president and other officers of the government.

Federalist-appointed judges soon had several Jeffersonian newspaper editors on trial. None of them could prove the insults and wild accusations they had flung at the president. The idea that a newspaper was supposed to tell the truth would not be accepted by most editors and reporters for another hundred years. The newspaper remained the "political engine" that President Adams had said it was twenty-five years earlier, on the eve of the Revolution.

Jeffersonian-Republican outrage soon produced an excess to counter this Federalist assault on a free press. Jefferson persuaded James Madison to join him in writing letters to the legislatures of Virginia and the new state of

Kentucky, urging them to protest this federal edict. Madison was temperate in his appeal. Jefferson was extreme. He assured the Kentucky legislature that a state could "nullify" any act of Congress, whenever it felt the law impinged on the rights or interests of its citizens.

Washington was so appalled, he appealed to Patrick Henry to emerge from retirement and persuade Virginia to disavow her allegiance to this ruinous doctrine. Henry died before he could respond to the summons. While Washington sought another spokesman, the grim reaper began stalking him too.[5]

. . .

In 1786, the Marquis de Lafayette had informed Washington that he had bought a plantation in the French South American colony of Cayenne (later French Guiana), where he planned to free a group of slaves and educate them to demonstrate to the world that blacks could live and work independently. He hoped Washington would join him in this enterprise. The older man wrote his adopted son a letter, praising "the benevolence of your heart," and warmly approved the experiment. But he did not accept Lafayette's invitation to become his partner. Instead, Washington sadly wished that "a like spirit would diffuse itself generally into the minds of the people of this country but I despair of seeing it."[6]

The cascade of violence and passion that the French Revolution unleashed in France soon claimed Lafayette as one of its victims. Parisian radicals—the infamous Jacobins—seized power and made him a candidate for the guillotine. The Marquis's property was confiscated and his plantation in Cayenne collapsed. He was forced to flee France, hoping to find refuge in America. But the Austrians, at war with the French, flung the Marquis into prison and ignored Washington's attempts to free him.

The Marquis's harsh fate almost certainly influenced Washington's attitude toward the French Revolution—and slavery. It reinforced his decision not to make a public statement about slavery while French extremism was dividing America. His desire to free his slaves was regretfully shelved for the foreseeable future.

•   •   •

As president, Washington displayed a grim realism about slavery when the issue intruded on his administration. In 1792, Southerners persuaded Congress to pass a bill requiring the federal government to help capture runaway slaves. Washington signed it without a comment. When Quakers, more and more militant about slavery, presented an emancipation proposal to Congress, Washington did not say a word in its support. Instead he made an approving comment to a friend when Congress ignored the plea.

The president apparently shared the negative opinion of Quakerism that most Americans had developed during the Revolution. The Quakers had refused to participate in the war, to the point of declining to pay taxes. To those who were risking their lives and property in this struggle for liberty, the sect seemed either cowardly or hypocritical or both. These mistakes had ruined any hope of the Quakers becoming an effective voice for emancipation.

Not even Benjamin Franklin, a man whom Washington admired, changed the president's mind about publicly backing emancipation. In the last year of his life, Franklin had become the leader of the Pennsylvania Society for Promoting the Abolition of Slavery and sent an emancipation plea to Congress. When Senator James Jackson of Georgia sneeringly dismissed it, claiming that American blacks were perfectly contented as slaves, Franklin responded with one of his best hoaxes.

He published a letter in the *Federal Gazette* saying that Jackson's speech reminded him of a similar argument by a Muslim ruler of Algiers a hundred years ago, as recorded in "Martin's Account of his consulship, anno 1687." The Muslim was responding to a plea to release the thousands of Christians toiling as slaves in his country. His reply marvelously paralleled Jackson's speech. He insisted that the slaves were needed to keep Algiers prosperous. He also maintained that the Christians were all perfectly happy and much more contented with their lives as obedient well-fed bondsmen than they had ever been in their Christian birthplaces, where they were required "to cut the throats of their fellow Christians" in their frequent wars. President Washington may well have chuckled about the jest in private; he enjoyed a good joke. But he said not a word in public. A year later the eighty-four-year-old Franklin's voice was silenced by death.[7]

. . .

During Washington's retirement years, an English visitor to Mount Vernon discussed slavery with him, off the record. The ex-president admitted black bondage looked like a crime, even an absurdity, in the light of the Declaration of Independence. But it was neither. "Till the mind of the slave has been educated to perceive what are the obligations of a state of freedom ... the gift would ensure its abuse. No man desires ... this event ... more heartily than I do. Not only do I pray for it on the score of human dignity, but I can clearly foresee that nothing but the rooting out of slavery can perpetuate the existence of our union by consolidating it in a common bond of principle."

Those words reveal that George Washington had travelled from complacent slave owner to believer in the humanity of black people to would-be emancipator. But he still saw no practical way to make emancipation work in Virginia or any other southern state.[8]

Several months later, the ex-president had an unnerving dream. He was sitting with Martha, chatting about their happy memories, when a "great light" suddenly surrounded them. From it emerged an angel who whispered in Martha's ear. Martha "suddenly turned pale and began to vanish" from his sight. The obvious interpretation was Martha's early death. But Washington told her that dreams often have opposite meanings. "I may soon leave you," he said.

Martha tried to make a joke of the dream, but Washington remained haunted by it. Soon Martha came across scraps of writing in his study that indicated he was composing his will. The document began with a very predictable sentence. He directed his executors to care for "my dearly beloved wife Martha" for the rest of her life. The second sentence revealed why Washington had made this abrupt decision, now. "Upon the death of my wife, it is my Will & desire that all the Slaves which I hold in my *own right* shall receive their freedom." Following that declaration were three pages of extremely explicit directives for his slaves' emancipation. He wanted them to be educated and trained to earn a living. Aging or ill slaves who could not leave Mount Vernon were to be supported there until their deaths.

The ex-president did not mince words. "I do hereby expressly forbid the sale . . . of any slave I may die possessed of, under any pretence whatsoever." Summing up, he commanded all concerned "to see that *this* clause respecting slaves and every part thereof be religiously fulfilled without evasion, neglect or delay."

In a South where many thought blacks should not be taught to read and write, or worse, that they could not be taught, Washington was calling for their education. He was also emancipating all his slaves in one stroke of his pen—something he clearly sensed his heirs would not like. If Martha had not been alive, he may well have freed them all immediately. Out of consideration for her, he delayed their emancipation until her death because so many of his slaves had intermarried with slaves that belonged to her.[9]

.   .   .

Six months later, in December 1799, Washington awoke with an alarming constriction in his throat, which made it extremely difficult for him to breathe. He awoke Martha and asked her to send for their family doctor. But there was little the physician or other doctors who were summoned could do with the primitive medical skills of their era. Already suffering from a bad cold, Washington had contracted an infection of his epiglottis, a cartilage just below his larynx. At the end of an agonizing day of struggling for breath, which he endured with remarkable stoicism, he died with Martha weeping beside him.

The news of Washington's death fell like a thunderclap from on high across the entire nation. The loss was so huge, so absolute, it seemed to alter everything from the nation's politics to its confidence in the future. The fact that he had emancipated his slaves dwindled to a blip in the context of the other meanings of his departure. His act of emancipation excited little or no comment. Part of the reason may have been the fact that the slaves all had to remain at Mount Vernon until Martha's death. There was no opportunity for newspaper stories of an exodus to freedom.

A year later, Martha freed all Washington's slaves unilaterally, and allowed them to leave Mount Vernon. Why? When President Adams's wife, Abigail, visited Mount Vernon on the first anniversary of Washington's death, Martha told her she feared one of the freed slaves might poison her to hasten their emancipation. Abigail, who described Martha's anxiety in a letter to her sister, thought it was doleful proof of "the banefull [*sic*] effects of slavery." Abigail's dislike of the institution had been visible in her letters to John even in 1776, when he was persuading the Continental Congress to vote for independence.[10]

Martha Washington's reaction revealed that emancipating slaves could be a complex business. Martha and most of her grandchildren (her four children were dead) did not agree with Washington's decision. Only her grandson, George Washington Parke Custis, honored Washington's example and freed his slaves at his death.

This disagreement was the reason for the tone of command in the emancipation pages of Washington's will. Even if Martha had agreed with her husband, she could not have freed her slaves. Under the terms of her first husband's will, they belonged to her only during her lifetime. At her death these "dower slaves" were to be handed on to her Custis descendants.[11]

George Washington's inability to convince the people closest to him, above all his beloved wife of forty years, was an ominous omen for the future of black freedom in the South. The second Emancipation Proclamation was as ignored and forgotten as the first one.

Fifty-eight years later, Washington's example would have an ironic resurrection. When George Washington Parke Custis died in 1857, the man who was responsible for freeing his slaves was his son-in-law, Lieutenant Colonel Robert E. Lee. The impact of the experience on this already famous soldier became a tragic turning point in American history.

CHAPTER 6

Thomas Jefferson's Nightmare

In 1800, the year after George Washington died, Thomas Jefferson was elected third president of the United States. One of the new chief executive's early visitors was Louis-André Pichon, the affable young chargé d'affaires of the new French republic. Jefferson greeted him warmly as the spokesman for a country that had long stirred his deepest political emotions.

Chargé Pichon asked what the president would do or say if Paris sent an army to the rebellious island of Saint-Domingue to restore it to French control. For over a century France had owned a third of the island. The Spanish, who owned the larger slice, called it Santo Domingo—the name that most Americans used.

The French section's sugar, coffee, and indigo plantations had made it France's most valuable overseas possession until the 1789 revolution in Paris triggered a civil war that had wrecked the economy. For American merchants, Saint-Domingue had been a prime customer. In 1790, U.S. exports to the island, mostly food and lumber, amounted to $3 million, second only to the $6.9 million in similar products that the Americans shipped to England.

The French Revolution's cry of liberty, equality, and fraternity had reached Saint-Domingue early in the 1790s. The precarious social mixture of royal officials, rich creole planters, middle class storekeepers and craftsmen, and free mulattoes was sitting on a potential volcano of 500,000 black slaves, whose toil on the plantations created the island's wealth. The mulattoes were almost as numerous as the whites and frequently as wealthy. They owned an estimated 100,000 slaves. But they were forbidden to dress like white men. They could not marry a white woman. They could not carry guns. If a mulatto struck a white man, his hand would be amputated. A white man could strike a mulatto and risk nothing but a fine.

The black slaves, called *noirs,* were kept under control with unspeakable brutalities. This cry of rage from a man who spent half his life as a *noir* is a grisly summary of French slave owners' tactics.

> Have they not hung up men with heads downward, drowned them in sacks, crucified them on planks, buried them alive, crushed them in mortars? Have they not forced them to eat shit? And, having flayed them with the lash, have they not cast them alive to be devoured by worms or on anthills or lashed them on stakes in the swamps to be devoured by mosquitos? Have they not thrown them into boiling cauldrons of cane syrup? Have they not put men and women into barrels studded with spikes and rolled them down mountainsides into the abyss? Have they not consigned these miserable blacks to man-eating dogs until the latter, sated by human flesh, left the mangled victims to be finished off by bayonet and poniard?[1]

As early as 1685, a French official wrote: "In the Negroes we have redoubtable domestic enemies." Hundreds of slaves fled into the mountains and became maroons, whose legends had inspired John Brown. Some of these communities lasted for decades, repeatedly repulsing or evading troops sent to destroy them. The most fearsome of these early rebels was one-armed Francois Macandal, who preached a terrifying doctrine: death to all whites.

When war erupted between Great Britain and Revolutionary France in 1793 and the Jacobins seized control of the French National Assembly, they issued a declaration freeing all the slaves in France's overseas dominions. The move was motivated only in part by a belief in universal liberty. The radicals also hoped to trigger slave revolts in Jamaica and other English colonies and in the United States. By that time President George Washington had declared America neutral in the global war—an act the French considered a betrayal of the treaty of alliance they had signed with the embryo United States in 1778.

When news of the Jacobin decree reached Saint-Domingue, a civil war of unbelievable ferocity exploded, with royalist whites fighting Jacobin whites and mulattos and blacks, compounded by the invasion of a British army. In the island's prosperous northern plain, slaves came out of the night to burn plantation houses and massacre their owners. All the equipment of sugar production, the boiling houses, the mills, the warehouses, was destroyed.

·   ·   ·

Out of this sanguinary turmoil had emerged a charismatic black leader, Toussaint Louverture, a short, wiry forty-seven-year-old former coachman and veterinarian on a plantation owned by the Comte de Breda. So thin he was nicknamed "the Broomstick," Toussaint could read and write—and think. He preached equality between blacks and whites and started creating a multiracial society.[2]

President John Adams and his secretary of state, Timothy Pickering, saw Louverture as an opportunity to frustrate British and French imperialism in the Caribbean and maintain America's lucrative trade with Saint-Domingue. They shipped supplies and ammunition to Louverture's army, and at Alexander Hamilton's suggestion they sent his boyhood friend Edward Stevens, born on the Danish island of St. Croix, to Saint-Domingue's major port, Cap Francois, where he became Louverture's trusted friend and advisor. The Adams administration even ordered the small American fleet in the Caribbean to show the flag at Cap Francois. Without quite saying it, they urged Louverture to declare independence.

Louverture routed the British army and became the de facto ruler of Saint-Domingue. His troops quickly conquered the Spanish part of the island as well. Edward Stevens asked Alexander Hamilton to advise the black leader on a constitution. True to his authoritarian instincts, Hamilton told Louverture to appoint himself governor general for life—and enroll every able-bodied man in the militia. An assembly was also added to the government's structure, but it had no power to initiate legislation.[3]

With driving energy, Louverture invited whites, blacks, and mulattoes to join him in restoring a semblance of prosperity to Saint-Domingue. He banned slavery forever but persuaded most of the former slaves to return to the plantations to work as paid draftees in the service of the state. Unfortunately, he never trusted the slave-owning Americans enough to declare independence. He retained a frequently expressed loyalty to Revolutionary France, which had given his race their freedom.

· · ·

In 1799, Napoleon Bonaparte seized power in Paris. One of his many careening ambitions was the restoration of France's colonial empire. This was the reason why Pichon visited President Jefferson to ask about Saint-Domingue. Jefferson's reply exceeded Pichon's most sanguine hopes. The new president urged Pichon to tell his government that America was eager to help restore French rule in Saint-Domingue. He welcomed France's proposal to send an army to crush the black rebels. "Nothing will be easier than [for us] to furnish your army and fleet with everything and to reduce Toussaint to starvation," Jefferson said.[4]

There was a reason for the urgency that Jefferson concealed in his reply. During the 1790s, the upheaval on Saint-Domingue had prompted more than a few white French planters to flee the island for the comparative safety of the United States, where they talked of their often harrowing experiences. Inevitably, American slaves overheard some of these stories and wondered if this triumph over slave owners might be repeated in America. As early as 1793, Virginian John Randolph claimed to have caught two slaves discussing plans for an uprising that would massacre the whites "as the blacks had killed the whites in the French islands." Other rumors and reports of black plots and threats had swirled through Virginia and other Southern states in succeeding years.[5]

In 1800, while Jefferson was running against incumbent John Adams for president, Virginia had been shaken by a slave revolt led by a twenty-five-year-old black preacher named Gabriel. Obviously inspired by events on Saint-Domingue, Gabriel had recruited over a thousand fellow slaves to march on Richmond on the night of August 30. There they planned to seize the state arsenal, arm themselves, and kill all the whites in the state except a handful of Quakers and Methodists who were "friendly to liberty."

Gabriel and his men had gathered at the appointed hour in woods about six miles from Richmond. Before they could march, a violent rainstorm pelted down, washing out bridges and submerging roads. The storm lasted most of the night, forcing the plotters to return to their plantations. The next day, a slave who had refused to join the conspiracy told his master what had almost happened. Governor James Monroe called out hundreds of well-armed state militia with orders to shoot to kill if necessary. Gabriel, his brother, and about thirty others were seized and sentenced to death.[6]

Governor Monroe wrote a full report on Virginia's narrow escape and sent a copy to Thomas Jefferson. Telling the grisly news to a Philadelphia friend, the presidential candidate said: "We are truly to be pitied."

Those anguished words reveal Jefferson's inner struggle over slavery, and his growing conviction that blacks and whites could never be reconciled. That ambivalence had made him ignore—or dismiss—Toussaint Louverture's attempt to create a multiracial society. Jefferson considered this an impossibility, and he was eager to see Louverture removed from power before his example inspired more Gabriels to rise in Virginia and other southern states.[7]

·   ·   ·

In Europe, Jefferson's election as president had coincided with the mutual exhaustion of France and Britain after eight years of global warfare. As peace negotiations began in November 1801, Napoleon shipped a 20,000-man army to Saint-Domingue, commanded by his brother-in-law, General Charles Leclerc.

Unknown to Jefferson, this expedition had another larger purpose. In March 1801, the "Man of Destiny," as Napoleon liked to be called, had browbeaten the reluctant Spanish king into retroceding the immense territory of Louisiana to France. It had been given to Spain in 1763 as compensation for her losses in the Seven Years' War. In secret orders, Bonaparte told Leclerc to transfer the bulk of his army to New Orleans as soon as he restored French supremacy in Saint-Domingue, a task that Bonaparte estimated would take only six weeks. The goal was the creation of a self-sufficient overseas empire.

Louisiana would supply Saint-Domingue and the other French West Indian islands with food at cut-rate prices, eliminating the need to buy from the Americans. The islands would continue to produce sugar, coffee, and indigo to swell France's depleted exchequer. Ships of other nations would be excluded from carrying this lucrative cargo.

A confident Leclerc arrived off the port of Cap Francois in February 1802 and promptly went to work on "the gilded Africans," as Napoleon contemptuously called the black rebels. The size of the French fleet and army made Louverture and his generals more than a little suspicious. It was much too large to be the escort of a delegation from Paris, reaffirming France's theoretical sovereignty. The French had sent several of these ambassadors during the previous tumultuous decade.

When Leclerc called on Jean Christophe, one of Louverture's best generals, to surrender the port city, he declined. Leclerc promptly attacked from land and sea. Christophe responded by burning Cap Francois and retreating into the countryside.

All-out war erupted throughout Saint-Domingue. At first it seemed to go well for the French. The Spanish section of the island was quickly occupied with the help of the resident white and mulatto population. Black garrisons in other ports surrendered to oncoming French brigades. In ten days Leclerc captured all the key ports and coastal forts and was preparing an offensive into the interior. But Toussaint Louverture remained beyond his grasp, and another black general, Jean-Jacques Dessalines, rampaged through the countryside, slaughtering every white person he found—and any black who tried to help them.

An attempt at negotiations failed, and on February 18, 1802, Leclerc launched an offensive against Louverture's interior stronghold, Gonaives. Advancing in four columns, the French discovered they had to wade through "fire and bayonets" for every foot of ground. Losses were heavy on both sides, but the offensive paid off when several black generals switched sides. Leclerc combined force with lavish offers of money and power to those who joined him in a pacified Saint-Domingue.

General Leclerc discovered a strange illness was creeping through the French part of his army. Soldiers weakened without warning; in a day they were too sick to walk. Then came black vomit, yellowing skin, convulsions, and death. The disease was yellow fever, inflicted by the bite of the female mosquito, *Aedes aegypti*. But the French commander, as determined and as ruthless as his imperious brother-in-law, pressed his offensive, and soon more black generals—notably the gifted Jean Christophe—switched sides.

.   .   .

On May 1, Toussaint Louverture suddenly agreed to peace terms. He would give up power and retire with a moderate-sized bodyguard to a plantation in the interior. His generals and officers would receive equivalent ranks in the French army, which became 50 percent black. Toussaint had learned that Napoleon had signed a definitive treaty of peace with the British at Amiens. This left him and his army at the mercy of Bonaparte's vastly superior numbers and weaponry. The black leader capitulated, hoping to get the best possible deal from Leclerc. Louverture's murderous second in command, Dessalines, sullenly accepted similar terms on May 6.[8]

The war was far from over. Guerilla resistance continued to flare throughout the interior of the island. Leclerc also confronted problems beyond Saint-Domingue's horizon. In the first months of 1802, Jefferson and his secretary of state, James Madison, learned that the French now owned Louisiana. Next, the American ambassador in London warned them of

Napoleon's plan to make Saint-Domingue a mere way station on Leclerc's voyage to New Orleans.

Jefferson's love affair with the French Revolution came to an abrupt halt under the influence of the cooler, more suspicious Madison. On Saint-Domingue, *Aedes aegypti* was still hard at work, decimating the French regiments. Noting Leclerc's growing weakness, a watchful Louverture began intriguing for a comeback.

Leclerc was watching him, too. Lured to a nearby plantation without his usual armed escort, the black leader was seized, thrown on a ship, and deported to France as a common criminal. There, Napoleon deposited him in a freezing fortress in the Jura Mountains, where Louverture would die a year later.

.   .   .

At this point Bonaparte made a ruinous blunder. Pressured by refugee planters from Saint-Domingue and by numerous merchants in Le Havre and other French ports who had grown rich on the slave trade, he decided to reimpose slavery on Saint-Domingue and other French islands. When word of this decision reached Saint-Domingue in June 1802, the black masses rose in fury against the French and the black soldiers allied with them. Captain-General Leclerc was stunned by the ferocity of the blacks' resistance. "These men die with an incredible fanaticism; they laugh at death; it is the same with the women," he said.

General Leclerc ordered Chargé Louis Pichon to obtain food and war materiel from America. He was even more eager for Jefferson and Madison to make good on their promise to starve the blacks into submission. The president and secretary of state informed the dismayed Pichon that they would not be able to starve the rebels after all. An agitated Pichon reported that he had found President Jefferson "very reserved and cold."[9]

Badly weakened by a growing food shortage and a lack of medical supplies, the French were unable to sustain their counteroffensive. Whole regiments began succumbing to yellow fever. Soon an appalling 60 percent of General Leclerc's staff was dead. On November 2, 1802, the French commander himself succumbed.

A grimly determined Napoleon poured in 15,000 replacements and continued the struggle. For a while the fresh troops seemed on the way to restoring French control of the island. But in Europe events were unfolding that soon turned these victories into hollow triumphs. The British decided that their experiment with a purportedly peace-loving Napoleon was not working. It soon became obvious that the war for world supremacy was about to resume.[10]

. . .

With that near certainty in mind, Napoleon rethought his plans for Louisiana. Bonaparte badly needed money for his war machine. When Ambassador Robert R. Livingston visited him in early 1803, Napoleon asked him how much he would be willing to pay for all of Louisiana. The amazed ambassador was soon joined by special envoy James Monroe, who could speak for President Jefferson. By July 1803, they had bought 868,000 square miles of North America—a third of the continent—for $15 million.

Napoleon continued the struggle to subdue Saint-Domingue, stirring fears that he might repudiate the Louisiana deal. But the moment news of the declaration of renewed war reached the Caribbean, the British West Indies fleet made Saint-Domingue target number one. The royal navy bombarded French-held seaports and smuggled guns and encouragement to the rebels. In November 1803, their army reduced to eight thousand men, the French retreated to Cap Francois and surrendered to a British fleet cruising offshore.

While France's hopes of colonial wealth and power vanished forever, triumph was the order of the day in Washington, DC. A special session of Congress confirmed President Jefferson's decision to pay Napoleon's price for New Orleans and the Louisiana Territory, doubling the size of the United States. Jefferson, with his gift for the electrifying phrase, declared the entire North American continent would soon become an "Empire of Liberty."[11]

. . .

General Jean-Jacques Dessalines, who had long since switched back to the rebel side, became the ruler of Saint-Domingue. He decided to begin the new year (1804) with a declaration of independence. A brigadier who acted as his secretary, Louis Felix Boisrond-Tonnerre, eagerly seconded the idea. What they needed in order to make the declaration authentic, Boisrond-Tonnerre roared, was "the skin of a white for parchment, his skull for an inkwell, his blood for ink, and a bayonet for a pen!"

A delighted Dessalines, who could not read or write, ordered Boisrond-Tonnerre to compose the declaration. "Make people know how I feel about the whites!" he said. He had long since made that clear by his merciless conduct on the battlefield. To underscore the new nation's policy, he picked up a French tricolor and cut the white strip out of it, creating a new national flag.

On January 1, 1804, a huge celebration took place at Toussaint Louverture's old stronghold, the inland town of Gonaives. After a day of feasting and dancing, General Dessalines mounted a platform draped in the new flags, and with a wave of his hand he silenced the pounding kettledrums and trumpets. The short stocky general proclaimed the island independent of France and declared it would henceforth be known by its Carib Indian name, Haiti. Then he summoned Boisrond-Tonnerre to read the Declaration of Independence.

It began with a war cry. "We must live free or we must die!" A paragraph exhorted the listeners to "look about you for your wives, husbands, brothers, sisters. Where have they gone? They have fallen prey to these vultures" (the whites). The rest of the document was a raging denunciation of France and French whites.

The mere news of this declaration inspired not a few Frenchmen to charter ships to send their families and moveable property elsewhere. But when they arrived at various ports to embark, armed soldiers blocked their paths and ordered them to return to their homes.

General Dessalines had decided Haiti must be cleansed of everyone white. On March 9 he marched into the port of Jeremie and dragged every white male in the city into the town square. Dessalines gazed contemptuously at them and snarled: "You whites of Jeremie—I know how you hate me . . . The blood of you all shall pay!"

Five doctors, an American visitor, and a few foreign merchants were shoved to the other side of the square. Next Dessalines offered amnesty to about four hundred men of property if they would pay substantial ransoms before sundown. The rest were hacked to death by ax-wielding execution-ers. The four hundred reprieved men paid their ransoms well before sun-down. But they were not released. During the night, they were all beheaded and their bodies left in a huge pile.

Dessalines marched to other cities and repeated this gruesome perfor-mance. Some of his generals, such as Jean Christophe, tried to dissuade him. They had become friendly with many of these doomed Frenchmen. They needed their help to restore Haiti's prosperity. But the new ruler was impla-cable. French men, women, and children died in the same merciless way.

In one or two ports, Dessalines's more compassionate lieutenants al-lowed some Frenchmen and their families to escape to nearby ships. A few foreign merchants used bribes and persuasion to help others flee. One Scot-tish merchant from Baltimore was later given a gold medal by French refu-gees in that city to express their gratitude.

Dessalines closed his campaign with a masterful final act of treachery. He issued a proclamation, calling on whites who had remained in hiding to emerge, guaranteeing them safe conduct to departing ships. A few dozen took him at his word—and met instant death from the waiting ax-men.[12]

· · ·

It is not hard to imagine what President Thomas Jefferson thought and felt when the story of the extermination of Haiti's whites reached Washington, DC, and other American cities in the spring of 1804. Instead of a prosper-ous multiracial nation under Toussaint Louverture, Jefferson had helped to create a wrecked and desolated island in the grip of an illiterate, half-mad despot. Haiti's blood-soaked birth made the ultimate meaning of the term *race war* an unforgettable nightmare. It was soon on its way to becoming a disease of the public mind in the southern states.

The horrified president could think of only one solution: Haiti had to be as isolated as possible from the United States of America. A few months after Dessalines had completed his slaughter, Jefferson's son-in-law, Congressman John W. Eppes, rose in the House of Representatives to introduce a resolution, calling on the United States to refuse to recognize Haiti's independence. Henceforth Americans would have no further political contact with the Republic of Haiti. Everyone knew this was a message from the president. It passed overwhelmingly.[13]

· · ·

Why did President Jefferson manage to escape without a word of reproach or criticism, both in the North and the South, for the awful fate he had helped to visit on Haiti? Few people besides James Madison knew about the president's approval of Napoleon's invasion. The public blame fell on France.

Even if the whole truth were known, there is another reason why most Americans would probably have found little fault with the president: the Louisiana Purchase. This diplomatic triumph had opened virtually endless acres of fertile western land to the nation's farmers and would-be farmers. The acquisition guaranteed Thomas Jefferson's popularity for decades to come. In 1804, he was reelected by an overwhelming majority. His Federalist opponent carried only two states.

But in Thomas Jefferson's troubled soul, the nightmare generated by Haiti never went away. On the contrary, it redoubled his fear that the problem of slavery in the South was insoluble and would eventually destroy the United States of America, either in a race war or in a civil war between North and South.

· · ·

A few months after General Dessalines ended his blood-soaked final campaign, he wrote a letter to President Jefferson, expressing the hope that an independent Haiti could establish diplomatic relations with the United States. Here was a moment that might have altered Haiti's tragic future.

The letter revealed that Dessalines's rage did not extend to all white men. It was the treacherous French whom he had hated and punished. He had conspicuously spared American lives in his final rampage. The dictator and his advisors were remembering the friendly relationship that Toussaint Louverture had enjoyed with America during President John Adams's administration.

For President Jefferson, the letter posed a stark political danger. It could lead to the exposure of his initial encouragement of the French attempt to reconquer Haiti and reimpose slavery. Jefferson never answered Dessalines. Haiti was cut adrift to reel through decades of instability and demoralizing poverty.

Other nations treated Haiti even more deplorably. Before resuming diplomatic and commercial relations, the French insisted on a huge indemnity for property destroyed or seized in the upheavals of the 1790s. Nevertheless, America's chance to alter Haiti's history—and perhaps eliminate the South's dread of a race war—was lost forever. President Thomas Jefferson's silence is one of those hidden turning points that leave historians brooding over what might have been.

CHAPTER 7

New England Preaches—and Almost Practices—Secession

While average citizens welcomed the Louisiana Purchase with enthusiasm and began voting for Thomas Jefferson and his Republican Party (often called "Democratic-Republican" by modern historians), the leaders of the defeated Federalist Party remained unreconciled. In Boston's *Columbian Centinel*, a Federalist spokesman voiced an angry fear of the future. "This unexplored empire, of the size of four or five European kingdoms," would destroy the balance of the Union. Louisiana was currently "a great waste, unpeopled with any beings besides wolves and wandering Indians." But in coming years it would be divided into states, all of whom would follow Virginia's political leadership.[1]

When the treaty approving the purchase was submitted to Congress, Federalist representative Roger Griswold of Connecticut declared the Constitution had no provision for acquiring new territory, and Louisiana would have to be governed as a colony, the way the British ruled Jamaica. Senator Timothy Pickering of Massachusetts, who had been secretary of state under President John Adams, went even further. He asserted Jefferson would need the unanimous approval of every state in the Union to sign the treaty. Senator John Breckinridge of the new state of Kentucky replied that if Congress rejected the treaty, Kentucky and Tennessee would secede from the Union and form a separate country.[2]

The Jeffersonians ignored the Federalists and the treaty was approved, thanks to the majorities they commanded in both houses of Congress. But the Federalists, led by Senator Pickering and former Congressman Fisher Ames, the party's leader in Massachusetts, continued to condemn the purchase of Louisiana. They predicted the prospect of cheap land would depopulate the East and lure badly needed workers from the new factories that were opening in New England. The only solution, as Ames saw it, was for the Federalists "to entrench themselves in the state governments and endeavor to make state justice and state power a shelter of the wise, the good and the rich from the wild destroying rage of the Southern Jacobins."

Pickering went further than Ames. He decided New England, and hopefully neighboring New York, to which thousands of New Englanders were emigrating, should secede from the Union, form a new country, and seek the protection and alliance of Great Britain to defend them against the Jacobinic Jeffersonians. He conferred with Vice President Aaron Burr, who had quarreled with the president and was unlikely to be on the ticket when Jefferson ran for reelection in 1804. Burr, a New Englander by blood, agreed to run for governor of New York with Federalist support. If he won, he would lead New York into the new nation.

The conspiracy again revealed the intensity of New England's conviction that they were the predestined leaders of an independent America. Their defiance of George III and his Parliament had triggered the American Revolution. Hadn't John Adams, the "Atlas of Independence" in the Continental Congress, selected George Washington to lead the army and Thomas Jefferson to write the Declaration of Independence? The Pilgrim fathers had seen Plymouth as "one small candle . . . [that] hath shone unto many, yea in some sort to our whole nation." The Puritans who founded Boston had prophesied it would be a "city upon a hill watched by the world." Now these arrogant Virginians were taking charge of the United States of America. It was intolerable![3]

Here were the seeds of a primary disease of the public mind, which would soon fuse with antislavery to create a hatred of the South and Southerners, with tragic consequences for America's future.[4]

. . .

Nothing came of Senator Pickering's plot. Slandered and smeared with special savagery by the Jeffersonian Republicans as a traitor to the party, Burr lost his race for governor of New York. Jefferson's landslide reelection in 1804 soon swept the Republican Party into power in Massachusetts. But the seeds of discontent and suspicion of Virginia's leadership had been planted in many minds. These burst into dangerous bloom in Jefferson's second term, when he confronted the threat of war with Great Britain over London's arrogant interference with American overseas commerce. The British insisted their blockade of France and her European allies entitled them to seize American ships and kidnap American sailors into the Royal Navy. The French were equally ready to assault American ships trading with Britain. Instead of war, the president declared an embargo against trade with Britain, France, and the rest of the civilized world.

The embargo had a devastating impact on New England, home of most of America's million-ton merchant fleet. Tens of thousands of restless, angry seamen were left idle in her ports. In Newburyport, once the third busiest harbor in Massachusetts, seventy ships rocked and rotted at their anchors. Merchants went bankrupt everywhere. One critic raged that it was like "cutting a man's throat to cure a nosebleed." In December 1808, on the first anniversary of the president's decree, down-at-the-heel sailors dragged a mastless ship along Newburyport's rundown streets, with a helmsman wearing a placard: "Which way shall I steer?"

Massachusetts Federalists used the embargo's distress to publish a warning: "A Separation of the States and its Consequences to New England." Led by Senator Pickering (Fisher Ames had died), the Federalists regularly condemned President Jefferson's supposed partiality to France. When some infuriated New Englanders began smuggling exports and imports to and from Canada in defiance of the embargo, the president asked Congress to pass a force bill, empowering him to make war on them with the U.S. Army and Navy.

This policy only deepened New England's sense of alienation. Connecticut's legislature, in a special session, declared that the state had the power to reject both the embargo and the force bill as unconstitutional. The state had a duty "to interpose a protecting shield between the rights and liberties of the people and the assumed powers of the federal government." A Vermont grand jury expressed outrage at the idea of the U.S. Army and local law officers enforcing the president's proclamation against trade with Canada. Rhode Island militiamen, called out by the governor, refused to arrest violators of the embargo. New England was giving the man who had said a state could nullify an act of Congress in 1798 (when the Federalists passed the Alien and Sedition Acts) a demoralizing taste of his own medicine.[5]

In the House of Representatives, Virginia's John Randolph, a Jefferson enemy, intoned that all of Europe—and most Americans—saw the United States as "a divided people, imbecile and distracted." Aghast at the widespread disgust with the embargo, the Republicans repealed it on President Jefferson's last day in office. It had accomplished little or nothing. But the Republican Party, still buoyed by the Louisiana Purchase, remained potent at the polls, electing James Madison as Jefferson's successor.

. . .

The uproar over the embargo proved to be only a warm-up for the War of 1812. President Madison struggled to achieve peace with France and England, but the two belligerents declined to cooperate. Republican congressmen from Kentucky and Tennessee, led by a gifted orator named Henry Clay, began calling for war with Britain. They were infected by a disease of the public mind that has led to many of America's wars: the illusion of an easy victory.

The British were locked in global combat with Napoleon Bonaparte, the ruler of Europe. The Congressional "War Hawks" argued it would be a simple matter to declare war and seize Canada's vast, mostly empty acres, which had only a miniscule British army to defend them. In 1812, Congress agreed—with almost every New England Federalist representative and senator voting against the declaration. As the Federalists saw it, Britain was defending the values of liberty and human rights against Napoleon Bonaparte's military dictatorship.

Within a few weeks, the Federalists in Congress, most of them New Englanders, issued "an address . . . to their Constituents on the subject of War with Great Britain." It was a blast of vituperation and condemnation of President Madison's government that might as well have been written by the prime minister of Britain. An abridged version of this ferocious document appeared in every major newspaper in the nation. The denunciation portrayed the Federalists as the party of peace, and the Jeffersonian Republicans as reckless warmongers.

On the heels of this assault came a broadside from the legislature of the state of Massachusetts, voicing even more hostile sentiments. The war was denounced as "outrageous to public opinion, [and] to the feelings and interests of the people." The conflict was motivated, the legislators declared, by President Madison's intent to "aggrandize the southern and western states at the expense of the Eastern section of the Union." The governor of Massachusetts followed this accusation with a call for a fast day, giving the state's clergymen a chance to join the chorus of deprecation and contempt. Connecticut's governor promptly imitated the Bay State.

Huge meetings in Boston and other towns and cities endorsed "without a single dissenting vote" the searing opinions voiced by the legislature. In Essex County, home of Timothy Pickering and other "high" or ultra Federalists, a new danger was denounced: a standing army. For good measure they threw in "mob rule."[6]

In Baltimore, Republicans soon validated the latter charge. They attacked a Federalist newspaper whose editor was equally vituperative in opposing the war. A handful of Federalists tried to protect the editor from physical harm. One of them was the editor's close friend, Henry Lee, the man President Washington had chosen to help suppress the Whiskey Rebellion. Lee had served three terms as the Federalist governor of Virginia.

Baltimore city officials persuaded the editor and his protectors to give up their weapons and retreat to the local jail before the mob erupted. A few hours later, an even bigger mob invaded the jail and beat and kicked the

Federalists, killing one of them and seriously injuring Henry Lee, leaving him a semi-invalid until he died in 1818. His son, Robert E. Lee, undoubtedly never forgot this example of how American politics could explode into mindless violence.[7]

Massachusetts Federalists called for the formation of committees of correspondence in all seventeen states to coordinate resistance to the "wanton, impolitic and unjust war." But the opposition to the war remained almost entirely in New England. There it soon became a serious matter. The governor of Connecticut refused to place the state's militia under the command of a federally appointed major general to defend the seacoast against an attack from a British fleet offshore. Massachusetts soon followed this example, refusing to summon forty-three companies of militiamen to defend the seacoast of their state and Rhode Island.[8]

The performance of the three federal armies that President Madison ordered to invade Canada in 1812 did not help matters. They were all repulsed; one army retreated to Detroit and surrendered to a much smaller enemy force. At home, Connecticut thwarted army recruiters by offering more money to volunteers who joined its state forces, which the governor refused to send beyond its borders.

·   ·   ·

Things did not go much better for American attempts to invade Canada in 1813. The British, sensing an opportunity to divide the Americans, decided not to blockade the ports of Massachusetts, Rhode Island, or New Hampshire. A thriving trade in British imports was soon in full swing, making Yankee merchants (and British exporters) rich. The Yankees rationalized this flirtation with treason by continuing to condemn the war as wanton and impolitic.

The British soon extended their divisive policy to the West Indies and Bermuda. The governors of these islands were ordered to limit imports from America to ships from New England. President Madison denounced the practice as an attempt to "dismember our confederated Republic." But no one in New England paid any attention to "Little Jemmy," the Federalist newspaper nickname for the nation's chief executive.

The embattled president had another weapon, which he soon utilized: an embargo on all trade, reinforced by the American navy. To no one's surprise, Massachusetts's governor declared it unconstitutional. In resolutions passed by the legislature and numerous towns, the law was also condemned as "slavery"—an echo of the accusation that the patriots of 1776 flung at the British.[9]

.   .   .

The Bay State's legislature now produced a report that took the slide to disunion in a new and more definite direction. Chaired by Harrison Grey Otis, one of the younger generation of Federalists, the committee declared that an "ardent attachment to the union" still beat in the hearts of the state's citizens. But since 1800 it had been "destroyed by a practical neglect of Constitutional principles." They traced this destruction to a desire to "harass and annihilate that spirit of commerce . . . the handmaid of civil and religious liberty." The villains did not have to be named: they were the Jeffersonian Republican citizens of the South and the West, who prospered largely through agriculture. There was no point in issuing more denunciations, Otis's committee declared. It was time to summon a convention "of the wise and good" of the oppressed New England states to decide what they should do about this situation.[10]

Meanwhile, the federal government was going broke. When it tried to float a loan of $25 million, the Federalists in Congress opposed it because the money was to fund "a war of invasion and conquest." New England banks, overflowing with cash thanks to the British imports trade, refused to lend them a penny. To cap the government's humiliation, the British fleet landed a small army, which routed American militia and burned Washington, DC.

Then came news that Napoleon Bonaparte had abandoned his invasion of Russia, which would have made him absolute master of Europe, and had retreated to Paris, where he confronted an overwhelming coalition of national armies and abdicated. That meant the United States now faced a war with a triumphant British fleet and army, untrammeled by commitments elsewhere.

The illusions behind the 1812 declaration of war had exploded in President Madison's face. Massachusetts called for his resignation. The demoralized Congress suggested transferring the fire-ravaged American capital elsewhere—perhaps back to Philadelphia. From New Orleans came reports that the British were preparing to assault the city with a fleet and army. If they captured it, they would control the Mississippi Valley.

On December 15, 1814, the New England convention met in Connecticut's capital, Hartford. In spite of the passionate rhetoric that summoned them, New Hampshire and Vermont decided not to attend. While delegates from Rhode Island, Massachusetts, and the host state met in secret sessions, an anxious President Madison and his advisors feared that the outcome would be secession and an alliance between New England and Great Britain. Federal troops were withdrawn from the Canadian border with orders to resist such a move and regard those who supported it as traitors. Civil war seemed a real possibility.[11]

. . .

Seldom has a new year begun with gloomier prospects for the United States of America than in 1815. But within two seemingly miraculous months, the storm clouds were transformed to sunshine and celebrations by news from distant quarters. First came the arrival of a treaty of peace, signed by American and British negotiators in Ghent, Belgium. Instead of demands for a swath of the Midwest and most of Maine—London's harsh opening terms—the British accepted a peace that left all America's borders intact. A few days later, a messenger arrived from New Orleans to tell the president that Major General Andrew Jackson of Tennessee had won a decisive victory, routing an army of British veterans with the loss of only seven men.

No one was more surprised than a delegation from the Hartford Convention, who had arrived in Washington with a set of demands that would give New England a special status within the Union, enabling them to defy or dismiss laws passed by the federal government. If the president refused to negotiate with them, a second convention would be called, which would vote to secede. President Madison, suddenly ten feet tall politically, never had to deal with this ultimatum. The delegates slunk out of Washington,

DC, while parades and speeches celebrated the end of the war in an aura of improbable victory.[12]

Two years later, another Virginian, James Monroe, became president. It was the death knell of the Federalist Party and the start of what a wry Yankee newspaperman called "the era of good feelings." Not all the feelings were entitled to that adjective, however. Triumphant Jeffersonian Republicans, both in New England and beyond its borders, made sure the men who had summoned the Hartford Convention were painted as would-be traitors and renegades in the newspapers. Their political careers came to an abrupt and unforgiving close. Henceforth New Englanders would have to find another way, outside of politics, to regain their lost leadership.

.   .   .

In this atmosphere of Jeffersonian Republican ascendancy, Southerners launched a campaign to solve the nation's largest remaining problem: slavery. The American Colonization Society appeared on the scene in 1816, backed by a chorus of approval from a who's who of the nation's politicians, including President James Monroe, ex-President James Madison, Henry Clay, John Randolph, and Supreme Court Justice Bushrod Washington, the late founder's nephew, who agreed to be its first president.

The ACS was proposed by two Presbyterian clergymen, Paul Finley and Samuel Mills, but their idea was obviously rooted in Thomas Jefferson's assumption that blacks could never achieve acceptance and true equality in America. The society proposed to raise money to purchase enough land in Africa to found a new nation for free blacks, to be called Liberia.[13]

They had no trouble selling the idea to mostly southern political leaders and their allies in the North. From 1800 to 1810, the number of free blacks in America had almost doubled, to 186,446. Philadelphia had the most thriving and prosperous black community. One of its leaders was James Forten, who had been born free and educated at a Quaker-funded school for blacks.

Forten had served aboard an American privateer during the Revolution. The warship had been captured and he had barely survived a year on one of the disease-ridden British prison ships in New York's harbor. Back in

Philadelphia, he went to work for a sailmaker, who steadily promoted him and eventually sold him the business.

Although Forten had cordial relations with many white Philadelphians in the business world, he was attracted to the idea of returning to Africa. Blacks were not welcome in many white Philadelphia homes, and they were barred from public schools. On the Fourth of July and other holidays, drunken patriots often beat them up and broke the windows of their homes. Forten was also acutely conscious of the huge number of blacks still enslaved in nearby Maryland and the other states of the South. He had organized an angry protest when Congress passed the act empowering federal marshals to pursue and arrest runaway slaves.

Forten's conversations with the American Colonization Society's spokesmen slowly disillusioned him. He sensed a racist undertone in the ACS approach. Their plan called for emancipating slaves only if they agreed to leave the country for the proposed refuge in Africa. Many of the leaders, notably Henry Clay and John Randolph, saw free blacks as potential fomenters of slave insurrections, and they did not conceal an eagerness to get them out of America. Perhaps most disturbing, the ACS did not say a word in their charter about eventually eliminating slavery.

Over three thousand Philadelphia blacks convened a protest meeting against the ACS. Speakers condemned Henry Clay's view that free people of color were "a dangerous and useless part of the community." Even stronger was their declaration that they would "never . . . separate ourselves voluntarily from the slave population of this country; they are our brethren by the ties of consanguinity, of suffering and of wrongs." The meeting convinced James Forten that colonization was a bad idea.

At one point, hoping to change his mind, the ACS offered to make Forten president of the proposed nation of Liberia. Forten replied that he would rather remain "a sail maker in Philadelphia than enjoy the highest offices" of Liberia. Once and for all, the United States had to understand that blacks were Americans too. "Here we were born, here we will live, here we will die."[14]

This opposition of the free blacks inflicted a serious wound on the ACS, but it would struggle on for decades, eventually founding Liberia and helping it become an independent nation. Native Africans did not welcome the Americans, and several times warfare broke out between the two groups. By 1830, fewer than 1,500 American blacks had chosen Liberia. Shocking numbers of the immigrants died of tropical diseases. But the ACS continued to receive strong support from clergymen, Quakers, and other idealists.

.   .   .

In 1819, Missouri applied for admission to the Union as a state that permitted slavery. Two other states with the same policy had already joined the growing Union: Mississippi and Alabama. They had been balanced by the admission of Illinois and Indiana, states without slavery, thanks to the Northwest Ordinance. Missouri would tip the balance in a proslavery direction, but no one thought this mattered at first. There were vast stretches of the Louisiana Territory west of the Mississippi waiting for settlement by Northerners. Leaders of the House of Representatives began preparing a routine enabling act, as they had done for the previous new states.

On February 13, 1819, while the act was being discussed, Congressman James Tallmadge of Poughkeepsie, New York, proposed two amendments. The first would bar the entrance of any more slaves into Missouri; the second would emancipate slave children born after the state joined the Union when they reached the age of twenty-five. Tallmadge based his reasoning on the Northwest Ordinance. Most of Missouri lay north of a line that extended west from the Ohio River.

A startling number of congressmen, many from New England, backed the proposal. Henry Clay and other Southerners attacked it as unconstitutional. The Northerners added injury to insult by winning a vote that passed the enabling act with Tallmadge's amendments. The Senate eliminated the amendments and sent the bill back to the House, which refused its approval. Congress adjourned with Missouri unadmitted, and the two sides prepared to renew their combat in the next session.

In December 1819, with the galleries packed, Congress reconvened, and it swiftly became evident that no minds had changed. A virulent debate exploded in the Senate. On the proslavery side was William Pinckney of Maryland, a quintessential southern gentleman who wore ruffled shirts and gloves, as if he wished to avoid dirtying his elegant hands with the opposition's arguments. He decried the idea that the federal government could interfere with slavery.

The leader of the antislavery battalion was Senator Rufus King of New York, a transplanted New Englander who condemned slavery as a loathsome violation of the Declaration of Independence's call for universal equality. "No human law, compact or compromise can establish or continue slavery," King insisted. "Such a law was contrary to the law of nature, which is the law of God."

The antislavery senators lost a roll call vote, but one of their group, Senator John Thomas from the new state of Illinois, submitted a resolution to bar slavery from all states north of 36 degrees 30 minutes north latitude—the line that ran west from the Ohio River. The amendment passed and the bill went to the House, where galleries were again packed and the debate made the Senate's clashes seem decorous. John Randolph spoke for four full days, repeatedly declaring slavery exempt from any and all federal regulation.

Sessions became all-night marathons. One exhausted congressman toppled to the floor, but his colleagues returned to their orating after he was carried out. Extremists on both sides took all-or-nothing positions. Finally, House Speaker Henry Clay of Kentucky brokered a compromise, which admitted Missouri and approved the Thomas amendment, thanks to a new provision. Maine had separated from Massachusetts and was applying for admission as a free state. This restored the balance of slave and free states and mollified the antislavery Northerners.

President Monroe signed the bill, and everyone hoped sectional peace had been restored. But a few months later, Missouri presented Congress with its constitution. Obviously the work of canny lawyers, the charter forbade the Missouri legislature to interfere with slavery, apparently making bondage perpetual within the Show-Me state's borders. It also barred free

African Americans from emigrating there, and emancipated slaves were required to leave the state.

Outrage was the order of the day among the northern members of Congress, and another six weeks of virulent debate shook the walls of the capitol. Again Henry Clay brokered a compromise. A joint House-Senate committee agreed to admit Missouri if the state agreed "to respect the rights of all citizens of the United States." The weary legislators did not give too much thought to what those words would mean in practice. Missouri was admitted and everyone went home to see if anything was left of the era of good feelings.[15]

·   ·   ·

Few followed this war of words with more intensity than the aging master of Monticello. From his mountaintop mansion, a distraught Thomas Jefferson saw the uproar as an impending disaster. "In the gloomiest moments of the Revolutionary War," he wrote in 1820, "I never had any apprehensions equal to what I feel from this source." He was especially disturbed to see New Englanders leading the antislavery forces in Congress. He accused them—including transplanted Yankees such as King and Senator Thomas of Illinois—of "taking advantage of the virtuous feelings of the people against slavery to effect a division of parties by a geographical line. They expect this will insure them . . . the majority they could never obtain on the principles of Federalism."

Jefferson feared that the old conflict between Federalists and Republicans would be fanaticized by this sectionalism. "The coincidence of a marked principle, [both] moral and political . . . would never more be obliterated from the [public] mind . . . it would be recurring on every occasion until it would kindle such mutual and mortal hatred as to render secession preferable to eternal discord." The triumph of the Republican Party in 1800—and the nation's near-miraculous victory in the War of 1812—had made him "among the most sanguine in believing that our union would be of long duration. I now doubt it very much." For Jefferson the Missouri Compromise was "like a fire bell in the night, signaling the death knell of the Union."

Jefferson was convinced that the antislavery men were politically motivated, but he admitted that some were no doubt honestly deluded by their
moral detestation of slavery. As a Southerner who had publicly condemned
the institution many times, Jefferson wondered why "they are wasting jer-
emiads [lamentations] on the miseries of the slave as if we were advocates of
it." Personally, he would willingly surrender all his "property" in slaves "if a
scheme of emancipation and expatriation could be effected. . . . But as it is, we
have the wolf by the ears, and we can neither hold him nor safely let him go."

The nightmare memory of Saint-Domingue's (now Haiti's) race war was
obviously still haunting Jefferson. "Are our slaves to be presented with freedom and a dagger?" he asked one of his favorite correspondents, ex-President
John Adams. If the antislavery restrictionists were right, and Congress could
regulate slavery in the new states, it could also declare all slaves free in current states. "In which case," he told another correspondent, "all the whites
south of the Potomac and the Ohio must evacuate their states, and most
fortunate will be those who can do it first."[16]

The more Jefferson thought about the Missouri debates, the more unhappy he became. Restricting the spread of slavery would not free a single
human being. It was pseudo morality, a feel-good policy motivated more by
hatred of southern whites than by concern for the slaves. He now thought it
was far better to spread slavery over the widest possible geographical area.
This would lighten the burden of future liberation "by bringing a greater
number of shoulders under it."

Here was irony: the original sponsor of the Northwest Ordinance was
now repudiating the idea of barring slavery in new states. Jefferson probably
changed his mind after a discussion with his right-hand man, James Madison. He was the one with the analytical mind, as he repeatedly displayed
throughout his remarkable career. Madison was now convinced that "diffusion" was the best hope of future emancipation. Thus far, the states that had
abolished slavery had a relative scarcity of blacks in their population.

The thinking of another Virginian, St. George Tucker, a professor of law
at the College of William and Mary, strongly influenced both men. In the
aftermath of the Haitian bloodbath, Tucker concluded that the "density" of

a slave population was intimately connected with the likelihood of insurrections. The numerous revolts in the West Indies, where the white-black imbalance frequently approached that of Saint-Domingue, was additional evidence supporting this conclusion.

Madison saw two routes to diffusion. One was the spread of slavery into new states; the other was an "external asylum for the colored race" beyond America's borders. For the moment, he was placing his hopes in the hands of the American Colonization Society. He recognized it was a weak reed, even though he became its president in the 1830s. At one point he asked some of his slaves whether they would consider going to Liberia, if he freed them. All expressed terror, even horror, at the idea.[17]

It was rapidly becoming evident that Africa was not the answer. Its unpopularity and the steady growth in the numbers of the southern slave population made it more and more obvious. That made diffusion into new states even more important. But the uproar over Missouri signaled that this would be difficult—perhaps impossible.

. . .

In 1822, South Carolina had almost as many blacks as whites in its population. A small minority of blacks were free; the vast majority were slaves. In 1799, a slave named Denmark Vesey paid six dollars for a ticket in the state lottery and won $1,500. He bought his freedom and became a carpenter. In his youth, he had served as a cabin boy aboard a ship captained by Joseph Vesey, which regularly sailed between Saint-Dominque and Charleston. The captain had sold him to a plantation owner on the island, but the buyer had demanded his money back, complaining that Denmark was subject to fits. Captain Vesey had made the young man a house servant in Charleston until Denmark won his freedom.

Vesey was an avid reader of the Bible and a member of Charleston's African Methodist Episcopal Church. The church had links to a black church of the same faith in Philadelphia, which often called for an end to slavery. Nervous Charleston officials had closed the local church in 1818. Vesey reportedly had become very angry about this decision. His anger was further fueled by coming across a pamphlet containing the antislavery speeches that Senator Rufus King had made during the controversy over Missouri.

Next, Vesey heard from one of the many black seamen who visited Charleston that Haiti had a new president, Jean-Pierre Boyer, who wanted American blacks to settle in his country and would pay their transportation costs. About six thousand blacks, many from Philadelphia, accepted this offer—four times as many as the American Colonization Society had been able to entice to Africa. Vesey wrote a letter to President Boyer, expressing interest in his invitation.

Meanwhile, Vesey began meeting secretly with several men who responded to his proposal that they seize the Charleston arsenal, arm their fellow blacks, slave and free, and kill all the whites. They would then set the city afire, seize a ship or ships, and sail to Haiti. They found hundreds of the city's blacks, some of them artisans, others seemingly devoted house servants, who were ready to join them. Soon messengers had enticed field hands on the plantations near Charleston into the plan. They promised to kill their masters and race into the city to guarantee that the whites were quickly overwhelmed.

The eruption was scheduled for July 14—Bastille Day, which was evidence that Vesey was well acquainted with the French Revolution and its influence in Haiti. Vesey told his followers "not to spare one white skin alive, as this was the plan they pursued in Santo Domingo."

As the climactic day approached, two blacks who had been invited to join the insurrection informed Charleston's mayor and other city authorities of the plot. Armed militia swiftly filled the streets and rounded up Vesey and his leading confederates. Ultimately, over 131 men were tried; 25 were sentenced to be hanged. The rest were shipped to the brutal slavery of the British West Indies sugar cane fields.

The shock waves generated by the size and murderous intent of Denmark Vesey's revolt sent shudders through the slave owners of the South. It validated everything they thought and imagined when they heard the words "Santo Domingo."[18]

CHAPTER 8

How Not to Abolish Slavery

On January 1, 1831, an unusual newspaper appeared in Boston. On the front page were four columns of dense type, topped by block capital letters that proclaimed its identity: THE LIBERATOR. Beneath it were the names of the publishers, William Lloyd Garrison and Isaac Knapp. On the next line was a motto: "OUR COUNTRY IS THE WORLD—OUR COUNTRYMEN MANKIND."

At the top of the first column, "Wm L. Garrison" identified himself as the editor. Below his name was a poem:

> *To date my being from the opening year*
> *I come, a stranger in this busy sphere*
> *Where some I meet perchance may pause and ask,*
> *What is my name, my purpose, or my task?*
>
> *My name is "LIBERATOR"! I propose*
> *To hurl my shafts at freedom's deadliest foes!*
> *My task is hard—for I am charged to save*
> *Man from his brother—to redeem the slave!*

The next ten stanzas urged the reader to feel sympathy for the suffering slave. "Art thou a parent?" How would you feel if someone sold your children? "Art thou a brother?" What would you feel if your sister were abused by a slave owner? "Art thou a sister?" How would you feel if you saw your brother shackled in chains? "Art thou a lover?" What would you do if your beloved was torn from your arms? Finally came an appeal:

> Aid me, New England, 'tis my hope in you
> Which gives me strength my purpose to pursue!
> Do you now hear your sister States respond?
> With Afric's cries to have her sons unbound?

In the second column, Garrison made his approach to slavery very clear—along with his belief in New England's moral superiority. He had explored publishing *The Liberator* in Washington, DC, but his efforts were "palsied by public indifference." The experience convinced him that America needed "a revolution in public sentiment." He had selected Boston for his home base because here he could "lift up the standard of emancipation in the eyes of the nation within sight of Bunker Hill and in the birth place of liberty."

Then came words that made *The Liberator* explosive: "I shall strenuously contend for the immediate enfranchisement of our slave population." Immediate emancipation with the right to vote. Garrison was rejecting the ideas of almost everyone who had struggled to find a peaceful solution to slavery, above all Thomas Jefferson.

Many people had already objected to "the severity of my language," Garrison continued on *The Liberator's* first page. He had been denouncing slavery in speeches and newspaper essays in Boston and other cities for more than two years. His answer to these critics was, "Is there not cause for severity?" Grimly he declared, "I will be as harsh as truth and as uncompromising as justice. On this subject, I do not wish to speak, or write, with moderation." Would you tell a man "to moderately rescue his wife from the hands of a ravisher? . . . I will not equivocate—I will not excuse—I will not retreat a single inch—AND I WILL BE HEARD." This comparison of slavery to rape would become one of his favorite themes.

Adding to the confrontational tone was Garrison's warning that unless slavery was abolished peacefully, there would be a resort to "the sword." This was all too clear in a poem he published in the first issue:

> *Though distant to the hour, yet come it must—*
> *Oh hasten it, in mercy, righteous heaven!*
> *When Afric's sons, uprising from the dust,*
> *Shall stand erect—their galling fetters riven. . . .*
>
> *Wo, if it comes with storm, and blood, and fire*
> *When midnight darkness veils the earth and sky!*
> *Wo to the innocent babe—the guilty sire—*
> *Stranger and citizen alike shall die!*
> *Red-handed Slaughter his revenge shall feed,*
> *And havoc yell his ominous death-cry.*

This grisly portrait was followed by a declaration that the editor of *The Liberator* opposed all forms of violence, and sincerely hoped that slavery could be abolished peacefully. The tone, the vocabulary, the attitude that preceded this claim virtually refuted it on the page. This did not mean that William Lloyd Garrison was a hypocrite. He was convinced that immediate abolition was the right policy because God had told him it was. He was equally convinced that God had inspired him to portray slavery as rape, and slaveholders as brutal barbarians.

From the start, some readers saw the fatal flaw in Garrison's approach. Francis Wayland, the president of Brown University, warned him that his "menacing and vindictive attitude toward slaveholders prejudiced their minds against a cool discussion of the subject." He reminded Garrison of the importance of preserving harmony in the Union. Another critic, a newspaper editor and erstwhile Garrison friend, suggested he could and should be indicted for sedition. Garrison asked him if he would have the same opinion if he were a whipped and branded slave.

The first issue of *The Liberator* had a press run of four hundred copies. Its readership did not extend beyond the city limits of Boston.[1]

.   .   .

William Lloyd Garrison was indifferent to the way American politics was acquiring a new shape in 1831. Three years earlier, Andrew Jackson of Tennessee, the hero of the Battle of New Orleans, had routed John Adams's son, President John Quincy Adams, in his bid for a second term in the White House. John Quincy had been Boston's last hope of national political leadership.

The men of the West, many of them originally Southerners, were joining forces with the South in a new entity called the Democratic Party, which would soon have adherents in New England. Opposing them was the emerging Whig Party, a mix of ex-Federalists and conservative Jeffersonian-Republicans, who chose the name hoping that some voters would remember the days of 1776, when rebel Whigs confronted loyalist Tories in the struggle for independence.

Garrison was unbothered by this new political alignment, which left New England an even weaker minority voice. From the start he reveled in being an outsider. He saw immediate emancipation as a triumph that would make political parties superfluous. "Nothing but extensive revivals of pure religion can save our country," Garrison wrote in April 1831, suggesting that he saw religion and politics as moral and spiritual opposites. In a prophetic mode, Garrison declared that America's redemption would come when Christian principles had triumphed in every soul. Then voters would change the name of the capital from the slave master Washington to Wilberforce.

Garrison was referring to William Wilberforce, the magnetic British orator and gifted politician who devoted forty years of his life to persuading Parliament to abolish slavery in the West Indies. Here was more evidence of Garrison's almost breathtaking indifference to realistic politics. Less than twenty years after British troops had burned Washington, DC, Garrison was proposing to rename America's capital after an Englishman![2]

It was by no means the last time Garrison denounced George Washington as a slave owner. He believed that the Father of the Country was writhing in the flames of hell, eternally damned for the sin of slavery. *The Liberator's* editor obviously knew nothing about Washington's emancipation of his slaves or his concern for the durability of the American Union.

Garrison's desire for a society where religion was the dominant force was an almost total repudiation of the principles on which the founders had created the American republic. One of their foremost goals had been the *separation* of religion from politics. They were not hostile to religion. They frequently affirmed its importance in the nation's social fabric. But they did not see it having a role in governance. Their historical awareness of the bloody wars religion had triggered in England and other European nations convinced them that politicized religion would destroy all hope of an enduring American union.

·   ·   ·

William Lloyd Garrison was born in 1805 in Newburyport, the third largest seaport in Massachusetts. His father, Abijah, was a moderately successful harbor pilot and occasional ship captain. On both sides, the family was Anglo-Canadian, having arrived in the New World in the 1760s and 1770s and settled on the border between Canada and Massachusetts. They had little or no roots in America's founding experience—and no political experience worth mentioning.

Newburyport's prosperity had attracted Abijah Garrison, and for a while he made a good living. But when the warring British and French began seizing American ships at sea, the number of voyages from Newburyport dwindled, leaving Abijah, a newcomer to the town, unemployed. President Thomas Jefferson's embargo was a far worse blow; it destroyed Newburyport's commerce. Abijah began drinking heavily, to the outrage of his sharp-tongued wife. One day in 1808 he walked out of their house on School Street and never returned.

His departure meant three-year-old Lloyd grew up as his mother's son. Fanny Lloyd Garrison was a passionate Baptist who had converted to this emotional faith in defiance of her Anglican father. She implanted in Lloyd a similar belief in the central importance of his relationship with a demanding God. Nothing else—politics, wealth, friendship—came close.

From Fanny, young Lloyd also contracted a fondness for correcting and exhorting the less religious portion of mankind. His mother enjoyed exerting power over people, even when the results—especially in her husband's case—were disastrous. Fanny had no better luck with her older son, James. He too began spending his time in waterfront bars, out of reach of his mother's hectoring tongue. Eventually he went to sea and disappeared from the family.

Fanny Garrison was by no means unusual in making religion the center of her life. Around 1800, Baptist and Methodist preachers began what historians now call "the Second Great Awakening"—a nationwide evangelical revival that swept through the older Protestant churches, putting many of their pastors out of business. This activist faith required a man or woman to prove his or her conversion with good works, preferably in a social cause that needed reform. Lloyd, as his mother called him, had chosen slavery.[3]

. . .

William Lloyd Garrison's embrace of New England was as rooted in his early life as his religious faith. Too poor even to imagine attending Harvard, he had become a printer's apprentice as a way to acquire at least a semblance of an education. From 1818 to 1825, young Lloyd toiled twelve hours a day in the offices of the *Newburyport Herald*, a newspaper that supported every and any attempt to breathe life into the moribund Federalist Party.

In the *Herald's* files was a veritable history of the party's losing struggle with the supposedly degenerate Jeffersonians, whom the Federalists saw as distorters and corrupters of the noble heritage of presidents George Washington and John Adams. Garrison read with delight and wonder the savage denunciations of Jefferson's party from the acid tongues of Timothy Pickering, Fisher Ames, and other Federalist leaders. Although the older men made only passing references to slavery, their rhetoric made it easy for the young Garrison to see the "peculiar institution," as it was beginning to be called, as a key element in the Jeffersonian-Republicans' supposedly immoral system of government.

Garrison also inherited another article of Federalist faith—the conviction that the South was determined to humiliate and injure New England for its resistance to their rule. This, rather than a noble attempt to find an alternative to war, was the motive they imputed for President Jefferson's embargo. Young Garrison had no difficulty accepting this doctrine. He had seen the tragic impact of the embargo on his own family.

Garrison subscribed wholeheartedly to the creed that was enunciated in a Boston newspaper in 1814. "The God of Nature, in his infinite wisdom, has made the people of New England excel every other people that existed in the world." With such a faith, how could he find fault with the three times that New England had flirted with secession and treason—in the quarrels over the Louisiana Purchase, the embargo, and the War of 1812?

Harrison Grey Otis, a chief organizer of the Hartford Convention, was one of Garrison's heroes. In 1823, Otis ran for governor of Massachusetts on the Federalist ticket. Garrison became his passionate advocate on the *Newburyport Herald*. He filled the paper's columns with invective against Otis's opponents, who were numerous and vocal. The Jeffersonian-Republicans, on their way to becoming Democrats, won in a landslide. Otis did not even carry Essex County, though he managed a majority in Newburyport.

In this election, Garrison found not a little of his voice and style. He did not analyze and refute his opponents' arguments; he denounced them, sneered at them, dismissed them. He found no conflict between this style and his religious beliefs because both nicely complemented the prevailing attitude of New England Federalists. They were inclined to believe in the moral depravity of anyone who disagreed with them.

This attitude was rooted deep in the New England soul, thanks to the sermons they and their ancestors had heard for the previous century. A Puritan preacher's favorite rhetorical form was the "jeremiad," a shorthand term for style and content inspired by the biblical prophet Jeremiah. Jeremaids combined lamentation and condemnation of the spiritual and moral short-comings of a people for their sinfulness and selfishness. Only a handful of mankind, stained by Adam's primary sin, would ever merit salvation.[4]

.   .   .

In the early years of *The Liberator*, Garrison was often short of cash. He had no money of his own, and his partner, Isaac Knapp, also a former appren-tice on the *Newburyport Herald*, had an equally empty wallet. Studying his subscription list, Garrison realized that he had only fifty white readers; the rest were free blacks. Garrison turned to these subscribers for help, and they responded with enthusiasm. James Forten became one of his strongest sup-porters, giving him serious amounts of money.

Garrison travelled to Philadelphia and New York to address black or-ganizations, many of them created to oppose the American Colonization Society. By the end of his first year, Garrison had acquired another five hun-dred black subscribers, and he published a pamphlet based on his speeches, *An Address to the Free People of Color*. He urged them to continue to speak against the inequality being inflicted on them in the northern states, and assured them that *The Liberator* would welcome protest statements and ar-ticles from them.

Garrison did not rely completely on his subscription list to spread *The Liberator*'s message. It was customary for newspapers to send free copies to other papers around the nation and receive complimentary copies in return. By the end of his first year, Garrison was exchanging *The Liberator* with over a hundred papers, many of them in the South. The editors of the latter pa-pers did not take kindly to *The Liberator*'s demand for immediate abolition or to Garrison's frequent comparison of slavery to rape. They reprinted ex-cerpts with furious refutations. Garrison gleefully reprinted these attacks and countered them with reprises of his own. This atmosphere of crisis and confrontation was exactly what he was hoping to achieve.[5]

.   .   .

In late August of 1831, a Virginia slave named Nat Turner gave Garrison's obscure publication an outburst of publicity that he could never have otherwise obtained. Stirred by an eclipse of the sun in February, Turner, a self-appointed black preacher, became convinced God had ordained him to free Virginia's slaves. On the night of August 22, he summoned several followers and approached the house of his owner, Joseph Travis. Later, Turner would admit that Travis was "a kind master." But his kindness did not prevent Turner or one of his followers from burying a hatchet in Travis's skull. Nor did the master's benevolence rescue Mrs. Travis and four other members of his family, including an infant, from a similar fate.

It was as if a chapter out of Santo Domingo's final slaughter under General Dessalines had somehow been reincarnated in Southampton County, a thinly populated rural region not far from Virginia's seacoast. Blacks outnumbered whites by more than a thousand, but most whites owned only two or three slaves and many owned none. Seizing horses from nearby farms, Nat Turner and his swelling band, soon numbering more than fifty men, rode from farmhouse to farmhouse, killing everyone with white skin.

Turner told his followers that by exterminating the whites, "they would achieve the happy effects of their brethren in St. Domingo . . . and establish a government of their own." The next day, whites who had managed to flee Turner's rampage sounded the alarm and Virginia called out hundreds of militiamen.

A reporter on a Richmond newspaper, who belonged to one of the militia units, described what he saw: "Whole families, father, mother, daughters, sons, sucking babes and school children butchered, thrown into heaps and left to be devoured by hogs and dogs or to putrefy on the spot." Especially horrendous was the discovery of a schoolteacher, Mrs. Levi Waller, and ten of her pupils "piled in one bleeding heap on the [classroom] floor." One quick-thinking child had ducked into the fireplace and survived.

Saddest of all was the story of one of the last families killed. At noon Turner and his followers approached the Vaughan farmhouse. By now most of the rebels had guns seized from pillaged houses. The hoofbeats of their horses alerted Rebecca Vaughan, who was in her garden selecting vegetables for dinner. She fled into the house. What could she do? Her husband was not at home. She rushed to a window and cried out that there was no one in the house but her and her children. A volley of shots killed her instantly.

Her fifteen-year-old son, Arthur, heard—and perhaps saw—his mother's murder and instinctively rushed to save her. He was riddled while climbing a nearby fence. Mrs. Vaughan's niece, fifteen-year-old Eliza Vaughan, ran out of the house, perhaps hoping that if she reached nearby woods, she might survive. Another volley ended her life, too.[6]

.   .   .

Forty miles away in Fortress Monroe, a U.S. Army bastion on the seacoast, Captain Robert E. Lee and his bride, Mary Custis Lee, considered themselves on an extended honeymoon. He had graduated second in his class from the U.S. Military Academy at West Point in 1829. The couple had been married on June 30, 1831, at Arlington. Mary's father, George Washington Parke Custis, had been delighted to welcome into the family the son of a soldier who had served with distinction under his step-grandfather. The wedding celebration had lasted a week, and they had spent much of the following month visiting relatives, enjoying more parties and showers of gifts and congratulations.

Arlington was crowded with Washington relics—portraits, his bookcase, the bed in which he had died. One of the house slaves, Caroline Branham, had been in the bedroom when the founder breathed his last. She had been one of Martha Washington's slaves, who had not been freed in the President's will. Lee's marriage, wrote a kinsman, "made Robert Lee the representative of the founder of American liberty."

It is not hard to imagine the shock and horror that swept through Fortress Monroe when the news of Nat Turner's insurrection reached its officers and men. For Mary Custis Lee, it must have seemed a ghastly intrusion on her happiness. The fort's commander immediately ordered the gates locked, barring the admittance of several dozen slave workmen who had been helping to rebuild part of the walls.

Three companies of regulars—perhaps 350 men—were ordered to march immediately to reinforce the militia sent to suppress Turner's revolt. Five additional companies were rushed to the fort. By the time the regulars reached Southampton County, Virginia militia had dispersed, killed, or captured Nat Turner's men. Only Turner himself escaped, remaining at large for another seven weeks.

As an engineering officer, Captain Lee did not accompany the dispatched regulars. But the stories that the Lees read in the newspapers or heard from fellow officers over the next several days must have left grisly memories. Rumor and terror swelled the insurrection's numbers into the hundreds and even the thousands.[7]

·   ·   ·

In Boston and elsewhere throughout the nation, newspaper headlines bellowed the story of Nat Turner: "INSURRECTION IN VIRGINIA!" William Lloyd Garrison pronounced himself "horror-struck." Looking back to the poem about coming violence he had published in his first issue, he wrote: "What was poetry—imagination—in January is now a bloody reality." Garrison invoked his professed pacifism to condemn the massacre, but he reminded his readers of the reason for it. "In his fury against the revolters, who will remember the wrongs?" he asked.

The answer to that question soon became evident: almost no one. Many of Turner's followers were beheaded on the spot when captured. Any slave suspected of collusion with them was likely to suffer a painful death. Over a hundred blacks died in the next month in a reaction marred by hysteria and cruelty in many ways worse than the insurrectionists had displayed. Garrison privately welcomed this retaliation. On October 19, 1831, he told one correspondent that he was pleased the "disturbances at the South still continue. The slaveholders are given over to destruction. They are determined to shut out the light."

Here was a signal revelation of the fundamental flaw in William Lloyd Garrison's character, a flaw that permeated the New England view of the rest of America: an almost total lack of empathy. Fellow Americans had just been exposed to an awful experience—a tragedy that dramatized in horrendous terms the problem of Southern slavery. Did Garrison express even a hint of sympathy or pity for these stunned, grieving families and their terrified neighbors? Did he confess that his immediate emancipation slogan was wrong, or at least in need of amendment? The only emotion Garrison permitted himself was thinly disguised gloating—and a call for sympathy for the slaves. No matter how much they deserved this emotion, was this the time to demand it?

. . .

Garrison soon found that slaveholders and many other people were determined to shut out *his* light. The *National Intelligencer* of Washington, DC, the closest thing the federal government had to a journalistic voice, accused him of "poisoning the waters of life" everywhere. The *Intelligencer* urged Boston authorities to shut down *The Liberator*. Garrison called this proof of "southern mendacity and folly."

Silencing Garrison was soon endorsed by other newspapers and politicians. The Georgia legislature offered $5,000 to anyone who delivered him to the state for trial on a charge of seditious libel. Garrison raged it was a "bribe to kidnappers" and cited the Bill of Rights as his protection. One South Carolinian warned Boston that toleration of "seditious" journalism would inflict serious damage on the pocketbooks of her merchants.

Ironically, the mayor of Boston happened to be Garrison's Federalist hero, Harrison Grey Otis. He soon received a letter from Nelly Custis, George Washington's step-granddaughter, telling him how upset she was by *The Liberator*, which she blamed for Nat Turner's eruption. She thought Garrison deserved to be hanged for his crimes. He had made her feel as if she were "living on the edge of a volcano."

Mayor Otis also received a letter from Senator Robert Y. Hayne of South Carolina, with whom he had served in Congress. The senator asked if Otis could or would suppress *The Liberator*. The mayor sent policemen to the paper's one-room office, in which Garrison and Knapp slept, ate, and worked. The police wanted to know if they were bothering Senator Hayne by sending him copies of their paper. Mayor Otis reported back to Senator Hayne that *The Liberator* was not worth suppressing. Garrison was a penniless malcontent who would never make the slightest impression on respectable people in Boston or anywhere else.[8]

. . .

Garrison began blaming most of his woes on the American Colonization Society. While its appeal to free American blacks remained minimal, the ACS's agents got a great deal of publicity in the newspapers, and they raised dismaying amounts of money. Even more irritating was the way they had won the backing of the established churches. The ACS's doctrine of gradual abolition gave thousands of vaguely antislavery whites the feeling that there was a way to end slavery with little or no pain or effort. Cash and patience were all that was needed.

Garrison decided to demolish this enemy of immediate abolition. By April 1832 he completed *Thoughts on African Colonization*, a book-length blast in his best denunciatory style. The American Colonization Society ignored the book, which sold little more than two thousand copies. Garrison learned that an ACS agent, Elliot Cresson, was in Britain raising money. The frustrated editor yearned to go there and challenge him—and win the blessing of his hero, William Wilberforce. He appealed for help from free blacks in Philadelphia and other communities, and soon had six hundred dollars in his bank account—more than enough to pay for a round trip.[9]

. . .

The editor of *The Liberator* arrived in England at an historic moment. The British abolitionists were on the brink of winning their forty-year struggle for the abolition of slavery in their West Indian colonies. Garrison's London host was a wealthy Quaker merchant, James Cropper, who escorted him to the crowded offices of the British Anti-slavery Society, where most of the leaders had gathered to receive hourly reports of the debate in Parliament.

Garrison visited the gallery of the House of Commons to hear the debates. Next he was invited to breakfast by Thomas Folwell Buxton, who had succeeded the aging William Wilberforce as abolition's chief spokesman in Parliament. The big burly politician stared at the editor in amazement for a full minute, leaving Garrison nonplused. Finally Buxton exclaimed, "My dear sir, I thought you were a black man!" It was an inadvertent commentary on how few white Americans spoke out against slavery. Garrison put Buxton at ease by replying that his words were a compliment he would never forget.

.   .   .

Garrison was in England when Parliament passed the final version of the bill that abolished slavery in the West Indies. The key provision that had broken the long deadlock was the decision to pay twenty million pounds to the slave owners as compensation for the value of their 850,000 slaves. That was a hundred million 1830s American dollars—the equivalent of perhaps $2 billion today. Garrison disapproved of this compromise, although he did not undertake to lecture the British abolitionists about it. He remarked that it did not give much satisfaction to either the winners or the losers. Like most idealists before and since, compromise was a dirty word to Garrison. In his report to *The Liberator*, he focused instead in the tremendous wave of antislavery petitions that had engulfed Parliament. One was signed by 800,000 women.[10]

Here was a moment when a different man—or a different reaction from Garrison—might have altered the course of American history. If Garrison had become a supporter of compensated emancipation, he might have found thousands of reasonable men agreeing with him. Instead he remained locked in his religious fervor, unaware that his New England–induced hatred of the South was distorting his crusade.

Unfortunately, this hostility was reinforced by British antislavery crusader George Thompson. He was about Garrison's age, and like him was largely self-educated. Thompson had been one of the youthful leaders in the 1831 decision to take a more aggressive attitude toward West Indies slave owners. Like Garrison, he had been converted to the cause by an evangelical experience and was convinced that "sin will lie at our door if we do not agitate, agitate, agitate." He swiftly became famous for his slashing platform style and the vituperation he flung at the slaveholders. Garrison considered him a soul brother and talked of inviting him to America.[11]

. . .

As the British antislavery societies celebrated, Garrison turned his attention to the agent of the ACS, Elliot Cresson. In a meeting with William Wilberforce, he persuaded the gravely ill hero to withdraw his endorsement of the ACS. *The Liberator's* editor used Wilberforce's words to demolish Cresson in a series of meetings arranged by other British antislavery leaders.

In the last of these clashes, carried away by the cheers and applause of the audience, Garrison confessed he was unhappy with America's current stance on slavery. His countrymen were "insulting the majesty of heaven" by tolerating slavery in their Constitution and hypocritically ignoring the great principles of the Declaration of Independence. In a follow-up article in a London newspaper, Garrison wrote that the U.S. Constitution would soon "be held in everlasting infamy by the friends of humanity and injustice throughout the world."

Garrison was apparently unaware that Elliott Cresson had allies in London, many of them visiting Americans. They were outraged to hear a fellow American denouncing his country in such reckless terms before a British audience, who loved every word of it. The Americans wrote furious letters to newspaper editors back home, urging them to tell their readers about Garrison's "treachery."[12]

. . .

Garrison returned to America in a state of euphoria. In his luggage was a letter signed by a gallery of British notables, including Wilberforce, denouncing the American Colonization Society. In New York, Arthur Tappan, a reformer who had supported Garrison with generous gifts of cash, was carried away by reports of Garrison's London triumphs and invited him to be the guest of honor at a mass meeting, announcing the formation of an American Anti-Slavery Society which would support a call for immediate abolition.

When Garrison debarked from his ship, he picked up a New York City newspaper on the dock and read an editorial that told readers "the notorious Garrison" was coming to the city. The paper urged New Yorkers to attend the antislavery meeting and tell the foul-mouthed betrayer of his country what they thought of him. The stunned Garrison made his way through the crowded streets to Clinton Hall, the site of the meeting. Unrecognized, he stood on the edge of an enraged crowd as they shouted denunciations of him and immediate abolition. The hall was dark and there was a notice on the door that the meeting had been moved elsewhere.

The crowd adjourned to a rally at nearby Tammany Hall, headquarters of the already notorious Democratic political machine. For a noisy hour, orators denounced abolitionists as the enemies of New York's southern friends, whose business was vital to the city's prosperity. Several thousand members of the audience, now totally infuriated, responded to news that the abolitionists were meeting at the Chatham Street Chapel near the docks, and charged into the streets again.

The rioters, many of them drunk, banged and kicked at the chapel's doors, shouting obscenities. Once more Garrison lingered nervously on the edge of the mob while the lights in the chapel went out and Gotham's handful of abolitionists fled for their lives. Soon the mob smashed in the chapel doors and swarmed inside.[13]

An appalled Garrison decided he would be safer in Boston, where he wrote a derring-do version of his narrow escape in *The Liberator*. Five thousand enemies of freedom had tried to tar and feather him, but he had eluded their evil clutches. "I regard them with mingled emotions of pity and contempt," he declared. He was ready to "brave any danger, even unto death." The words may have won him some sympathy in Boston, where opinions of money-grubbing New Yorkers had never been high. But it remained clear that the nation's largest and richest city was unimpressed by Garrison's supposed triumphs in Britain.[14]

New Yorkers also did not think much of the British abolition of slavery in the West Indies. Freeing 850,000 slaves who were three thousand miles away was simply not the same as the immediate liberation of 2,000,000 blacks in the American South. Virginia, the nation's largest slave state, was only three hundred miles away. What was to stop tens of thousands of ex-slaves from heading for New York and competing with white workers for jobs? If employment was not forthcoming, they would have to be fed and clothed by the city or state government to prevent an insurrection that would make Nat Turner's eruption a mere skirmish. William Lloyd Garrison and his followers remained tragically blind to this crucial difference between British and American slavery.

CHAPTER 9

New England Rediscovers the Sacred Union

While William Lloyd Garrison was learning that his love affair with British abolitionists was meaningless, American politicians had other things on their minds. The Industrial Revolution in Britain and parts of the United States—notably New England—was beginning to transform the world. To protect the new factories, Congress began passing tariff bills that shielded America's manufacturers from competitive British products.

At first many southerners supported the tariff; they expected to industrialize too. South Carolina was especially optimistic. They had water power, and their plantations were producing cotton by the ton. But few southerners had the technical background to run a mill, and imported Yankees proved poor managers of slave labor. The cotton growers decided they could make more money by expanding their plantations. Many of the most ambitious planters headed west to bigger farms and richer soil in Alabama and Mississippi. South Carolina slid into a slow but unmistakable economic stagnation.

In 1819, the stock market had crashed and a recession stifled the American economy everywhere. By the mid-1820s, South Carolina was looking at the tariff as a burden rather than a benefit. Their hostility was deepened by a cotton surplus that triggered a sharp drop in the price paid by British and New England mills. The state began to see the tariff as a sinister policy aimed at enriching greedy Yankees and impoverishing genteel southern aristocrats.[1]

In 1827, this persecution complex was exacerbated by finding a Yankee, John Quincy Adams, in the White House backing a new and even steeper levy on consumer goods from Britain. President Adams was hoping to raise money for canals, highways, and other public works projects that the country needed. South Carolina's politicians dismissed these ideas and denounced "the tariff of abominations."

Virginia's John Randolph, always ready to create an uproar, accused the New Englanders of building their factories with dollars pilfered from the pockets of the South. Charleston began hosting mass protest meetings where politicians wondered aloud whether there was any point in staying in a Union that was bankrupting them. The North, cried one man, veering toward a metaphor everyone instantly recognized, acted as if they were the masters and the Southerners were their humble "tributaries."[2]

In Washington, DC, South Carolina's John C. Calhoun, vice president under President Adams, paid close attention to these growls of discontent. Calhoun decided it was time to borrow a leaf from Thomas Jefferson's playbook and resort to the ominous word, nullification. At this point Calhoun was considered a likely prospect for the presidency. Strikingly handsome, he was a superb orator and a politician who seemed adept at working with Northerners and Westerners. He had been a well-regarded secretary of war under President Monroe. But he was extremely sensitive to the growing hostility to slavery in the northern states.

Soon there was something called "the Exposition of 1828," a treatise secretly written by the vice president and approved by the South Carolina legislature. It declared that the Constitution was a compact between the states, each of whom still retained an ineradicable sovereignty. This meant a state had the right to nullify any act of Congress if its legislature thought the law exceeded federal powers. Some politicians in Virginia and other southern states applauded this idea. Seventy-six-year-old James Madison, still very much alive in his Virginia mansion, Montpelier, said the argument was preposterous and nothing in the Constitution countenanced it. The nullifiers dismissed him as a senile has-been.[3]

These tensions did not diminish when Andrew Jackson defeated President Adams's run for reelection. The ex-general had no quarrel with high tariffs. They did not bother many people in his home state, prosperous Tennessee. But the West wanted a better deal on the government's sale of public lands. Would she get help from the South or the North? The debate swiftly became a confrontation between the two older sections.

In December 1829, a Jackson-hating Connecticut senator introduced a proposal to put a hold on selling any more western land. Senator Thomas Hart Benton of Missouri called the idea a "scheme to injure the West and South" by keeping "pauperized" factory workers in the East. Senator Robert Y. Hayne saw an opportunity to score points for the South. The slim, handsome orator attacked the proposal as a typical example of New England's habit of putting self-interest ahead of the nation. This charge led readily to a condemnation of the Yankees' role in promoting ever-higher tariffs, forcing South Carolina to consider leaving the Union.

Senator Daniel Webster of Massachusetts rose to deplore Senator Haynes's hostility to New England and his habit of speaking of the Union "in terms of indifference, even of disparagement." Too many Southerners talked this way. Webster challenged Hayne to a debate on whether there was any justification for his condemnation of New England—and dared him to prove a state could legally disobey a law passed by Congress, such as a tariff.

Hayne accepted the terms of this verbal duel, and he began by attempting to prove New England's hostility to the West. Webster replied that the claim was absurd. Tens of thousands of New Englanders had already migrated to the growing states of Ohio, Indiana, and Illinois. The retort was superficially effective but largely beside the point. Already the northern tiers of these states was called "the Yankee Midwest." The settlers brought with them their New England traditions and loyalties, which included hostility to the Southerners who inhabited the lower half of these states—and to the rest of the South.

Senator Hayne replied with a speech that lasted two days. He attacked New England's record of disloyalty to the federal government, culminating in the Hartford Convention, and defended the Calhoun view that a state's rights transcends the authority of the Constitution. By now the small circular Senate chamber was packed with spectators. They filled the gallery and the aisles on the floor below. People sensed that the future of the nation was being debated.

·   ·   ·

Daniel Webster rose to rescue New England from the obloquy of its secessionist flirtations. The senator had begun his political career as a combative Federalist congressman and had graduated to the Senate in 1827 under the banner of the proto-Whig National Republican Party. A large, imposing man, Webster's craggy brow seemed to darken like an impending thunderstorm as he assailed Senator Hayne for his betrayal of Washington's and Madison's ideal of an indissoluble Union. Hour after hour Webster's rhetoric engulfed the Senate. He was alternately witty, sarcastic, angry—and ultimately, solemn. He called on the Senate and the rest of the nation to dedicate America to the founders' faith that the Union was eternal.

> I have not accustomed myself to hang over the precipice of disunion, to see whether, with my short sight, I can fathom the abyss below; nor could I regard him as a safe counselor in the affairs of this government, whose thoughts should be bent mainly on considering, not how the Union may be preserved, but how tolerable might be the condition of the people when it should be broken up and destroyed.

What did these disunionists want? Webster thundered. "A land rent with civil feuds and drenched, it may be, in fraternal blood?" For him there was only one answer to such a prospect. The flag as it now soared above American soil, "honored by all the nations of the earth"; the flag without a single star or stripe "erased and polluted," with its motto what it has always been and always should be. Not "words of delusion and folly" such as what is this all worth? Or Liberty first and Union afterwards. "No, there can only be one sentiment, dear to every American heart: Liberty and Union, now and forever, one and inseparable!"

If these magnificent words had been spoken by anyone but a senator from Massachusetts, they might have made the Union as unbreakable as the biblical rock of the ages. Webster's subsequent career would demonstrate he was deeply sincere. But in 1830, Southerners heard his speech as a hypocritical attempt to obfuscate the way New England had repeatedly ignored George Washington's plea in his farewell address to avoid any and all political posturing that endangered the Union. On the other hand, Westerners, most of them passionate nationalists, applauded Webster. President Andrew Jackson, that quintessential Man of the West, agreed with every syllable.[4]

·   ·   ·

A few months later, on Thomas Jefferson's birthday, President Jackson was the guest of honor at a public dinner celebrating the famed Virginian, who had died four years earlier. Calhoun—now Jackson's vice president—and some of his allies attempted to trap the president with a series of toasts that reminded everyone that Jefferson had endorsed the idea of nullification.

The plotters were confident of winning this not-so-subtle confrontation. Andrew Jackson had been born in South Carolina. His life had been molded by southern traditions. He was a rebel by instinct, with a long history of quarrels with his superiors. Perhaps most important, he was the virtual opposite of a political theorist; he had no education worth mentioning.

Finally, it was Jackson's turn to offer a toast. He raised his glass and riveted his flinty eyes on Vice President Calhoun. "Our federal Union," he growled. "It *must* be preserved!"

The vice president replied with a defiant countertoast: "The Union—next to our liberty, the most dear!"

Those words ended all possibility of John C. Calhoun serving another term as vice president. In 1832, with Martin Van Buren of New York as his running mate, Jackson won a second term on a tidal wave of votes. He also signed a new tariff bill, which lowered some of the 1828 duties but still retained high rates on textiles and other materials, such as iron, that South Carolina needed. The state's infuriated politicians summoned a convention that declared the law null and void. No federal officer would be permitted to collect a penny on imports in Charleston after February 1, 1833.[5]

·   ·   ·

The cavaliers of the Palmetto State were unaware that President Jackson was conferring almost daily with the man who had written much of the Constitution—James Madison. One of Jackson's aides, Nicholas Trist, had been Thomas Jefferson's secretary for the last two years of his life. (Trist had married a Jefferson granddaughter.) While at Monticello, he also became friendly with Madison. When the nullification crisis erupted, Trist asked Madison to advise President Jackson. The aged founder told Old Hickory he could and should condemn the nullifiers, and if they attempted to carry out their threat to secede from the Union, he should crush their revolt with all the force and authority of his presidential powers.

One of Jackson's old soldier friends, General Sam Dale of Mississippi, visited the White House not long after South Carolina had announced its nullification of the tariff. The two men discussed the situation over a decanter of whiskey. "Sam," Jackson said. "They are trying me here. But by the God in heaven, I will uphold the laws."

General Dale said he hoped things would go right.

"They shall go right, sir!" roared Old Hickory, and smashed his fist down on the table so hard he broke one of his clay pipes.

On December 10, 1832, President Jackson issued a proclamation to the people of South Carolina, warning them that their nullification decree was an absurdity. If they tried to support it with force, it would become disunion and treason. Jackson began sending South Carolina unionists grenades and rockets for street fighting. "Nullification means insurrection" he wrote to one of the unionist leaders. "I will meet it at the threshold and have the leaders arraigned for treason. In forty days I can have within the limits of South Carolina fifty thousand men and in forty days another fifty thousand."

Senator Robert Y. Hayne had become South Carolina's governor. He defiantly made plans for a ten-thousand-man army and declared he would maintain the state's sovereignty or "perish beneath its ruins." The nullifiers called on other southern states for support. Virginia, Georgia, and Alabama replied that they abhorred nullification, but Georgia proposed a Southern convention to discuss the situation.

In Washington, Vice President Martin Van Buren and other cautious politicians urged Jackson to go slowly. "Your policy," Old Hickory replied, "would destroy all confidence in our government at home and abroad. I expect soon to hear a civil war has commenced. If the leaders are surrounded by twelve thousand bayonets, our [federal] marshal shall be aided by twenty four thousand and arrest them in the midst thereof."

The president grimly directed Congress to prepare a force bill that would authorize him to invade South Carolina. But Jackson was a man who had seen war and loathed its death and destruction. He warned "the citizens of my native state" that as president he could not "avoid the performance of his duty." He also announced his approval of a congressional revision of the tariff, to lower some of the rates that were distressing South Carolina.

The two bills passed almost simultaneously. The South Carolinians repealed the nullification ordinance—and voted to nullify the force bill. The president ignored this empty gesture of defiance and accepted a precarious peace. "I thought I would have to hang some of them," Jackson said with more than a hint of regret. He feared the next time the nullification monster reared its head, "It will be the Negro, or slavery question."[6]

CHAPTER 10

Another Thomas Jefferson Urges Virginia to Abolish Slavery

While South Carolina veered toward rebellion against the tariff, the future of slavery was agitating Virginia. The Old Dominion was still one of the nation's three largest states, with 1,211,405 people, including 469,737 slaves. In a dozen eastern counties the bondsmen heavily outnumbered whites. Nat Turner's rebellion had prompted Governor William Floyd to propose a select committee to examine "the subject of slaves, free Negroes and the melancholy occurrences growing out of the tragical massacre in Southampton County." The committee was duly organized, with only a vague idea of how to proceed. Privately, Floyd confided to his diary his hope that they would find a way to gradually abolish slavery in the state.[1]

William Henry Roane, a grandson of Patrick Henry, submitted a Quaker petition calling for emancipation as a topic the committee should discuss. A violent debate erupted, with not a few lawmakers demanding that the subject be banned from the committee's agenda. They claimed that the mere mention of the word was likely to foment a larger and more horrendous replay of Nat Turner's rampage.

Committee Chairman William Henry Broadnax, a blunt-spoken slave owner from Dinwiddie County in eastern Virginia, was shocked by this proposed evasion. He asked the members if they wanted the rest of America to conclude that Virginia was unwilling or afraid to consider how to find "an ultimate delivery from the greatest curse that God in his wrath ever inflicted upon a people." The legislature voted by a three-to-one majority to accept the Quaker proposal—and were soon wondering if they had made a mistake.

The lawmakers were flooded with pro and con petitions and resolutions. Emancipation was a topic that obviously stirred deep emotions. Once more the alarmists rose to demand an end of the discussion. Their slaves, one man warned, "were not unconscious of what was going on here." There was no hope of finding a practical plan for freeing them. A debate on the topic would only create massive unhappiness and very possibly another outbreak of violence.[2]

A new delegate stepped forward with a plan. Six feet four, with the shoulders of a champion wrestler, thirty-nine-year-old Thomas Jefferson Randolph was the founder's oldest grandson. He was deeply devoted to his grandfather. "Jefferson," as the family called him, was in the midst of paying all the debts that the bankrupt Master of Monticello had left on his ledgers. It would take Randolph and his wife another twenty years of painful sacrifices, but the money would ultimately be paid, to the last penny.

Randolph had run for the legislature to present a plan for gradual emancipation and realize his grandfather's yearning to solve the problem that had tormented his old age. Another reason for his presence as a delegate was the anxiety Nat Turner had stirred in Randolph's wife, Jane. Like many Virginia women her age, a fear of slave violence had all but vanished from her mind. But Turner's eruption had aroused her anxiety "to the most agonizing degree." In a way, slavery, too, was an inherited debt that Thomas Jefferson Randolph wanted to remove from his family's escutcheon.

Another spur was a letter from Edward Coles, a Virginia neighbor who had written to Thomas Jefferson in 1814, urging him to lead a crusade against slavery. Jefferson had replied that he was too old to undertake such a huge task but assured Coles and fellow idealists of his generation that they had his blessing. Coles had transported his slaves to Illinois and freed them. In the 1820s, when proslavery men in that state tried to persuade the legislature to repeal the Northwest Ordinance, Coles had run for governor and defeated them. Now Coles urged Thomas Jefferson Randolph to take the lead in ridding Virginia of slavery. It was a virtual command the younger man could not ignore.[3]

Slowly, earnestly, Randolph presented his plan: Starting on July 4, 1840, all the slaves born in Virginia would become the property of the state government when they reached maturity. Before they matured, their owners would be free to sell them to masters in other southern states. Those who remained would be hired out to earn the cost of transporting them "beyond the limits of the United States."[4]

The huge number of Virginia's slaves made the cost of sending the slaves to another country almost prohibitive. Randolph was clinging to his grandfather's solution, but time had rendered it dubious. The speech left much to be desired in other ways. Later Randolph would confess that the brave words marching through his head as he rose to speak had somehow vanished "as mist before the sun." He had inherited his grandfather's limitations as a public speaker. The best he could do was close by reading Thomas Jefferson's reply to Edward Coles, proving that he passionately wished to see slavery vanish from Virginia.

Another fierce debate exploded. Sharpening tempers was a not-so-secret division in the legislature between delegates from western Virginia, where slaves were few, and the east, where the original settlers had created large plantations, some with hundreds of bondsmen. The westerners had recently demanded more delegates to the legislature, based on a count of white voters. The easterners insisted on counting their slaves and retained a majority. To no one's surprise, the westerners were far more willing to consider a proposal to eliminate the evil institution. They did not even blink when one delegate called slavery "a calamity" and predicted Virginia was heading for a "servile" war, with the extermination of one of the races the outcome. Santo Domingo was obviously still a nightmare in many memories.

The candor and passion with which these men spoke was remarkable proof of the desire to solve the problem. James MacDowell expressed his dread of a "ruptured brotherhood" and the creation of two sections of their formerly united country, each hunched behind barriers of mutual hatred. Virginians were in danger of being held up as "common enemies of man whom it will be a duty to overthrow and justice to despoil." A century later, those words drew an anguished exclamation from a veteran historian. For "prophetic vision," he wrote, those words were "never surpassed by anyone who opposed the holding of Negroes in bondage!"[5]

Eastern Virginians, living in the midst of thousands of slaves, were far less likely to favor emancipation. One spokesman for the eastern delegates called Randolph's plan "monstrous and unconstitutional." Some of them dismissed Turner's revolt as a minor tragedy, triggered by an "ignorant religious fanatic." Others claimed Virginia's slaves were "as happy a laboring class as exists upon the habitable globe." At this point in the industrial revolution, these words were hardly a tribute to slavery. Workers in British and New England factories were toiling twelve hours a day for starvation wages. But it was a way of portraying slave owners as no worse than other businessmen.

Another eastern delegate rejected the whole idea of debating the "abstract" question of slavery's morality. Didn't these antislavery do-gooders know the nation's founders owned slaves? he asked. Not a word was said by anyone about George Washington freeing his slaves—more evidence that this gesture had made little impact on the public mind, even in Virginia. Growing heated, the speaker predicted that if this plan of future emancipation passed the legislature, it would ignite a race war and destroy the liberty and justice for which the founders had fought.

Finally, Committee Chairman William Broadnax intervened. They were getting nowhere, he said. There was little chance of the committee endorsing a plan as explicit and far-reaching as Thomas Jefferson Randolph's. But he strongly disagreed with the delegates who were saying slavery should not even be discussed. It was agitating people around the world. (Britain was in the midst of her West Indies abolition debates.) Broadnax said he also disagreed strongly with the people who claimed slavery was not immoral. As it was practiced in Virginia, the institution was a "transcendent evil."

If anything was to be done about it, Broadnax continued, it had to meet three requirements: freed slaves had to be removed from the state as soon as possible; the inviolability of private property had to be respected; no owner should be forced to part with a slave without "ample compensation" for his or her value. Thomas Jefferson Randolph's plan did not pass this test, and Broadnax dismissed it as "nauseous to the palate."

The committee chairman now revealed his own agenda. He thought there was little hope of figuring out what to do about the state's hundreds of thousands of slaves. It was more important to find a solution to Virginia's fifty thousand free blacks, who were far more dangerous. Many of them could read and write, and they had access to abolitionist literature. He recommended a program to deport six thousand free blacks a year to Liberia. That would take only a decade, and the cost would be minimal—even a bargain, compared to buying the freedom of the slaves. It would give the legislators time for further thought about the conundrum of the enslaved blacks.

With very little further discussion, the committee accepted the chairman's solution. Their report's preamble declared it was "inexpedient" for them to enact any legislation for the abolition of slavery. A wry western delegate jumped up to recommend changing "inexpedient" to "expedient." The motion lost by 15 votes. Thomas Jefferson Randolph was one of the few eastern delegates who voted for it. The preamble—and by implication, the entire report—was accepted by a vote of 67 to 60, with Randolph again voting against it. Not a few people were amazed by the closeness of the vote. A shift of opinion by four delegates would have defeated the measure.[6]

The legislature spent most of the next weeks concocting a plan to force free blacks to leave Virginia, either by the colonization route, or by migration to a free state. Another bill denied them the right to a trial by jury; if they were convicted of a crime, they could be reenslaved and sold out of the state. No black could attend a religious service unless there were whites in the audience, making it unlikely that the preacher would utter any insurrectionary ideas.[7]

.   .   .

Watching this reversal of his hopes, Thomas Jefferson Randolph became more and more distressed. He finally exploded in a speech that was reprinted in the *Richmond Enquirer*. He scoffed at this attempt to make another slave insurrection unlikely. Without any hope of abolition for themselves or their children, Virginia's slaves were certain to revolt on a scale far larger than Nat Turner's berserk band. That would almost inevitably lead to another tragedy that his grandfather had predicted to him and to the public: the dissolution of the federal Union.

That would mean civil war, Randolph predicted, and an invasion of Virginia by a northern army. In their ranks would be black troops, determined to achieve "the liberation of their race." There would be no place for white Virginians to hide when that happened. Nothing would save "your wives and your children from destruction."[8]

Thomas Jefferson Randolph went back to Albemarle County, determined to continue his fight for gradual abolition in his grandfather's name. He stood for the legislature again and defeated a former U.S. congressman who ran against him on a proslavery platform. But Randolph soon grew discouraged and abandoned his campaign. Forty-two years later, in a bitter letter written after the Civil War had reduced him and his family to poverty, Randolph told how Virginia had been inundated with an avalanche of abolitionist propaganda that revealed a "morbid hatred of the southern white man" and blackened his character "with obscene malignity." Before long, enraged Virginians would not tolerate a discussion of how to eliminate slavery because abolitionism had become synonymous with hatred and contempt for their way of life, as well as a word that stirred their deepest fear—a race war.[9]

CHAPTER 11

The Abolitionist
Who Lost His Faith

The man behind this outburst of abolitionist animosity was not William Lloyd Garrison. Thanks largely to his combative ways and offensive language, his impact was limited outside his small circle of New England followers; the circulation of *The Liberator* remained small. The new vigor emanated from the New York–based American Anti-Slavery Society, financed by Arthur Tappan and his circle of well-to-do philanthropists. Their energies were divided by enthusiasm for numerous good causes. But they found a man in upstate New York who became their dynamic spokesman against slavery: Theodore Dwight Weld.

A Connecticut-born minister's son in search of a life-fulfilling mission, Weld was Garrison's opposite in many ways. He was a big, muscular man with a rough-hewn face and streaming unkempt hair. Unlike the fastidious Garrison, Weld was proud of his "bearish" style and sometimes described himself as a "backwoodsman untamed." When he was invited to speak in Boston, he declined, saying he was much too "shaggy" for their elegant tastes.

This was the language of a consummate actor, playing a role to please an audience. The man behind the persona was a much more complex human being, as his followers would eventually discover. Weld's audience was the tens of thousands of Yankees who had streamed into New York and then into the midwestern states. They brought with them their New England Protestant faith with its roots in Puritanism. Almost all of Weld's followers had experienced the spiritual drama of the Second Great Awakening and were ready to listen to new ways of winning the approval of their stern Old Testament God.

Some embraced temperance in the hope of abolishing alcoholism, a plague that was ruining countless families. Their version of temperance quickly became an absolute ban on even a single drink of alcohol, including beer or wine. Others assailed Roman Catholicism as a creeping menace to American liberty. Still others crusaded against the Masonic Order for its secretive, supposedly evil ways. Even more turned to abolition—and Theodore Dwight Weld became their heaven-sent prophet.[1]

· · ·

Instead of publishing a newspaper sent to unseen readers, Weld sent himself. He began his career as a protégé of a famous revivalist in upstate New York but soon transferred his abilities to Ohio. There he entered Lane Seminary in Cincinnati, and in a few months he convened an eighteen-day discussion with his fellow seminarians that persuaded them slavery was America's most ghastly sin. They called on Lane to start admitting Cincinnati's free Negroes to some of their classes. Lane's trustees objected; they were sensitive to the city's proximity to Kentucky with its 250,000 slaves. Lane's president, a glowering former New Englander named Lyman Beecher, was also opposed. He thought the Roman Catholic Church was the nation's premier evil.[2]

Weld led a revolt that virtually emptied the seminary of students. Many of them became Weld's collaborators in a campaign to awaken antislavery fervor in Ohio. Another large group transferred to Oberlin College, which was run by outspoken abolitionists and was already admitting blacks. Others flung themselves into educating and uplifting Cincinnati's free blacks, who lived in a segregated "Little Africa" community.[3]

From town to town Weld and his followers travelled, preaching their message of slavery's sinfulness and the guilt that every American man and woman shared for this ongoing defiance of God's will. They used the techniques of the revival meeting to stir emotions; they challenged their listeners to put themselves in the slave's place, to imagine how he felt when he saw his wife lashed or raped by a sadistic owner, or his children sold to a slave trader who took them, shackled and forlorn, to Memphis or New Orleans. Garrison said similar things in *The Liberator*, but words on paper were pale lifeless things compared to the impact an impassioned Weld and his disciples achieved in person.

Weld was the most indefatigable of these crusaders by far. He would arrive in a town, introduce himself to the local minister, and sometimes board with him and his family. Meanwhile he would rent a hall and preach day and night, as many as eighteen times in one place. He was not always welcome. More than once, he found himself the target of flung stones and pods of manure and mud. In Circleview, Ohio, a rock struck him in the head while he was preaching. Dazed but unfazed, he got up and finished the sermon. Most of the time, audiences succumbed to his call for action; when he departed a town, he usually left behind an antislavery society.

The pace at which the Weld wing of the abolitionist movement grew under his leadership was phenomenal. In four years of campaigning, often to the point of physical and emotional collapse, he and his followers created 1,346 local antislavery societies, and they raised enough money to hire seventy full-time paid agents to continue the crusade. To appreciate this achievement, a comparison to the British antislavery campaign is instructive. At the climax of their forty-year struggle, they had only six paid agents.

Energized by Weld, the American Anti-slavery Society also began distributing over a million publications—pamphlets, sermons, petitions to Congress and state legislatures—each year. These became the paper avalanche that deluged and infuriated Virginia.[4]

One of the keys to Weld's success was his almost mystical appeal to women. They sent him stories of dreams he had inspired, in which his stentorian voice and charismatic figure is mingled with the power of God. One woman told him he had moved her "like the quivering throb of a lacerated limb, the convulsive throb of a crushed bosom." Women became the prime distributors of antislavery publications. They jammed Weld's meetings, wept and cried out at his oratorical flights, and soon gave Weld the illusion that he was invincible. He told one man that he now thought slavery would be vanquished in five years.[5]

"God's terrors begin to blaze upon the guilty nation," he told one fellow campaigner. "If repentance, speedy and deep and *national*, does not forestall Jehovah's judgment . . . the voice of a brother's blood crying from the ground will peal against the wrathful heavens and shake down ruin like a fig tree casteth her untimely fruit."

These apocalyptic words terrified and uplifted most of Weld's listeners. But some people began asking tough questions. Most of Ohio, western Pennsylvania, and northern New York were in an abolitionist turmoil. But had all this excitement freed a single slave in the South?

It began to dawn on many abolitionists that America was not and never would be England. No matter how many people they converted and how many antislavery petitions they generated, they had little or no impact on the politicians in the state and federal governments. Even more daunting was the realization that they were changing almost no minds in the South, where the power to free or not to free the slaves resided. For Weld, such doubts were troubling and his experience in northern New York further darkened these questions in his mind and heart.

Weld was not welcomed in this turbulent section of the Empire State. He swiftly became "the most mobbed man in the United States." Usually he demanded and got police protection. But at Troy, Weld collided with a hostile community—and public officials—not unlike those he would encounter if he ventured into the South. A mob shut down the church where he and an associate were planning to preach. The mayor of the city said things that encouraged the demonstrators. When Weld found another church that gave him its pulpit, the mob stormed into the place and tried to drag him into the street. It soon became apparent that if he so much as ventured outside his boarding house, he was going to be assaulted by rocks and epithets. His body became "one general painful bruise."[6]

In a letter to a Rhode Island believer who was urging him to quit Troy, Weld declared that every abolitionist had to find out if he were willing to "lie upon the rack" for the cause. But the mayor of Troy did not give him an opportunity to make this sacrifice. He told Weld to leave the city or he would use force to deport him.[7]

This defeat inflicted a serious psychological wound on Weld. For a while, he continued to play a leadership role at the American Anti-Slavery Society. To energize their paid agents, they held a convention in New York and asked Weld to preside over it. For seventeen days in November and December of 1836, he did so with his usual vigor, meeting with these eager crusaders for eight hours every day and often toiling until three a.m. preparing his remarks for the following day. By the last session, his mighty voice had been reduced to a croak. No one realized that they would not hear Theodore Dwight Weld speak again for another decade.[8]

. . .

During the next years, Weld turned to a new role in the crusade. He became a writer and editor for the American Anti-Slavery Society and a resident of New York, where he fell in love with a remarkable woman, Angelina Grimké. She and her older sister, Sarah, were the daughters of a wealthy Charleston slave owner. They had decided slavery was evil, broken with their family and friends, and moved north. Angelina and her sister were also passionate advocates of women's rights. When Angelina married Theodore in 1838, instead of the usual ceremonial words about love and obedience, she required a promise that he would always treat her as an equal.

The Grimkés' firsthand stories of the cruelties inflicted on slaves in South Carolina mesmerized Weld. For the first time he realized that he and other abolitionists had been contending with a general idea of slavery as wrong in principle. They devoted most of their speeches to what freedom could accomplish in a slave's soul. They had little or no acquaintance with slavery as a day-to-day reality. Weld decided they needed a book that would prove slavery was wrong in practice. Day after day for the next six months, he and the Grimkés went through twenty thousand copies of southern newspapers, clipping stories that proved slavery's almost daily cruelty.

The Grimkés added to this collection their personal memories. Angelina told of talking to the female slave of a wealthy Charleston woman, who had been sent to the "treadmill" where disobedient or defiant slaves were flogged. The slave revealed gashes on her back so deep, Angelina said, "I might have laid my whole finger in them." Another victim, a disobedient boy, had been whipped so ferociously he could barely walk. These were typical of the examples that filled the pages of Weld's book, *Slavery As It Is.*

In Weld's introduction to the book, he urged each reader to sit as a juror and bring in "an honest verdict" on slavery and slave owners. When a reader finished the book, Weld was sure, he or she would no longer believe slave owners who claimed to treat their slaves as human beings. Here was proof that slaves' "ears are often cut off, their eyes knocked out, their bones broken, their flesh branded with red hot irons; that they are maimed, mutilated and burned to death over slow fires; All these things and more, and worse, we shall *prove.*"

Slavery As It Is was an instant publishing success. It sold a hundred thousand copies in its first year and continued to sell for another decade. But it did not solve the personal problems that were troubling Theodore Weld— or the future of the stalled abolition movement. Not a few of Weld's friends objected to the harsh tone of his book. Others accused him of worsening the threat of a civil war. The Grimkés' relations in South Carolina considered the book a personal insult. One of Angelina's sisters accused her of hastening their mother's death.[9]

Weld followed this book with a report on the impact of abolition in the British West Indies. He claimed that contrary to the dread inspired by Santo Domingo, emancipation had gone smoothly there. Subsequent developments would prove this was anything but the case. But it was undoubtedly true that the freed slaves had not turned on their ex-masters with machetes and muskets.

.   .   .

Over the next few years, Theodore Weld became dubious about abolitionism as a way of life. He was enormously disturbed by two scandals in the movement. One was the discovery that a leader in the Midwest had pilfered funds from Oberlin College. The evildoer had also seduced and impregnated a woman acquaintance, forced her to abort the child, and married another woman. Even more shocking was the revelation that the minister of an abolitionist church in Brooklyn had sexually abused at least ten young girls.

Weld began to wonder whether abolitionism was the path to personal holiness and true contact with God. Compounding these doubts were angry clashes with abolitionists and their critics in many parts of the nation. A series of visits to Washington, DC, where Weld worked with antislavery members of the new Whig Party, added to his disillusionment. He saw firsthand the rage that abolitionism stirred in Southerners, who accused its proponents of being indifferent to—or even eager for—a slave insurrection and a race war in which thousands of women and children would be slaughtered. Was this the way to achieve God's heaven on earth? Weld wondered.

His doubts exploded in a speech Weld gave in 1844, "God's Hinderances." He asked his audience—and himself—a question: Could any person or group of persons hope to reform the American world in any fundamental way by calling slave owners vicious names? Were Christian charity and any hope of mutual respect being destroyed by abolitionism? Weld's reply was a mournful yes, and he withdrew from the abolitionist crusade.[10]

CHAPTER 12

Abolitionism Divides and Conquers Itself

While abolitionism lost its strongest voice with Theodore Weld's withdrawal, the William Lloyd Garrison wing of the movement was undergoing its own upheavals. Much of the trouble was caused by the founder's tendency to attack established churches for their lukewarm approach to antislavery and their continuing fondness for colonization. He also viewed with disapproval any antislavery society that was not pledged to his demand for immediate emancipation. When his followers won a vote in the 1840 annual meeting of the American Anti-Slavery Society, a large part of the membership seceded to form a separate society, opposed to this all-or-nothing approach.[1]

New causes and beliefs further divided potential recruits. Many people became convinced that they did not need a church or a minister to discover God's truth. Prayer and an intense reading of the Bible would guide them. This led to a bewildering variety of Christian faiths preached at camp meetings. Upstate New York was the home for many of these new beliefs. It soon acquired the nickname "The Burned Over District," suggesting that many souls had caught fire so often, they no longer had the energy to deal with any cause in a systematic way.

One of the most explosive ideas came from a lay preacher named William Miller. He grew convinced that Christ would return to earth and the world would end in the next few years, making abolitionism and other crusades irrelevant. Millerism swept New York and New England and even found roots in distant Britain. Various dates for Christ's return were proposed by a veritable babble of Bible readers. Miller himself remained reluctant to specify a single day. Gradually, however, a consensus emerged that October 21, 1844, would be the day of the "Great Hope."

Some people sold their farms and gave away their money, convinced that only the poor in fact as well as in spirit would achieve salvation. On the appointed day, hundreds gathered on mountaintops in northern New York to welcome the Savior. When Jesus failed to appear, not a few people were unable to deal with the "Great Disappointment" and began wailing and babbling hysterically. In some towns angry mobs stormed the churches where the true believers had met, smashing and burning them. Occasionally the disenchanted wielded clubs and knives. In Toronto, Canada, the punishment was tar and feathers.[2]

.   .   .

Further confusing the abolitionist movement were the extreme doctrines Garrison began to embrace. He wondered aloud if people needed a government, which only seemed to corrupt them into passive tolerance of evils like slavery. One of his followers, Nathaniel Peabody Rogers, began preaching not only no government, but also no organizations of any kind—a forerunner of the ideology of anarchism that would agitate the closing years of the nineteenth century. This was too much even for Garrison, and he silenced Rogers by seizing control of the newspaper he was publishing, *Herald of Freedom.*

In the mid-1830s, the opposition to abolitionism both in the North and South became stronger when a mass of antislavery pamphlets mailed from

Boston was discovered in the Charleston post office. Indignation swept the South, and Harrison Gray Otis was one of several prominent Bostonians who convened a mass meeting to "vindicate the fair name" of their city. The seventy-year-old Otis gave one of the most vehement speeches of his career, calling on respectable people to unite against the abolitionists, who were creating so much turmoil in the nation. Speaking as a man who knew many Southerners well, he predicted that if Garrison and his friends were not checked, they were going to start a devastating civil war, in which the South would fight to protect the safety of their women and children.[3]

.　　.　　.

Boston responded to Otis's plea by coming very close to lynching William Lloyd Garrison. When the newspapers announced that Garrison had invited the English abolitionist George Thompson to the city, a mob poured into the streets to tell the Englishman to go home. Thompson fled, but the mob found Garrison and paraded him through the city with a rope around his neck. For a while it looked as if they were going to do him serious harm. But some friends joined local policemen who rescued the almost-victim and whisked him to the safety of the city jail.[4]

Watching from the sidelines was a young Boston aristocrat named Wendell Phillips. Harvard educated, he had shared the low opinion most of the Boston establishment had toward Garrison. A combination of sympathy for the menaced reformer and disdain for the mostly lower class mob that attacked him worked a transformation in Phillips. From that day in 1835, he became an abolitionist with a taste for violent solutions. In a few years he was urging slaves to "at least try to cut your master's throat."[5]

.　　.　　.

In Alton, Illinois, a Presbyterian minister from Maine, Elijah Lovejoy, was daring to do something that Garrison and most abolitionist leaders had hitherto avoided: telling slave owners and proslavery Southerners to their faces that they were committing a terrible wrong by keeping blacks in bondage.

This was dangerous work. Lovejoy had tried to publish his newspaper in St. Louis, Missouri. Angry mobs attacked his office and threw his press into the nearby Mississippi River not once but three times.

Lovejoy moved across the river to Alton. Why he thought this transfer would improve his reception remains mysterious. Alton and the counties in its vicinity had been settled by Southerners. The atmosphere there was not much friendlier to abolitionism than in St. Louis. Alton's city officials claimed they lacked the resources to protect Lovejoy. Instead they deputized the minister and his handful of supporters, authorizing them to defend their crusade with gunfire.

Lovejoy bought a fourth printing press and again opened for business. It did not take long for a mob to gather. Lovejoy and his friends opened fire on them, the rioters fired back, and Lovejoy died with a half dozen bullets in his body.[6]

William Lloyd Garrison decided to make Lovejoy a martyr, although he severely disapproved of Lovejoy's reliance on violence. He called on Boston to express its disapproval of the minister's murder. On December 8, 1837, over five thousand Bostonians jammed Faneuil Hall. Some came to protest Lovejoy's death, others to condemn abolitionism. The meeting was run by William Ellery Channing, a leading Boston churchman and outspoken foe of Garrison.

The stated goal was a protest against the violation of Lovejoy's civil rights—above all freedom of speech. The attorney general of Massachusetts, James T. Austin, set the tone when he condemned Lovejoy and his fellow abolitionists for trying to turn slaves loose on unoffending Southerners. Austin declared that the protestors were patriots, defending the American Union from the ruinous rupture that the abolitionists were hoping to achieve.

Up sprang Wendell Phillips to tell Austin that he did not know what he was talking about. He insisted that Lovejoy was a martyr to America's ideals, no different from the men who died in the Boston Massacre. A burst of applause made this a pivotal moment in the abolitionist crusade. A delighted Garrison pronounced the meeting "a signal triumph for our side."

Garrison still insisted that Lovejoy's death with a gun in his hand disqual-ified him as a "Christian abolitionist." With Theodore Weld on the sidelines, there is little doubt that if the abolitionist crusade had been left in Garrison's hands, it would have remained a minority movement, out of touch with the mainstream of American politics. That probability was about to change, thanks to a most unlikely recruit.[7]

CHAPTER 13

Enter Old Man Eloquent

Defeated for reelection in 1828, President John Quincy Adams was dismayed at the thought of going home to Massachusetts and turning into a replica of his embittered father, John Adams, whose defeat by Thomas Jefferson had stripped New England of its original dream of leading the American nation. In 1831 John Quincy decided to run for Congress and was easily elected. He soon found himself embroiled in the quarrel over slavery, an issue that he had done his best to avoid during his previous political career.

In the aftermath of Nat Turner's 1831 uprising, Southerners became determined to intercept antislavery newspapers, pamphlets, and books that abolitionists sent to free blacks and sympathetic whites in the South. Antislavery societies also began sending petitions to Congress urging the lawmakers to demonstrate a federal disapproval of black bondage. These appeals were equally unpopular below the Mason-Dixon line.

The petitioners wanted to amend or even ban the 1790s law that gave federal marshals the power to seize runaway slaves and return them to their owners. The law was being abused by professional slave catchers who were much more diligent than the average marshal. In the 1830s, a man could earn two hundred dollars by catching a runaway slave; that was several times the yearly salary of a common laborer. For that kind of money, these profession- als soon became ready to seize free blacks as runaways and smuggle them South aboard ships or trains.[1]

New England poet John Greenleaf Whittier summed up the abolitionists' growing anger in a poem that proclaimed:

> *No slave-hunt in our borders—no pirate on our strand!*
> *No fetters in the Bay State—no slave upon our land!*[2]

Another abolitionist cause was a ban on slavery in Washington, DC, which was governed by Congress. The abolitionists argued that if slavery was as great an evil as even many Southerners admitted, it was a disgrace to have blacks bought and sold and shackled virtually in the shadow of the capitol, with Old Glory rippling in the breeze above their heads.

Other petitions called for a ban on the interstate slave trade, which en- abled Virginia, Maryland, and other states in the upper South to sell surplus blacks to the plantations in the deep South, where the cotton crop was be- coming an ever-more-lucrative product. Numerous petitioners adopted Wil- liam Lloyd Garrison's extremism and called on Congress to give every slave his or her freedom immediately. All heaped scorn on the nation's tolerance of this terrible institution. Southern legislators reacted to these requests with outrage, and John Quincy Adams's life as a congressman became very complicated.[3]

. . .

Adams's thinking about slavery was complex. Early in his political career he had abandoned the Federalist Party and become a Jeffersonian Republi- can. That virtually guaranteed he would say nothing against slavery publicly. Privately, however, he loathed the institution. During the Missouri Com- promise crisis in 1819 and 1820, when he was President James Monroe's secretary of state, he had taken no part in the controversy but confided some revealing thoughts to his diary:

If slavery be the destined sword in the hand of the destroying angel which is to sever the ties of this Union, the same sword will cut in sunder the bonds of slavery itself. A dissolution of the Union . . . for the cause of slavery would be followed by a servile war in the slave holding states, combined with a war between the two severed portions of the Union. It seems to me that its result must be the extirpation of slavery from this whole continent; and, calamitous and desolating as this course of events . . . must be, so glorious would be its final issue, that, as God shall judge me, I dare not say it is not to be desired.[4]

A few days before Adams returned to Washington, DC, as a congressman, he had a talk with a young French writer, Alexis de Tocqueville, who was researching a book about the United States that would make him famous—*Democracy in America.* De Tocqueville asked Adams if he thought slavery was a great evil for the nation. "Yes, unquestionably," Adams replied. "It's in slavery that are to be found all the embarrassments of the present and fears of the future." But Adams also made it clear that his view of blacks made him dubious about freeing them immediately, as his fellow New Englander William Lloyd Garrison was demanding.

Speaking from his experience as a resident of Washington, DC, for almost two decades, Adams said: "I know nothing more insolent than a black when he is not speaking to his master and is not afraid of being beaten." Black women slaves were even worse. He had seen them "make frequent abuse of the kindness of their mistresses. They know that it isn't customary to inflict bodily punishment on them."[5]

·　·　·

Slowly, reluctantly, Congressman Adams was stirred to action by the measures that Southerners demanded as their anger at abolitionism increased. They wanted changes in the postal laws that would enable southern postmasters to weed out antislavery literature. They called for better enforcement of the Fugitive Slave Law. They wrathfully refused to consider abolitionist petitions to Congress. No one said a word about their underlying fear of a slave insurrection. More and more, they declaimed that they had a right to own slaves, thanks to the compromises in the Constitutional Convention that had won Southern support for the national charter.

As Adams sat at his desk in the House of Representatives listening to these tirades, he wrote a plaintive letter to his son Charles: "The voice of freedom has not yet been heard, and I am earnestly urged to speak in her name. She will be trampled under foot if I do not, and I shall be trampled under foot if I do. . . . What can I do?"

Those words suggest that Adams felt impelled to oppose the southern readiness to stifle freedom of speech—one of the fundamental rights that James Otis and John Adams and the other men of their Revolutionary generation had vowed to defend. But Adams the politician, who still hungered for another term in the White House, said little as Congress authorized postmasters to search the mail for antislavery pamphlets or books and dismissed proposals to ban slavery in the District of Columbia.

Senator John C. Calhoun summed up the South's view on the latter point in a stentorian declaration: meddling with slavery in the nation's capital would be "a foul slander on nearly one half the states of the Union." Calhoun's stance underscored another significant shift in the Southern attitude toward slavery. Instead of apologizing for it as an evil necessity, the South Carolina senator and many others began claiming there was nothing morally wrong with it.[6]

·   ·   ·

In spite of his inner hesitations, Congressman Adams became one of the most inveterate introducers of antislavery petitions, even though few of the dozens he presented in each session of Congress came from the voters who had elected him. His fame as an ex-president made him a favorite recipient for many petitioners. By 1836 he was on his feet almost daily, urging Congress to at least give these citizens the courtesy of considering some of their requests. "Over head and ears in debate," he wrote to Charles. "I have taken up the glove . . . I had no alternative left."

Although he was tormented by sciatica and lumbago, which deprived him of badly needed sleep, the aging ex-president found the combat strangely invigorating. "A skirmishing day," Adams told Charles in another letter. He had made a point of reading aloud each of three petitions to the last line, while Southerners, trapped by the House rules, impotently growled and grumbled.

After his reading, Adams sat down and listened almost cheerfully to the ferocious rebuttals and denunciations of his defiance of the majority's wishes. He knew that "one hundred members of the House represent slaves." An additional forty members from nonslave states sided with their fellow Democrats. The other hundred and twenty representatives ranged from cold to lukewarm on antislavery and "are ready to desert me at the very first scintillation of indiscretion on my part."[7]

Only a handful of congressmen from New England and their Midwest diaspora supported Adams. This huge imbalance emboldened the Southerners to make a serious blunder. In May 1836, a committee headed by Henry Laurens Pinckney of South Carolina introduced three resolutions. The first declared Congress could never interfere with slavery in any state. The second was a resolution to bar future Congresses from interfering with slavery in the District of Columbia. Adams surprised everyone by voting for both proposals.

Then came the resolution that brought the ex-president to his feet, ablaze with protest. "All petitions memorials, resolutions or papers relating in any way or to any extent whatsoever, to the subject of slavery or the abolition of slavery, shall, without either being printed or referred, be laid on the table, and that no further action shall be taken thereon." Soon called "the gag rule," the idea had the tacit approval of Speaker of the House James K. Polk of Tennessee, who cut off attempts to debate it.

Congressman Adams repeatedly broke into discussions of other matters to denounce the idea of violating free speech in this brutal way. On May 26, 1836, the House voted on the gag rule. When the clerk of the House called: "Congressman Adams?" the ex-president roared: "I hold the resolution to be a direct violation of the Constitution of the United States, of the Rules of this House, and of the rights of my Constituents!" The House voted in favor of the proposal, 117 to 69.

The gag-rulers' victory only made Adams resolve to resist it as long as he had breath and voice. He convinced himself that he would be fighting for the preservation of the Union. "This is the cause upon which I am entering the last stage of my life," he told a friend.[8]

.   .   .

Usually, the Senate was not influenced by the agitations of the House of Representatives. Pennsylvania's James Buchanan did not foresee any fuss when he introduced a petition from Quakers calling for the abolition of slavery in the District of Columbia. Buchanan quickly added that he did not share the opinion, but felt it was his duty to present it. Everyone understood what the freshman senator meant. Quakers were a significant portion of the electorate in Pennsylvania. Buchanan, who had spent a decade in the House, knew his state's political geography.

"Buck" Buchanan was a tall, heavy-set man with a strangely lopsided face, due to an eye problem that caused him to tilt his head to the left. His close friendship with Alabama's Senator William Rufus Devane King was already prompting covert smiles. President Andrew Jackson, among others, had called the fastidious King a "Miss Nancy." Some historians have suggested—or wondered if—Buchanan was gay. Others have cited a tragic youthful romance with an attractive woman who died suddenly, prompting him to vow never to marry.

As a bachelor, Buchanan had gravitated to southern politicians who often left their wives on their plantations and lived in Washington hotels and boarding houses. He roomed with Senator King until he died after a long struggle with tuberculosis in 1853. Other southern senators also became close friends.

Buchanan had made a fortune as a lawyer and investor and supported a remarkable number of orphaned nieces, nephews, and cousins, all of whom swirled through and around his mansion, "Wheatland," outside Lancaster, Pennsylvania. He had made his opinion of slavery clear in a speech in the

House of Representatives. He saw it as a political and moral evil that could not be remedied without the introduction of "evils infinitely greater." For him, abolition was virtually synonymous with a race war against "high-minded . . . southern men."

Senator Buchanan was more than a little shaken when Senator John C. Calhoun responded to his antislavery petition by angrily urging the Senate to institute its own gag rule. The debate raged for two months without reaching anything close to a majority backing the South Carolina senator. Buchanan was appalled by the rancor on both sides. Slavery was obviously a topic that virtually annihilated the Senate's tradition of courtesy and mutual respect. It is easy to see why Senator Buchanan became convinced that abolitionism was a disease in the public mind. Alas, his southern sympathies made it impossible for him to see that other diseases spawned by slavery were distorting the public mind of the South.[9]

• • •

John Quincy Adams rapidly became the most powerful Washington, DC, voice opposing Senator Calhoun and his fellow defenders of slavery. Daniel Webster, distracted by his desire to become president, struggled to find some middle ground between proslavery and antislavery and fell far behind him. People began calling the former president "Old Man Eloquent"—a title lifted from a poem by John Milton. The nickname must have galled Webster, who saw himself as Congress's great orator.

Adams was soon galling the Southerners in the House of Representatives far more with his relentless opposition to the gag rule. The abolitionists gleefully cooperated with him. In the years 1837 and 1838, they deluged Congress with petitions—130,200 for banning slavery from the District of Columbia, 32,000 for the repeal of the gag rule. Each petition had hundreds and often thousands of signatures on it. Other antislavery causes also drew large numbers of petitions. By violating the right to free speech with their gag rule, Southerners had added tens of thousands of people to the antislavery cause.

The abolitionists devised other ways to exacerbate the damage. They persuaded thousands of women to petition for their civil rights. Would the

Southern Democrats and their Northern allies dare to gag them too? Adams promptly put the Democrats to the test. When a Georgia congressman protested against Adams's presentation of a rights petition from the women of Dorchester, Massachusetts, the ex-president claimed to be shocked. Would southern gentlemen dare to extend the ban already inflicted on another group of "pure and virtuous citizens"—abolitionists—to women? It was almost tantamount to insulting their own presumably virtuous mothers!

Speaker of the House Polk ruled that Adams had a right to describe the contents of the petition. When the ex-president proceeded to read almost every word of the lengthy document, he was ordered to sit down. He did so, still reading in a defiant, declamatory voice.[10]

On another day, Adams asked the speaker if he could present a petition from nine ladies of Fredericksburg, Virginia, who seemed to be protesting the slave trade in the District of Columbia. The congressman said he was not sure whether the petitioners were slaves or free mulattoes. The petition was not clearly worded. But it was encouraging to see women engaging in such a worthy cause. This move sent Southern tempers soaring to volcanic proportions.

A South Carolina congressman called for indicting Adams for encouraging slaves to revolt. An Alabamian demanded a vote of censure. A Virginian reproached Adams for consorting with mulattoes, who by virtual definition were not respectable women. A New York Democrat tried sarcasm, urging his fellow members to be gentle with this old gentleman, who obviously did not have full command of his faculties. Otherwise how could he disturb the decorum of the House with such a ridiculous petition?

Adams finally got a chance to reply. He pointed out that he had only asked the speaker for permission to submit the petition. He had been as polite and respectful as possible. Why couldn't these critical gentlemen reply in the same decorous fashion? Moreover, he was not at all sure what these female slaves—or free mulattoes—were saying. After further discussion it became apparent that the petition was *against* the abolition of the slave trade. Someone had sent it to Adams as a hoax, hoping to embarrass him. But he had turned the joke against the jokers, with devastating results.

Adams proceeded to make a speech that lashed the Southerners like an overseer's whip. He said he was amazed that they would object to the mere idea of a petition from slaves. The most odious tyrants in the history of the human race had felt obligated to hear petitions from "the poorest of the meanest of human creatures."

He went on to say that even if the petitioners were mulattoes, and supposedly not respectable, did that mean they had no right to petition? Since when had petitioners been required to meet a character test? Moreover, who was responsible for their reputations? Wasn't it well known in the South that that there were often "great resemblances" between the progeny of colored people and the white men who claimed possession of them?

The House of Representatives Register of Debates now recorded the words: "Great agitation in the house!" Even this was an understatement. Dixon Lewis of Alabama, who weighed more than four hundred pounds, rose to roar that the House should "punish severely such an infraction of its decorum and its rules." If the House refused, he recommended that "every member from the slave states should immediately, in a body, quit this House, and go home to their constituents. We no longer have any business here."

"I will second the motion for punishment," shouted a congressman from Georgia, "And go all lengths for it."

Others bellowed, "Expel him!"

"No, no!" shouted others.

Julius Alford of Georgia seized the floor and declared: "As an act of justice to the South, the petition should be taken from the House and burnt!"

Waddy Thompson of South Carolina made a formal motion to censure Adams for "gross disrespect for the House" and called for him to be "brought to the bar to receive the severe censure of the Speaker."[11]

Here was political obtuseness wafted by outrage and anxiety to the ultimate extreme. The Southerners were talking to each other, with little or no awareness that the rest of the nation was watching and listening. They were abusing and threatening a former president of the United States who was the son of a former president. They were endowing Old Man Eloquent with a popularity in the northern states that he had never come close to achieving before.

It was only human for Adams to relish this burst of fame. But the satisfaction had its dark side. Most of his new admirers were abolitionists, and Adams's comments on mulattoes resembling their owners was a lurch in their vindictive, Southerner-slandering direction that carried him a long way from his original intent to protest the gag rule as a violation of the right of free speech.

Adams had personal reasons to dislike Southerners. They had elected Jefferson and ended his father's political career on a note of repudiation. John Quincy had hoped his reelection for a second term would compensate for the stain and pain of his father's defeat. Instead, he had been ousted from the White House by Tennessee's Andrew Jackson with the help of southern votes. Old Hickory's role as a slave owner was mostly a coincidence. But in the atmosphere of rancor and hatred created by the abolitionists and the South's reaction to them, it was difficult if not impossible for Adams to avoid thinking and feeling with an abolitionist vocabulary.

·   ·   ·

Beyond heated and abusive oratory on both sides, nothing came of the first southern attempt to censure John Quincy Adams. He continued to agitate Congress with petitions and declamations against the gag rule. In 1839, fate handed Adams an opportunity to strike a blow against slavery that won him even more national attention. A Spanish slave ship, the *Amistad*, was transporting fifty-three blacks to a Cuban port when the unwilling passengers revolted, killed the captain and most of the crew, and ordered a surviving white officer to sail back to Africa. Instead he sailed to America, where a U.S. warship captured the *Amistad* and guided it into New Haven, Connecticut's harbor.

Spain demanded that the slaves be returned to Cuba, where they would be tried for piracy. President Van Buren was inclined to give them up, and more than a few southern members of Congress supported him. But abolitionists rushed to defend them; their newspapers portrayed the slaves' leader, Cinque, as a hero. A violent legal tangle exploded in the Connecticut courts. The case soon reached the U.S. Supreme Court, where John Quincy Adams volunteered to represent the slaves. Although the court had a majority of Southerners on its bench, they listened respectfully to Adams's argument that the slaves should be released because both Spain and the United States had outlawed the slave trade. The Supreme Court freed the slaves and they returned to Africa accompanied by five Christian missionaries.[12]

. . .

Back in Boston, William Lloyd Garrison was drifting toward a new variation of his extremist views—a dissolution of the Union. He began denouncing the Constitution for the bargain the founders had made with slave owners. He called on people of the North "to demand the repeal of the Union or the abolition of slavery."

Garrison claimed the North would be forever sinful if they ignored this moral ultimatum. Some forty-five citizens of Haverhill, Massachusetts, decided to send Congressman Adams a petition asking Congress to begin working out "measures peaceably to dissolve the union of these states." They did not mention slavery; they claimed to be writing as taxpayers. In their opinion they were not getting their money's worth from the federal arrangement.

When Adams introduced this petition, southern congressman by the dozens lost their tempers. One man declared his intention to get rid of a certain member,

> *Who in the course of one revolving moon*
> *Was poet, fiddler, statesman and buffoon.*[13]

A motion for censure was swiftly voted and approved by a majority of Adams's own Whig Party. The Southern Democrats were equally ferocious, of course. But the Whigs had decided that getting rid of Adams was a good way to bolster the link between the northern and southern sections of their unstable political enterprise. The man whom the Whigs selected to submit the resolution was Thomas F. Marshall of Kentucky, the nephew of the late

Chief Justice John Marshall, a man whose reputation as an interpreter of the Constitution had no equal.

Adams welcomed the opportunity to defend himself. For the next two weeks, he held the floor, day after day, flinging abuse and argument with a vehemence and persistence that stunned his opponents. He told Thomas Marshall to resign from Congress and enroll in some law school that might teach him about "the rights of the citizens of these states and the members of this House." He also hoped that Marshall would learn to control his fondness for alcohol. Again and again Adams ridiculed Southerners for having a double standard—crying disloyalty to the Union at Northern citizens for their petitions against slavery while holding the nation hostage to tolerating slavery with similar threats of secession.

His assaults regularly contained the sort of personal barb that left Thomas Marshall red-faced with chagrin. Adams asked Congressman Henry A. Wise, the future governor of Virginia, how he could have the nerve to attack him. Everyone knew Wise had encouraged a Kentucky congressman to challenge a new Maine member to a duel for supposedly insulting him. The Kentuckian had killed the New Englander, and some members had wanted to censure Wise, but Adams had defended him because a censure trial would have violated his constitutional rights. "Is it possible I saved this blood-stained man," Adams roared, "although his hands were reeking with the blood of murder?"[14]

All this and much more appeared in the daily papers. People in every state in the North read Adams's words with growing fascination. In Boston, a huge meeting convened in storied Faneuil Hall with William Lloyd Garrison presiding. It was jammed with Boston's so-called "best people," who a few short years before would cross the street rather than pass Garrison on the sidewalk. It was electrifying evidence of the impact Old Man Eloquent was having in New England.

At the end of Adams's two weeks of oratory against his censure, the battered southern Whigs said nothing while their anxious northern brethren proposed a motion to table the measure. An ecstatic Garrison gloated in *The Liberator* that Adams had "frightened the boastful South almost out of her wits." Theodore Weld had worked behind the scenes to supply Adams with material for his daily harangues. In a burst of optimism he would repudiate a few years later, Weld told his wife Angelina that from this "first victory over the slaveowners in a body . . . their downfall takes its date."[15]

. . .

Adams sensed he was close to an even bigger victory—the defeat of the gag rule. One of his Midwest supporters, Congressman Joshua Giddings of Ohio, submitted a resolution opposing the southern argument for regaining some Virginia slaves who had revolted aboard the ship *Creole* while en route to New Orleans. The slaves had sailed the ship to the Bahamas, where the British freed them. Without permitting any of the apparatus of debate that Adams had exploited, the southern Whigs censured Giddings. He resigned from Congress and immediately ran for reelection, winning in a landslide.

Sensing a shift in public opinion, Adams's son Charles, having won a seat in the Massachusetts legislature, drafted a resolution that called on Congress to draw up a constitutional amendment that would eliminate the provision entitling Southerners to count five slaves as three men in apportioning representatives to Congress.

On the defensive now, the House's majority created a select committee to consider the proposal and made John Quincy Adams the chairman. It was a sign that they had learned a hard lesson from the censure debacle. The rulers of the House made sure the rest of the committee was chosen with a view to making rejection a certainty. When they submitted their negative report, the House adopted it by a huge majority.

Undaunted, Massachusetts submitted the resolution three more times in the next year (1844). It went nowhere, of course. Some Southerners called it "the Hartford Convention Amendment," implying that they had not forgotten New England's flirtation with secession in 1814. The House refused even to print copies of the later submissions to circulate among the members. But the onslaught made some southern members wish they had never made an enemy of Old Man Eloquent.[16]

Adams waited until the first session of the next Congress in 1845 to introduce a resolution to abandon the gag rule. Congress approved it 105 to 80 with virtually no debate. A startling number of northern Democrats supported Adams—evidence of the growing strength of antislavery sentiment in that section of the country. In his diary, John Quincy Adams wrote: "Blessed, ever blessed be the name of God." There was little doubt that he now saw himself exclusively as a warrior for righteousness, in the style of William Lloyd Garrison—the opposite of the judicious politician he had once been.[17]

CHAPTER 14

The Slave Patrols

Is there evidence unmentioned in the bitter debates that engulfed Congress in the 1830s and 1840s that demonstrates how seriously Southerners took the danger of slave insurrections—the reason they gave for their angry determination to suppress petitions calling for the emancipation of their slaves?

Probably the best answer to that question is a civic duty performed by thousands of southern men. Every night, in almost every county in the South, armed riders patrolled the roads, challenging every black man they encountered, demanding to know his name, where he was going, and why. If the man did not have a letter from his master justifying his journey, he was given fifteen strokes of the lash. If he was defiant or tried to run away, the number was raised to thirty-nine.

If these midnight riders saw a group of blacks meeting in a field or woods off the road, they immediately dispersed them and detained a half dozen for questioning. They often searched slave cabins for weapons or stolen goods. They had the power to question whites too, and enter their homes without a warrant. The riders were drawn from the local militia in each county and were paid for their time.[1]

This was the world of the South's slave patrols. A visitor to Charleston in the 1850s was astonished by the way patrols "pass through the city at all hours." When he inquired about them, he was told that Charleston had many criminals who needed watching. But the visitor soon concluded that the real reason for the patrols was "the slave population." One letter writer to a South Carolina newspaper remarked that "in this country at least, no arguments will be necessary to prove the necessity of such a police."

Slave insurrections, real or rumored, were not the only reason slave patrols were vigilant. In the 1830s, an incendiary book written by an ex-slave, David Walker, triggered widespread anxiety throughout the South. The North Carolina legislature created a new committee, whose only duty was the supervision of slave patrols. Three men in each county were given semi-judicial authority to dismiss inept or unreliable patrollers and hear complaints about them.

In some places where slaves outnumbered whites by large ratios, private patrols were also organized. Planters in St. Matthew's Parish, South Carolina, created a Vigilant Society with about twenty members. Their chief worry was not an insurrection but the steep rise in theft from their plantations. Slaves stole jewelry, clothing—anything portable—and headed for the local railroad station. Blacks working for the railroad gave them money and sold the stolen goods somewhere up the line.

On Edisto Island, an auxiliary association also recruited members to supplement the regular slave patrollers. The residents of the island had a special reason to be worried. Blacks outnumbered whites fifteen to one. Too often "the midnight incendiary has escaped with impunity and the assassin has perfected his schemes of horror," one jittery white resident said. The auxiliary association asked the state to give them the same legal authority as the official patrollers. Sometimes these spontaneous associations agreed that they would whip only their own slaves. If a patroller whipped a slave so violently that he was unable to work, his owner could sue the patroller.

If several years passed without a serious disturbance, the discipline of the patrols tended to deteriorate. The newspapers carried frequent complaints about the carelessness and inefficiency of some patrols. But these cries of alarm only underscored the intensity of the South's anxiety about slave in-surrections. People who refused an order to serve in a patrol could be fined and even jailed.

Joining a slave patrol was serious business in other ways. The new arrival had to go before a justice of the peace and take a solemn oath:

> I [patroller's name] do solemnly swear that I will search for guns, swords and other weapons among the slaves of my district, and as faithfully and as privately as I can, discharge the trust reposed in me as the law directs, to the best of my power. So help me God.

The specificity of the patroller's task leaves little room for doubt about the reason for his promise to serve. The word "privately" also reduced the pos-sibility that a patroller might talk to a newspaper.[2]

Slave patrols were sometimes good at tracking down runaway slaves before they left their district. In this respect, they often competed with professional slave catchers, who searched for runaways expecting suitable compensation for their time and trouble. Some patrollers became so adept that they made slave-catching a full-time job. One man moved to New York and advertised in southern papers about his ability to seize runaways in that city.

Most of the time patrolling was tedious work, not unlike contemporary policing. Some bored patrollers felt free to drink while on the job. Often, the captain of the patrol was expected to furnish the alcohol as well as food, such as an oyster supper, paying for these pleasures out of his own pocket.

In a crisis, state and county boundaries were ignored. The first militia to arrive after Nat Turner's revolt in Virginia came from North Carolina, only a few miles away. State governors and other officials corresponded frequently about rumors of insurrectionary plots.

When the news of the first large-scale rebellion on Saint-Domingue reached South Carolina, the state organized coastal patrols to make sure blacks from the rebellious island did not reach its shores. Slave patrols were expanded everywhere from militia reserves.

The patrols played a curious and paradoxical role in southern life. Their existence more or less admitted that the slaves were unhappy and often deeply resentful of their bondage and were a constant threat to white lives. Simultaneously the patrols assuaged these fears and enabled people to go about their daily routines with no more than passing qualms. Any attempt to use the patrols as an argument that slavery should be eliminated was dismissed with scorn. But in the hours of darkness, more than one Southerner, in the words of the best historian of the patrols, still "dreamed vivid racial nightmares."[3]

Slave patrols are convincing evidence that Thomas Jefferson's nightmare—the dread of a race war—had become a fixture in the southern public mind.

CHAPTER 15

The Trouble with Texas

Congressman John Quincy Adams and his southern antagonists were soon deep in an argument much larger than the gag rule: the admission of Texas into the Union. The idea had on its side something far more powerful than constitutional contentions about slavery. North, South, and West, the American public mind of the 1840s was in the grip of an idea that united most of the country: Manifest Destiny. Numerous journalists, many of them spokesmen for the Democratic Party, foresaw an America that stretched from the Atlantic to the Pacific shores, absorbing the parts of the continent that lay beyond the boundaries of Thomas Jefferson's Louisiana Purchase.[1]

No one had been a more enthusiastic proponent of this idea than John Quincy Adams before he became embroiled with the issue of slavery. At a time when there already were three quarters of a million slaves in the nation, he predicted God had destined the United States "to be the most populous and most powerful people ever combined under one social compact." When he was president, he had tried to buy Texas from a disorganized, unstable Mexico, which had won independence from Spain in 1821.[2]

President Andrew Jackson had continued the attempt to purchase this huge swath of prairie and plateau, stretching 750 miles from the Sabine River to the border of California, and almost as lengthy from the panhandle to the Rio Grande. Its loamy black soil promised riches for cotton growers and almost as much wealth for grain farmers. Larger than France, Texas was peopled only by a few Indian tribes and a scattering of small Mexican settlements. The mantra of Manifest Destiny lured thousands of Americans, often with the encouragement of the erratic Mexican government. By 1835 these pioneers numbered fifty thousand. The majority were Southerners, who had brought with them some five thousand slaves.[3]

Mexican authority grew more and more unpredictable as revolutionary governments came and went. When a one-legged dictator named General Antonio López de Santa Anna seized power and abolished all state governments, the Texans revolted and won America's attention with their heroic stand in a fort named the Alamo, facing a Mexican army that outnumbered them 30 to 1. Santa Anna's slaughter of wounded captives galvanized Texan resistance.

Within a year, an army led by an Andrew Jackson disciple, General Sam Houston, smashed the dictator's battalions in the 1836 battle of San Jacinto and captured him. Texas declared her independence, and cheering Americans deluged Washington, DC, with demands for immediate recognition. Most people had little doubt that this was only a necessary first step for Texas to join the Union.[4]

Instead of celebrating with the rest of the nation, several antislavery spokesmen viewed with horror the prospect of admitting another slave state to the Union. Into this emotionally charged political brew the abolitionists flung a new phrase, "The Slave Power." They claimed that the whole process—the massive immigration, the importation of slaves, Houston's role as a Jackson emissary—was part of a long-range plot hatched by the South to take complete control of the United States government.[5]

Soon no American politician was doing more to popularize the use of "The Slave Power" than John Quincy Adams. To a confidential correspondent in Massachusetts, Adams stated his position: "There is no valid or permanent objection to the acquisition of Texas but the indelible stain of slavery." Adams ignored the way this claim contradicted his previous political principles. In 1803, Senator Adams had backed President Jefferson's right to buy Louisiana by treaty, to the outrage of not a few people in Massachusetts. In 1819, Secretary of State Adams had bought Florida from Spain by treaty. In both cases, slaves were involved. Now Adams told a skeptical House of Representatives that acquiring Texas and its few thousand slaves by treaty with Mexico was unconstitutional.[6]

For three weeks in the summer of 1838, Adams used his procedural skills to hold the floor of the House, frustrating Congress's hopes of achieving a quick vote to annex Texas. In the course of this filibuster he went public with his new political creed: "I believe that slavery is a sin before the sight of God, and that is the reason and the only insurmountable reason why we should not annex Texas to this union!"

It need hardly be added that "sin" is not an idea that can be found in the U.S. Constitution. Religion had invaded American politics in a totally unexpected way. It was not, as William Lloyd Garrison had hoped, by a mass conversion, but as the justification for flinging hatred at fellow Americans.

Old Man Eloquent was still holding the floor when Congress adjourned, and that meant he would have the floor when it reconvened for its next session in December. By that time, President Martin Van Buren had become so discouraged by the deluge of petitions and angry sermons against annexing Texas emanating from New England and the Yankee Midwest that he abandoned the idea as politically ruinous to his hopes for a second term.[7]

Abolitionists hailed this retreat as a victory over The Slave Power. But Texas was too big and its potential too huge to go away. Angry southern Democrats and southern Whigs became determined to make it part of the Union, no matter what the abolitionists—or the Mexicans—thought. Their determination increased exponentially when they learned that the British were negotiating with the Texas government, offering them recognition if they agreed to abolish slavery. London even proposed the sort of compensation for the Texans' freed slaves that had persuaded the West Indian planters to accept emancipation.

The British claimed the offer was part of their policy to eliminate slavery around the world. Not a few people saw it as a continuation of their previous attempts to restrict America's growth toward world power status. Not even John Quincy Adams favored it. He told two antislavery men who were going to a World Anti-Slavery Convention in London that he distrusted "the sincerity of the present British administration in the antislavery cause."[8]

. . .

An unprecedented clash between a new president and Congress finally brought Texas into the Union as a slave state. In 1841, John Tyler became the first vice president to succeed a president who had died in office. His predecessor, William Henry Harrison, had been a Whig who expired after only a month in the White House. Tyler was a Virginia Democrat with a distinguished lineage. His father, also named John, had been Thomas Jefferson's roommate at the college of William and Mary and a three-term governor of Virginia. No one was surprised when the younger Tyler became Virginia's governor in his mid-thirties and a senator at thirty-seven. He had voted with the Whigs to protest Andrew Jackson's tendency to ignore Congress and rely on his presidential powers to run the government. The Whigs had added Tyler to their presidential ticket to attract wavering members of the larger Democratic Party.

When the Whigs, led by Senator Henry Clay, attempted to launch a program of expensive public works projects, they collided with Tyler's Democratic roots. Convinced that federal power should be kept to a strict minimum, he relentlessly vetoed their bills. The Whigs lacked the two-thirds Congressional majority needed to override him. Whig rage at Tyler reached epic proportions. He was regularly burned in effigy in the North and South. At one point his entire Whig cabinet, except Secretary of State Daniel Webster, resigned in a body.

Eager to be elected president in his own right, Tyler looked for an issue that would attract both Whigs and Democrats. There sat Texas, all but begging for his embrace. The idea coalesced with one of Tyler's deepest political convictions: expansion was the key to America's continuing political peace and economic prosperity. He also saw expansion as the eventual answer to the problem of slavery. He had inherited this belief in diffusion from James Madison.

President Tyler first tried to annex Texas by treaty with Mexico. That prompted Secretary of State Daniel Webster to resign. Tyler made Senator Calhoun Webster's successor and chief negotiator. The president also persuaded Andrew Jackson to write an open letter urging annexation, lest Texas "be thrown into the arms of England." The treaty failed to get a two-thirds vote in the Senate. In the political conventions for the election of 1844, both the Whigs and the Democrats refused to nominate the "accidental president," as Tyler was often called.[9]

This rejection only made Tyler more determined to bring Texas into the Union. Soon after the voters chose a pro-admission Democrat, James K. Polk, as the new president, Tyler announced that Texas could be annexed by a joint resolution of both houses of Congress. He argued this move would only ratify the expressed will of the American people in their choice of Polk, a disciple of Andrew Jackson. The proposal outraged John Quincy Adams and his small band of antislavery supporters in Congress. They had already issued an address to the people of the United States warning that the annexation of Texas was a "slaveholders' plot"—fresh evidence of how Slave Power paranoia was gaining a grip on their minds.

Adams had also tried to persuade the House Foreign Affairs Committee, of which he was chairman, to approve a resolution declaring that any attempt to annex Texas by Congress would be null and void. He argued that it violated the Constitution, and the people of the free states should refuse to accept it. Adams followed this up with a tour of northern New York and the Midwest. Everywhere he called for "the extinction of slavery from the face of the earth." But he offered no proposals on how this goal could be achieved. Instead, his speeches were drenched with hate-filled rants about The Slave Power.[10]

In Washington, DC, Senator Calhoun issued a reply to Adams's campaign. He said American slavery was drastically different from the brutal version that the British had abolished in the West Indies. He even praised the British for this "wise and humane" decision. In America, slavery was a reasonable, rational political institution, whose "employees" were far better off than the factory workers of England and New England. Slavery was vital to the "peace, safety and prosperity" of the southern states. There was therefore no reason why it should not thrive in the state on their present border, Texas.

The statement added vigor to this new disease of the public mind, which would soon became epidemic in the South. It had just enough truth in it to seem persuasive to men and women of the 1840s. American plantation owners were more humane than the British and French planters in the West Indies, who resorted to horrendous cruelties to intimidate slaves and worked them to death as a matter of policy. But Calhoun's refusal to consider slaves as human beings with a natural longing for freedom nullified his argument.[11]

· · ·

President Tyler was the personification of self-confidence as he pressed forward with his proposal to annex Texas by a majority vote in Congress. His attractive second wife, Julia, wooed Congressional votes with spectacular White House receptions and dinners. The president flourished another statement by Andrew Jackson, issued, it soon became apparent, from his deathbed. "You might as well try to turn the current of the Mississippi," the ex-president declared, "as to turn the Democracy [the Democratic Party] from the annexation of Texas." With this endorsement, and a Democratic majority looming in Congress after the 1844 elections, Tyler had good reason to be confident.

John Quincy Adams could only sit helplessly in the House of Representatives, watching the pro-Texas momentum build to avalanche proportions. On January 24, 1844, he made a last despairing speech against it. He even said he would applaud Texas in the Union, but only if it were purged of slavery. No one even bothered to answer Old Man Eloquent. President Tyler ordered the issue to a vote, and it passed overwhelmingly in the House of Representatives. In the Senate the vote was much closer, 27 to 25, revealing the growth of antislavery hostility in the northern states. The delighted

Tyler immediately dispatched a courier to Texas with the news. He returned with Texan acceptance by a unanimous vote of the legislature.[12]

In Boston, the Massachusetts legislature declared the annexation of Texas unconstitutional. They had never delegated to Congress the power to accept a "foreign country" into the United States, and the Bay State would never agree to such an idea if slavery was in the equation. Nor would they agree to permit any future state to join the Union unless slavery had been abolished within its borders.

In Congress, John Quincy Adams predicted that Texas was only a first step in the imperial plans of The Slave Power. After Texas would come the conquest of Mexico, then Canada. In a letter to a friend he added that these triumphs would be followed by an invasion of South America, while in Washington a Caesar would arise to rule a third of the world with guns and bayonets. Adams was too old to do anything about this dark vision. He told his friends—and his son, Charles Francis Adams, now a power in the Massachusetts legislature—that it would be the task of the younger generation to arm themselves and prepare for immense sacrifices to prevent this crucifixion of "freedom and truth."[13]

.   .   .

Was President James Polk, a slave owner like Andrew Jackson, part of a Slave Power conspiracy? Fortunately, this question can be answered. Along with a legacy of dynamic presidential leadership, Polk left a diary that has given historians insights into his private thoughts and feelings. Slavery was simply not that important in his view of the American future. It was Manifest Destiny that gripped the new president's mind.

Polk saw a West growing ever stronger and more populous as settlers poured into it, peopling California and Oregon as well as Texas. When a thriving America stretched from sea to sea, she would have the leisure and the wealth to summon her native ingenuity and find a peaceful solution to slavery.

With remarkable energy and diligence, Polk tackled his presidency with his eyes on these western goals. California was another vast territory, with

only six thousand Mexicans and a few Indian tribes inhabiting a natural won-
derland of unspoiled forests and primeval valleys. The territory included the
future states of New Mexico, Arizona, Utah, and Nevada, all virtually unpeopled. To its north, the Oregon territory was entangled with a foreign claim-
ant, Great Britain, acting on Canada's behalf. The British disputed America's
claim that it stretched to the fifty-fourth parallel of latitude—the border of
Russian-owned Alaska. After running for president on a slogan of "Fifty four
forty or fight," Polk avoided a war with a compromise, accepting the forty-
ninth parallel as Oregon's northern border in negotiations with Britain.

At first the president hoped he could acquire California and confirm
American annexation of Texas without a war with Mexico. His envoy to
Mexico City offered large sums for peaceful possession of both territories.
Polk wanted to extend the Texas border to the Rio Grande, a far more natu-
ral dividing line than the wandering Nueces River, which had been the Texas
border for a long time. He was ready to pay generously for this concession.

Unfortunately, bankrupt Mexico did not have a government. It was a
shifting sands of competing politicians, some inclined to pragmatism, others to virulent hatred of the Yankee colossus to the north. On New Year's
Day 1846, a Mexican general named Mariano Paredes overthrew the legally
elected president, accusing him of a willingness to make a "treasonable"
bargain with the Americans. The Yankee-haters were in control, and they
marched an army to the Rio Grande with talk of reconquering Texas. Polk
ordered Brigadier General Zachary Taylor to advance to the same contested
border with 3,554 men—almost half the 7,200-man American army.[14]

· · ·

On April 24, 1846, General Taylor ordered a cavalry captain and his troop of
dragoons to investigate a rumor that 1,600 Mexican horsemen had crossed
the Rio Grande. Two days later, the Mexican guide who had accompanied
the troopers stumbled into camp and reported they had been ambushed.
Sixteen had been killed, the rest captured. General Taylor rushed a message
to President Polk: "Hostilities may now be considered as commenced."

The news reached Washington in two weeks, lightning speed for those days, and Polk asked Congress to agree that "war exists by act of Mexico." Both houses concurred with massive majorities. Only two Whig senators from New England and fourteen Whig Congressman, led by John Quincy Adams, voted no.

Now came the much larger question: Could the Americans win this war? Many people in the United States and outside it had grave doubts. The tiny American army had fought no one but a few Indian tribes since 1815. The Mexican army was 32,000 strong, and many of these soldiers were veterans, thanks to Mexico's numerous revolutions.

The Americans had a secret weapon that virtually no one appreciated. Since the War of 1812, when their untrained militia armies had floundered to disaster in Canada, the U.S. Military Academy at West Point had produced over a thousand graduates. Not a few of them were in the American regular army. Still others returned from civilian life to officer regiments in the fifty thousand volunteers that Polk persuaded Congress to raise.[15]

.   .   .

Even before President Polk wrote his war message and the volunteers arrived to support the regulars, West Pointers in Taylor's little army demonstrated what professional soldiers could achieve. In two hard-fought battles, they inflicted shattering defeats on the much larger Mexican army. Meanwhile the energetic Polk launched smaller armies into what are now the states of Arizona, New Mexico, and California. In the next year they would conquer these territories with virtually no gunfire or bloodshed.

The battlefield victories on the Rio Grande and the prospect of conquering the other territories thrilled most Americans. Men rushed to enlist in the volunteer regiments. Two thirds came from the western states, where Manifest Destiny was virtually an article of faith. Almost no fighting men came from New England. There the war was denounced and damned as a plot of The Slave Power. James Russell Lowell summed up their attitude in his satiric poem, *The Biglow Papers.*

They just want this Californy
So's to lug new slave states in
To abuse ye and to scorn ye,
An' to plunder ye like sin.[16]

·   ·   ·

In spite of the opening defeats, the Mexicans refused to negotiate. General Taylor led an army of regulars and volunteers into Mexico and captured Monterrey in a bloody battle. Polk, still hoping for an early peace, smuggled General Santa Anna into Mexico—he had been living in exile in Cuba—on the promise that he would sign a peace treaty. Instead Santa Anna seized control of the government and attacked Taylor's army at Buena Vista. Again the Americans won a victory thanks largely to the West Pointers in their ranks, notably the artillerymen. Still the Mexicans refused to negotiate.

President Polk ordered another ten-thousand-man army under the command of General Winfield Scott to invade Mexico at Vera Cruz and march to Mexico City to dictate peace. This was a high-risk gamble. Could ten thousand men conquer a country of eight million? Military experts in Europe, including the Duke of Wellington, predicted disaster.

Scott staffed his army with as many West Pointers as he could obtain. In particular, he asked for a soft-spoken Virginia captain named Robert E. Lee. In the ensuing campaign, Lee became the most talked-about soldier in the American army. Again and again, he found ways to outflank and outwit Santa Anna's larger army.

Confronted by a twelve-thousand-man force on Cerro Gordo, a conical thousand-foot ridge guarding the only pass into the Mexican interior, Captain Lee ventured alone into the surrounding underbrush and found a path that enabled the Americans to attack the Mexican rear.

The next day General Scott routed the stunned Mexicans. During the assault, Captain Lee led a brigade around the enemy flank to seize a road through a crucial pass behind the Mexican lines. The panicked enemy fled down narrow footpaths, their army disintegrating into a mob.[17]

Advancing over the mountains into the magnificent Valley of Mexico, Scott and his men confronted another daunting combination of man-made and natural defenses. One of the most formidable was the Pedregal, an immense lava field that stretched for miles along the left flank of the fortified village of Contreras. There was nothing in this wilderness of jutting rocks but a few stunted shrubs and a winding mule path. General Scott asked Captain Lee to see if there was a way across this stony desert.

Lee returned with a sketch of a possible road. Scott immediately put five hundred men to work building it under the captain's supervision. The result was a flank attack that swept the Mexicans out of Contreras in seventeen minutes. The commander in chief called Lee's night trips across the Pedregal "the greatest feat of physical and moral courage performed by any individual . . . in the campaign." The forty-year-old captain was promoted to brevet lieutenant colonel on the spot.[18]

The Americans captured Mexico City in a final assault, with Lieutenant Colonel Lee again working out maneuvers and troop dispositions designed to maximize surprise and minimize casualties. At a victory dinner in the capital, General Scott declared that without Lee and his fellow West Pointers, "this army multiplied by four" could not have conquered Mexico.

Many other graduates had distinguished themselves in the war's battles. At Buena Vista, Colonel Jefferson Davis and his three-hundred-man regiment of Mississippi rifleman stopped the charging Mexican cavalry and infantry three times, saving Zachary Taylor's outnumbered army from destruction. In an attack on the fortress of Chapultepec, outside Mexico City, artillery Lieutenant Thomas Jackson led a "one gun charge" up the road, ignoring blizzards of Mexican bullets and cannonballs. But no one came close to matching Robert E. Lee's accomplishments. Back in the United States, General Scott called him "the very best soldier that I ever saw in the field." At another point, when someone speculated that America and Britain were likely to go to war again because of London's imperialistic ambitions, Scott said the government should insure the life of Lieutenant Colonel Lee, even if the cost was $5 million a year.[19]

Throughout the next decade, an awareness of Lee's talents spread from the army to the general public. In 1852 he was appointed superintendent of the U.S. Military Academy. There he distinguished himself by doing his utmost to keep sectional conflict to a minimum. Again and again, he stressed that the academy was a "band of brothers" who should not allow the dispute over slavery to rupture the harmony of the cadet corps—and by implication, the unity of the nation.

. . .

In 1846 a Pennsylvania Democratic congressman named David Wilmot introduced a resolution into a fundraising bill, declaring that slavery should be banned in every single foot of territory acquired from Mexico. One of Wilmot's motives was resentment against President Polk for taking the Democratic nomination away from Martin Van Buren in 1844. Another motive was to become the mantra of many northern politicians: no quarrel with slavery where it existed but opposition to letting it spread. Wilmot called his proposal "the White Man's Proviso." With almost breathtaking candor, he added: "I want to have nothing to do either with the free Negro or the slave Negro. We wish to settle the territories with free white men." In many ways Wilmot was more racist than John C. Calhoun.[20]

William Lloyd Garrison adored the Wilmot Proviso. He said it was proof that antislavery was marching forward with "irresistible power." John Quincy Adams and the small circle of abolition-minded Whigs who supported him in Congress did everything in their power to sustain the proviso. They focused on the prohibition against slavery and tried to ignore its racist underpinning. Slave-owning border states, Missouri, Kentucky, and Tennessee, who had contributed most of the fighting men to the war with Mexico, rose in fury against the idea. The southern states were almost as outraged; they argued that the Constitution permitted them to bring slaves into any American state or territory.

. . .

In 1846 antiwar voters had given the Whigs a slim majority in the House, bringing to Congress a tall Illinois lawyer named Abraham Lincoln. Originally a supporter of the war with Mexico, the elongated (six-foot-four) attorney joined enthusiastically in the Whig campaign, led by Senator Henry Clay, to label President Polk a warmonger who had "invaded" Mexican territory. Their partisan reasoning was lost on most Americans, who refused to forget that it was the Mexicans who had ambushed and killed American soldiers to start the war.

Of far more significance was a bill that Congressman Lincoln submitted for the approval of the House. It called for the emancipation of the slaves in the District of Columbia. But instead of condemning slave owners with imprecations like William Lloyd Garrison and John Quincy Adams, Lincoln proposed that the "treasury of the United States" should pay the owners "the full value for his or her slave." It demonstrated the (seemingly) uneducated prairie lawyer's independence from the mounting abolitionist frenzy.

Compensated emancipation had psychological and spiritual dimensions as well as an economic side. It brushed aside the abolitionists' hatred of slave owners based on their religious conviction that slavery was a sin. Instead, it recognized that slavery was a system that the South had inherited two centuries ago. The current generation of slave owners was not guilty. They had not invented the system, and not a few of them admitted it was evil. It also recognized that, by the same accident of history, slaves were valuable property, even if the idea grated on some sensibilities.

Alas, Lincoln's bill never reached the floor of the House and sank into oblivion. But the *New York Tribune* praised the congressman as "a strong but judicious enemy of slavery."[21]

. . .

On Monday, February 21, 1848, John Quincy Adams rode to the capitol in his carriage. A stroke had left him a ghost of his previously fiery self, but his opinion of the Mexican War had not changed. When a motion was made to allow Congress to vote their thanks to Winfield Scott and other generals for their exploits in the war, Adams voted a loud and emphatic NO. The motion won by a huge majority.

His defeat only hardened Adams's determination to vote even more emphatically against a third and final reading of the resolution. Before the roll call reached him, a rush of blood colored his temples and Adams slumped in his chair, unconscious. A nearby congressman caught him before he crashed to the floor. He was carried to a sofa in the speaker's office and died two days later.

As a patriot whose lineage and experience reached back to the days of 1776, John Quincy Adams was mourned by Democrats and Whigs alike; even a South Carolina congressman spoke of him with respect and sorrow. The citizens of Washington, DC, praised him at a public meeting. He lay in state in a silver embossed coffin while funeral services were conducted by the chaplain of the House of Representatives.

The praise was unquestionably deserved. In his youth Adams had been an outstanding diplomat. As President George Washington left office, he had urged incoming president John Adams not to feel the least uneasiness about promoting his son to even more responsible foreign tasks. John Quincy had been a key player in negotiating the treaty that ended the War of 1812. As secretary of state under James Monroe, he had written the Monroe Doctrine, which did much to end European intrusions in South America. Few men were more qualified to become president in 1824.

If John Quincy Adams had capped this magnificent career by healing the breach between the North and South, it would have been his greatest accomplishment. As a first step, Adams might have rebuked Garrison and his fellow extremists with their impossible demands for immediate abolition. Next, he might have become an advocate for compensated emancipation, a crucial part of a practical solution, as the British had demonstrated in the West Indies. If a virtually self-educated Illinois congressman named Lincoln saw this ingredient as part of the answer, a Harvard graduate of John Quincy's intellectual stature could have—and should have—grasped its value at a glance.

Like Lincoln, Adams could have started small, proposing compensation for the slaves of the District of Columbia. Other men might have applied it to border states such as Delaware and Maryland, where slavery was already dwindling. Adams might have reached out to Thomas Jefferson Randolph and helped him persuade Virginia to accept the solution. There were strong unionist sentiments among a large percentage of southern voters, but they were inhibited by the fear that emancipation meant a race war. There were ways to reduce this fear that might have been acceptable to both sections. A bond issue might have been floated to raise money to station troops in parts of southern states where the density of the black population made a revolt a possibility. The British had followed this policy in the West Indies. At the very least it would have been meaningful to hear an ex-president from New England say he understood and sympathized with the South's fears and as a fellow American wanted to join them in a search for a solution.

As a former president, John Quincy Adams had once been a spokesman for all the people of America and should have felt a compelling loyalty to the central idea of the American republic, the Union. When he was elected to Congress, he had declared he would be the representative of the entire nation. He had spoken out strongly, even fiercely, against John C. Calhoun's doctrine of nullification. Adams had once admired George Washington so deeply that he had named his firstborn son after him (to the dismay of his parents). Instead, Congressman Adams had closed his career ignoring Washington's plea to regard the Union as a sacred trust above all others. The congressman abandoned the principles that had once made him a national leader and become another snarling Southerner-hating New England voice of disunity.

Of all the victims of this disease of the public mind that distorted the noble cause of antislavery, John Quincy Adams is the saddest, most regrettable story. Far more powerfully than his southern counterpart, Thomas Jefferson Randolph, Adams had the potential to alter the debate and remind Americans of the 1830s and 1840s of the heritage they were in danger of forgetting. Among the many might-have-beens on the twisting road to the Civil War, the seeming success—and hidden failure—of Old Man Eloquent was the one in which a change of mind or heart might have made a huge difference.

CHAPTER 16

Slave Power Paranoia

By the time the Mexican War ended, paranoia about The Slave Power was virulent throughout New England and among her Midwest emigrants. The original abolitionist hope that they could change the minds of Southerners through "missionary work" had expired. William Lloyd Garrison now called the idea "a useless waste of time." No longer would they deluge the South with pamphlets or bury Congress in blizzards of petitions. Instead, they hoped to "abolitionize the North" by portraying The Slave Power as a corrupt and decadent society whose inequity had to be trumpeted to the world.

The abolitionists convinced themselves, based on their evangelical experiences, that smearing the South's reputation in every possible way would create the "anxiety" that would lead to a mass conversion of the North to their crusade. In an analogy that was tortured at best, and blasphemous at worst, the South was portrayed as a province ruled by Satan that would consume the North's soul if her citizens did not vow to expunge the sin of slavery. It was the evangelical camp meeting on a national scale, accusing the South of four unforgiveable sins: violence, drunkenness, laziness, and sexual depravity.[1]

Abolitionists declared that the South's "lust for power" was built into the system because from boyhood Southerners learned to tyrannize their male slaves and exploit defenseless female slaves. That was why the South had become "an erotic society" which encouraged whites to "all the vicious gratifications that unrestrained lust can amalgamate." From Richmond to New Orleans, "the Southern states are one great Sodom."[2]

This absorption with pleasure had supposedly produced a society that regarded work as degrading. Southerners saw it as something that only slaves performed. Free white laborers in the South were almost as worthless as slave labor, which everyone knew was inferior because it was unrewarded. Presiding over this swamp of decadence and degradation were the great planters, who looked down with scorn on the "mud-sills" of society, white and black, and devoted their days to loathsome pleasures.

Abolitionist clergymen developed a jeremiad on The Slave Power. They identified it as the anti-Christ, come to terrifying life in America after their Protestant ancestors had defeated this evil being in a centuries-long struggle with the Catholic Church in Europe. The South was "the apocalyptic dragon" of the book of Revelations, rising to strangle freedom in the North as it had already extinguished it in the South.[3]

No one loved this rhetoric more than William Lloyd Garrison. "The spirit of southern slavery," he declared, "is a spirit of EXTERMINATION against all those who represent it as a dishonor to our country, rebellion against God and treason to the liberties of mankind." Senator William Sumner of Massachusetts summed up this rampaging hatred with three questions he roared at a rapt audience in Boston's Faneuil Hall. "Are you for freedom? Or are you for slavery? Are you for God or the Devil?"[4]

Others saw Slave Power plots in the early history of the republic. First came the concessions southern spokesmen demanded at the Constitutional Convention. Then they acquired the immense territory of Louisiana for slavery's expansion. Next came Jefferson's embargo, which crippled New England's commercial power. In the War of 1812, southern generals had

John Brown grew this beard to hide his identity while reconnoitering Harpers Ferry for his 1859 raid. He was wanted for murdering five defenseless men in Kansas and ordering his sons to chop up their bodies with swords, while their horrified wives and children watched. Brown regularly denied his guilt for this atrocity. *Library of Congress*

Here is the John Brown that the beard concealed. Note the grim mouth and glaring eyes of the fanatic. One can almost hear his war cry: "Without the shedding of blood there can be no remission of sin." *Library of Congress*

Many Virginians considered Captain Robert E. Lee to be George Washington's heir. He was married to Mary Custis, the founder's step great-granddaughter. In the war with Mexico, Lee won promotion to lieutenant colonel for his daring and leadership. President Lincoln offered him command of the Union Army in 1861. In one of the hidden turning points of American history, Lee refused the offer. *National Archives*

Quaker John Woolman urged slavery's abolition through patience, prayer, and gentle reproaches. Hatred was foreign to what one biographer has called his "beautiful soul." Woolman died in England, urging the British to free the slaves of the West Indies. The seed he planted led to peaceful emancipation in 1833.

Phillis Wheatley arrived in Boston on a slave ship in 1761 at the age of seven. She learned to read and write almost immediately and in 1773 published a book of poems. In 1775, she dedicated a poem to General Washington. He paid tribute to her "great poetical talents" and invited her to visit him. It was a first glimpse of the remarkable freedom from race prejudice that led Washington to free all his slaves in his will. *Library of Congress*

Colonel John Laurens persuaded George Washington to back his proposal to free 3,000 slaves to serve in the Continental Army. The Continental Congress voted its approval. Some historians have called their vote the first emancipation proclamation. Sadly, Laurens was killed in a skirmish and the idea died with him. *National Park Service*

When President Thomas Jefferson approved Napoleon Bonaparte's invasion of St. Domingue (Haiti) in 1802 to restore French rule, he created a nightmare that became a disease of the Southern mind—fear of a race war. Yellow fever destroyed the French army and the enraged Haitians killed almost every white man, woman, and child on the island. *From* France Militaire, *1833*

Short, stocky Jean Jacques Dessalines was the black general who fought Napoleon's invasion of Haiti and ordered the slaughter of the surviving French men and women on the island. But his hatred extended only to French whites. In 1804, he sought American recognition of Haiti's independence. President Jefferson persuaded Congress to reject his letter. The next president to send a diplomat to Haiti was Abraham Lincoln in 1862.

In 1822, inspired by the example of Haiti, Denmark Vesey proposed to kill all the whites in Charleston, South Carolina, seize ships in the harbor, and flee. Some blacks revealed the plot the day before the rebels were to strike. Vesey and many of his followers were hanged. The South's fear of a race war grew deeper.

In 1831, William Lloyd Garrison launched *The Liberator*, a newspaper that demanded the immediate emancipation of the South's slaves. Although he claimed to be inspired by God, Garrison repeatedly compared slavery to rape and preached hatred of slave owners and "The Slave Power"—his name for the southern states. Almost single-handedly he created a disease in the public mind. *Library of Congress*

Ex-President John Quincy Adams was elected to Congress soon after Andrew Jackson defeated him in his bid for a second term. Although Congressman Adams promised to represent "all the people," he gradually became an outspoken foe of "The Slave Power" and helped turn abolitionism into a political movement. *Library of Congress*

Thomas Jefferson Randolph was Thomas Jefferson's oldest grandson. In 1833, he called for the gradual emancipation of Virginia's slaves and participated in a ferocious debate on the issue in the state legislature. Numerous Virginians admitted slavery was a great evil. Randolph's proposal lost by only five votes. *Thomas Jefferson Foundation*

Theodore Dwight Weld was a brilliant preacher who converted thousands to the cause of abolitionism. But he gradually realized he was contradicting his belief in a loving God by preaching hatred of slave owners. He quit the crusade he had done so much to create. *Library of Congress*

On almost every road in every county of the South, armed men patrolled each night, challenging every black man or woman they met, to make sure they were not plotting a revolt. Above is a slave patrol operating near New Orleans. These patrols underscored the South's constant fear of a race war. *From* Frank Leslie's Illustrated History of the Civil War, *1895*

In Southampton County, Virginia, in the summer of 1831, a black preacher named Nat Turner launched a race war that killed more than sixty white men, women, and children. He called on his followers to imitate the example of "Santo Domingo"—as Haiti was called at that time. *From* Authentic and Impartial Narrative of the Tragical Scene which Was Witnessed in Southampton County, *1831*

Harriet Beecher Stowe often amazed people by denying she wrote *Uncle Tom's Cabin*. "Who wrote it?" they asked. "God," Mrs. Stowe replied. When President Abraham Lincoln met her in 1862, he supposedly said: "So you're the little lady who wrote the book that made this great war." *Library of Congress*

Josiah Henson was the real Uncle Tom—the Maryland-born slave whose story gave Harriet Beecher Stowe the idea for *Uncle Tom's Cabin*. But Stowe's Uncle Tom had very little resemblance to the tough, shrewd, independent man of business that Henson became. *Library of Congress*

Horace Greeley was the editor of the New York *Tribune*, America's leading anti-slavery newspaper. When Civil War loomed, he was horrified. But he could not control his managing editor, Charles Dana, who repeatedly called for war in fiery headlines. *Library of Congress*

Frederick Douglass escaped from slavery and became a leading voice calling for abolition. In the 1850s he met John Brown, who urged him to join the raid on Harpers Ferry. Douglass warned Brown that it would end in disaster. After the Civil War, Douglass worked with President Ulysses Grant to win civil rights for the freed slaves. *Library of Congress*

Dred Scott was a Missouri slave whose master took him to Illinois, a free state. Scott claimed this made him and his wife and two daughters free. In 1857, the Supreme Court ruled that as a slave Scott was not a citizen and could not sue in federal court. Three months later, Scott's owners freed him and his family. The court's decision convinced many northerners that the judges were under the evil influence of "The Slave Power." *Library of Congress*

In 1861, ex-President John Tyler proposed a peace conference to avoid an imminent civil war. He argued that diffusion—the spread of slavery into the western territories—was the only way to avoid a bloody clash. Already slaves were 40 percent of the South's population. Confining them to the Southern states forced the South to choose between a civil war and a race war. When President-elect Lincoln rejected Tyler's proposal, the ex-president called for Virginia's secession. *Library of Congress*

In this illustration, John Brown and his men fire on citizens of Harpers Ferry from the doorway of the federal armory. Hundreds of militiamen responded to the town's call for help and took cover in nearby buildings and on the looming heights. Harpers Ferry became a trap for Brown and his raiders. *From Frank Leslie's Illustrated Newspaper, 1859*

A New York *Tribune* reporter concocted this story of John Brown kissing a black child on his way to his execution. "Faking it" was a well-established custom in American newspapers until the early twentieth century. This became one of the many abolitionist myths about Brown that made Ralph Waldo Emerson and others compare him to Jesus Christ. *Library of Congress*

Few people are aware that the first battle of the Civil War was fought in the streets of Baltimore. The Sixth Massachusetts regiment was attacked as they marched through the city to board a train to Washington, DC. The regiment suffered four dead and seventeen wounded. In return, they killed twelve rioters and wounded dozens. Marylanders blamed the abolitionists of Massachusetts for starting the war. *Library of Congress*

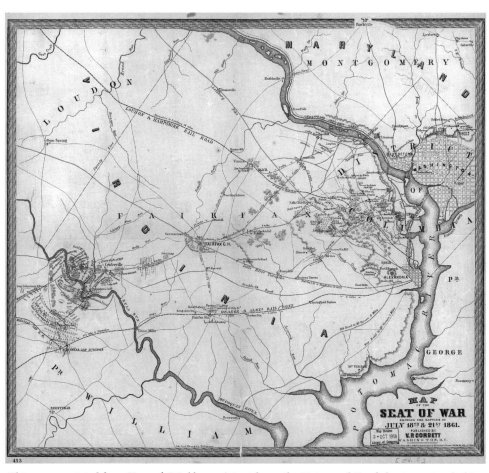

This map, reprinted from *Harper's Weekly* magazine, shows the Union and Confederate armies clashing at Manassas Junction, with Bull Run Creek flowing through the battlefield. General Lee was the unseen planner of the battle. Thanks to his foresight, fresh Southern troops arrived by railroad to overwhelm the weary Union men.

On July 22, 1862, President Lincoln read his first draft of the Emancipation Proclamation to his cabinet. Secretary of State William Seward is on the president's left, Secretary of War Edwin Stanton sits midway down the table on the right. Seward persuaded Lincoln not to issue the epochal statement until the Union had won a victory, lest it seem like "the last shriek" of an exhausted government. *Library of Congress*

Taken in February 1865, this picture shows the deep weariness that the war inflicted on Abraham Lincoln. But when a senator visited him on April 14, he was amazed by the cheerful, energetic man who shook his hand. The war was virtually over and "The Tycoon," as his aides called Lincoln, was preparing to forge a peace of reconciliation. Alas, that night he went to the theater. *Library of Congress*

prevented "the brave soldiers of New England and New York from capturing Canada." These were, of course, the same New England soldiers who had refused to serve beyond the borders of their states, in defiance of "Mr. Madison's War."

Paranoid history is indifferent to facts. The Slave Power preachers told their followers that the South had fallen far behind the North in wealth—the exact opposite of the truth. By playing off the two political parties against each other, they claimed the slavocrats had elected presidents and congressmen and senators and chosen judges of the Supreme Court. The Slave Power had caused the financial panic of 1837 by draining the wealth of the North into endless needless expansion exemplified by the Mexican War. For a final touch, there were invented quotations attributed to John C. Calhoun: "The North must be shorn of her natural strength when needful, that slavery may preserve her balance of power."

Perhaps the most amazing—and dismaying—aspect of this raging final stage of the abolitionist disease in the public mind was the relatively small number of men who perpetrated it. One of slavery's best historians estimates that the paranoid phase of the campaign was launched by little more than twenty-five people.[5]

.   .   .

Did the campaign of slander about the South's sexual exploitation of its slaves have any basis in fact? The mulatto population of the South, as recorded in the censuses of 1850 and 1860, suggests a rather low rate of miscegenation. In the nation as a whole, the census takers of 1850 counted 406,000 "visibly mulatto" people out of a black population of 3,639,000, which is 11.2 percent of the total. About 350,000 mulattoes lived south of the Mason-Dixon line.[6]

These figures make it clear that there was a considerable amount of sexual activity between the two races, even if it was a long way from meriting the term "unrestrained lust." There were many factors that kept the percentage relatively low. A master who recklessly seduced his slaves would demoralize his plantation. A white overseer exhibiting such a tendency would usually be fired. Slaves were accustomed to making stable marriages. The average age at which a slave woman gave birth to her first child was 22.5. This does not suggest teenage girls having wild sex by the tens of thousands.

A strong religious faith persuaded many Southerners to take their marriage vows seriously. At least as important was the genuine love that existed between most husbands and wives. At the same time, slaves were subject people. A master who wanted to assert his dominance undoubtedly possessed the power, and there are more than a few examples of men who did so.

One of the most deplorable cases is James Henry Hammond of South Carolina. A governor, congressman, and senator, he was semifamous as one of the first who declared, "Cotton is king!" Over three hundred slaves toiled on his ten-thousand-acre Silver Bluff plantation. Hammond regarded stable marriages among his slaves as crucial to the good order of the plantation. A slave who committed adultery was liable to severe punishment.

Nevertheless, for twenty years Hammond maintained a *ménage á trois* with two black women, Sally Johnson and her daughter Louisa, who worked in his mansion as servants. He had children by both of them, and in his will he begged his oldest son to care for the women and their offspring. His wife discovered the truth early in their marriage, but she seemed powerless to do more than berate him and treat the defenseless black women with livid hostility.[7]

Was Hammond typical of slave owners? Apparently not. Was his example lurid enough to "prove" the wildest fantasies of the abolitionists? Unquestionably, yes.

.   .   .

In the South, Senator John C. Calhoun was telling people, "We have borne the wrongs and insults of the North long enough." He called for a southern convention that would, like the Hartford Convention of 1814, put George Washington's sacred Union out of business by forming a separate confederacy. Calhoun had a pretext more serious than abolitionist smears—the threat of admitting California to the Union as a free state, barring slavery.

Calhoun's fellow senator, Henry Clay of Kentucky, disagreed. Speaking as a fellow Southerner, he asked Calhoun if there was anything the South had demanded in the previous decades that she had not obtained. President Polk had lowered the tariff to the vanishing point, to the chagrin of New England's textile magnates. Slavery still flourished in the nation's capital. Florida, the Louisiana Territory, and now Texas had created opportunities for an enormous expansion of their peculiar institution.

All true enough. But Calhoun and his followers felt that they were surrounded by enemies. A British naval squadron cruised the Atlantic, seizing ships that attempted to transport slaves from Africa. Urged by British diplomats, every other nation and colony in South America except Brazil and Cuba had freed their slaves. On nearby Jamaica and other West Indian islands, freed slaves seemed to be living peacefully with their former masters, undermining the assumption that emancipation meant insurrection. More and more, it looked as if the South would soon become an isolated community, despised for their refusal to consider some form of gradual emancipation.

To counter this isolation, Southerners like Calhoun began yearning for an empire. Their purple dream had ironic similarity to the fantasy John Quincy Adams created in one of his early rants against The Slave Power. It would stretch from the Potomac River to California and extend into the Caribbean, with slave-owning Cuba a first and obvious prize. At the close of the Mexican War, many people in the northern Mexican states had expressed a desire to join the United States. Why not occupy them and convert them into slave states? Each year, the price of cotton increased, as England's and New England's mills prospered and grew. Why should the South be limited by lines drawn on a map by the aging architects of the Missouri Compromise?[8]

. . .

This purple dream redoubled the South's rage at the slanderous abuse they were receiving from the North. Soon there was a flourishing paranoid conviction that the abolitionists were a conspiracy aimed at destroying the South. This belief was intensified by the slaves who fled to the northern states with the help of an abolitionist creation, the Underground Railroad. The members of this organization, many of them courageous free blacks, helped runaways dodge federal marshals and professional slave catchers until they were across the border into Canada and settled in free communities.

Compared to the three and a half million men and women living in slavery, the actual number of these escapees was trivial—about two thousand a year. Almost all came from the border states of the upper South. But the symbolic impact of these fugitives was large. When a runaway was caught, abolitionists and their sympathizers began defying the U.S. Supreme Court, which had ruled in 1842 that state laws providing jury trials to determine a runaway's status were invalid. Northern state legislatures passed new laws, forbidding their officials from cooperating in any way with federal pursuers.

Then there was California. Thanks to the discovery of gold in 1848, its population had multiplied almost overnight. A cry for statehood soon produced a constitution that barred slavery. Next came a governor and a legislature, asking for admission to the Union. When the new president, Mexican War hero General Zachary Taylor, took office in 1849, he recommended in his first message to Congress that California be admitted immediately. Southerners were infuriated and all but shouted secession in his face. The old soldier replied that he would personally take charge of the federal army and smash any such venture without mercy, a la Andrew Jackson.[9]

. . .

Meanwhile, slavery was paralyzing that crucial arm of the federal government, Congress. When the legislators gathered for their first session under the new president, it took sixty-three ballots to elect a speaker of the House of Representatives. The contest was between the previous speaker, Whig Robert Winthrop of Massachusetts, and Howell Cobb, a Georgia Democrat, with eight other candidates churning on the fringes. For three weeks the House's walls vibrated with furious oratory. The Whig Party virtually dissolved in the cauldron, as southern Whigs deserted in favor of Cobb. Finally, for the first time in its history, the House voted to accept someone who won by a plurality, rather than a majority, and Cobb became the speaker.

So rancid was the antagonism between proslavery and antislavery congressmen, even the most trivial jobs, such as doorkeeper of the House, became a contest that depended on the applicant's allegiance. With Cobb in command of appointing committee chairmen, a congressional revolt was soon fermenting. The admission of California would tip the balance of free versus slave states, sixteen to fifteen, in the Senate.

It was time for desperate measures, and seventy-three-year-old Senator Henry Clay of Kentucky summoned his dwindling strength and undertook the rescue of the imperiled Union. With masterful oratory and even more masterful backstairs negotiations, Clay asked Daniel Webster and John C. Calhoun to join him in a package of compromises that would, he hoped, settle the issue of slavery without bloodshed or further divisive rancor.

California would be admitted as a free state. As for New Mexico and Utah, two territories that were within California's borders when conquered and then purchased from Mexico, Clay urged that they remain neutral on slavery for the time being, in spite of the Wilmot Proviso (which had never been approved by Congress). Next came a tough new fugitive slave law that would provide both money and legal machinery to capture runaways. Finally, the slave trade, but not slavery, would be abolished in the District of Columbia.

To the amazement of many people, southern congressmen displayed little enthusiasm for defending the Washington, DC, slave trade. The slave pens in the vicinity of the White House were to be dismantled. For the first time, the free blacks of the district would live without fear of being kidnapped and sold south.[10]

. . .

For abolitionists, especially of the Garrison sort, compromise was still a filthy word. They unanimously denounced Clay's political package. This surprised no one, of course. More unexpected was a speech by Senator Clay. Speaking as a Kentuckian, he issued a warning to his fellow Southerners. Secession was not and never would be a peaceful solution. The Americans of the Midwest, of which Kentucky was a geographic neighbor, would never

tolerate the idea of letting a foreign state control New Orleans and the immense commerce from their farms that flowed down the Mississippi River
for export to a hungry world. Webster followed Clay with a speech extolling
the vital importance of the Union. The abolitionists condemned him as a
traitor to New England.

Calhoun, too ill to speak, let a Virginia senator read his speech, while he
glared out at the Senate with the angry eyes of a man who accepted nothing,
including his imminent death. (He would expire of chronic lung conges-
tion four weeks later.) His words declared he accepted the compromise but
warned it would never work unless Congress and the president "did justice
to the South" by guaranteeing her the right to bring slaves into all the remaining western territories. Even more important must be an absolute and
total end to "the agitation of the slave question."

These three famous voices did not by any means stifle further debate on
the compromise. The oratory lasted for weeks. But sheer exhaustion began
to play a part in a growing sentiment to accept these four proposals. This
willingness was somewhat ironically accelerated by the sudden death of
President Taylor from a stomach disorder and the ascent of mild-mannered
Vice President Millard Fillmore of New York. Partly at his suggestion, the
package was broken into four separate bills and passed individually, under the leadership of a strong new voice in the Senate, Democrat Stephen
Douglas of Illinois.

It would take another year to learn whether the South would accept the
compromises of 1850. In the state elections of 1851, the two political parties, Democrats and Whigs, were temporarily irrelevant. The contest was
between unionists, who were in favor of the compromise, and secessionists.
The unionists met their opponents with a steady and frequently steely denial that secession was a constitutional right. Backed by Henry Clay's warning, James Madison's denunciation of nullification and secession came back
to life with surprising force. The unionists won in every state except South
Carolina, which remained loyal to its lost prophet, John C. Calhoun.[11]

•   •   •

In the North, where Slave Power paranoia remained strong, the compromise of 1850 proved to be a temporary truce. The revised fugitive slave law rapidly became unacceptable in New England. Even aloof Ralph Waldo Emerson, the nation's best known writer, who strove to avoid all types of extremism, was enraged. (He had urged abolitionists to love their southern neighbors more and their colored brethren a little less in the name of civic peace.) "This filthy enactment was made in the Nineteenth Century, by people who could read and write. I will not obey it, by God!" declared The Sage of Concord.

The law empowered federal officials to draft northern citizens to assist them in catching and detaining runaway slaves. If a local federal marshal refused to pursue the fugitive, he could be fined $1,000. Any citizen who aided or concealed the runaway was liable to the same fine. All the slave catcher needed was an affidavit from a slave's owner to seize a runaway. Jury trials were banned. A hearing before a federal judge was the only legal procedure permitted.

In states where abolitionist sentiment was strong, there were legal counterattacks. The Wisconsin Supreme Court declared the law unconstitutional, freeing a fugitive slave named Joshua Glover. Vermont's legislature passed a "habeas corpus law" that required state officials to do everything in their power to assist a captured runaway. In other states, local juries regularly acquitted men arrested for helping runaways. An infuriated President Fillmore threatened to send the U.S. Army to support federal authority.

The most sensational challenge to the law came in 1853 in Boston, where a Virginia runaway, twenty-year-old Anthony Burns, was arrested. New Hampshire–born President Franklin Pierce, elected by the Democrats in 1852, made it clear that he was going to enforce the law in the name of sectional peace. Undeterred, an enraged crowd stormed the courthouse and battled with fists, clubs, and knives against outnumbered U.S. marshals. In the melee, a deputy marshal was fatally stabbed. But the lawmen finally drove the protestors into the street.

A grimly determined President Pierce rushed hundreds of troops to Boston and a hearing was conducted before Judge Edward G. Loring, who served as commissioner of the federal circuit court in the state. His ruling was a foregone conclusion—Burns must be returned to his owner. While a huge crowd screamed insults, the soldiers lined the streets from the courthouse to the harbor, where a ship waited to take Burns back to Virginia. One Bostonian said he and his friends "went to bed one night old fashioned conservative compromise Whigs and woke up stark mad abolitionists."

Not long after Burns left Boston, William Lloyd Garrison presided over a huge protest meeting, at which he burned copies of the Fugitive Slave Act and the U.S. Constitution. Abolitionists launched a movement to dismiss Judge Loring. After another three years of agitation in and out of the legislature, a new Massachusetts governor fired the jurist. The new Democratic president, James Buchanan, promptly gave him an appointment in the federal government.

Among the manic antislavery crusaders in New England and the Midwest, this rescue only confirmed the virtual omnipotence of The Slave Power.[12]

CHAPTER 17

From Uncle Tom
to John Brown

The uproar over the Fugitive Slave Act inspired a woman to begin writing a novel that she first published, in the custom of the day, as a serial in a newspaper. Her choice was *The National Era*, Washington, DC's abolitionist paper. Harriet Beecher Stowe was the daughter of the anti-Catholic crusader, the Reverend Lyman Beecher, and the brother of the Reverend Henry Ward Beecher, a passionate abolitionist. She called the novel *Uncle Tom's Cabin, or Life Among the Lowly.*

The book sold 300,000 copies in the first year of its publication (1852). It also inspired dramatic versions that were soon playing on stages all over America. The instant success of *Uncle Tom's Cabin* is often described as a kind of miracle. But few books have ever been published with more built-in publicity, courtesy of the federal government and the infuriated voices of thousands of abolitionists protesting the Fugitive Slave Law. Central to the book's drama is the flight of slaves to the North and to Canada.

One of the most mesmerizing escapees is the mulatto slave Eliza Harris, who crosses the frozen Ohio River by leaping from ice floe to ice floe with her five-year-old child in her arms. Eliza was one of two slaves that Arthur Shelby decided to sell to save his Kentucky plantation from debt. The other was Uncle Tom, who rapidly became the most famous African American in real or imagined history. Described as tall and husky, with a wife and family from whom he was cruelly separated, Uncle Tom had a deep Christian faith that inspired him to love and forgive the whites who treated him abominably. He even forgives his last and worst owner, Simon Legree, who whips him to death in a fiendish attempt to break his spirit.

For twentieth- and twenty-first-century readers, Uncle Tom has been too noble to understand or accept. His name has become shorthand for a black man or woman who is ready to knuckle under to white prejudice and abuse. This criticism is an exaggeration, as some contemporary scholars are eager to maintain. They point out that Tom refuses Legree's orders to whip a fellow slave. He also refuses to betray the hiding places of some runaways. But Tom's faith in God's ultimate love, and his anticipation of a reward in heaven if he forgives his persecutors, are not ideas that find much acceptance today.[1]

The problem of understanding Tom's extraordinary spiritual life is compounded by the dialect in which he speaks, which seems to underscore his inferiority, if not his simplemindedness. As he parts with his wife, Chloe, who is angry at Arthur Shelby for separating Tom from her and their children, Tom says: "Chloe! Now if ye love me, ye won't talk so, when perhaps jest the last time we'll ever have together. And I tell ye, Chloe, it goes agin me to hear one word agin Mas'r. Wan't he put in my arms a baby?—it's natur I should think a heap of him."

These words, even at their dialect-distorted worst, are still very important. Harriet Beecher Stowe was adding a dimension to the abolitionist crusade—personal love, or at least pity—for one of the South's slaves. Unfortunately, Uncle Tom's message was also tragically racist. Mrs. Stowe revealed this sad fact in her own words, in *The Key to Uncle Tom's Cabin*, a book she wrote after the novel's success. "The Negro race is confessedly more simple, docile, childlike, and affectionate than other races," she declared.

Stowe's judgment was based on her religious convictions. "The divine graces of love and faith . . . in-breathed by the Holy Spirit, find in the [Negro's] natural temperament a more congenial atmosphere." She presented

Eliza Harris and her husband George as far more ready to revolt and challenge slavery in language and action. Stowe attributed their defiance to the white blood in their mulatto veins. With unconscious complacency, Harriet Beecher Stowe created a huge wave of sympathy for slaves—and reinforced white convictions about their own racial superiority.[2]

Another interesting aspect of the novel is the almost complete absence of sneering snarling abolitionists like William Lloyd Garrison or Wendell Phillips in its text. The only antislavery Northerners the reader sees are kindly Quakers in Ohio, who conceal Eliza Harris and help her escape to Canada. There may be an implied critique in this omission, but it probably was not deliberate. The writing of a novel is a complex psychological process, and the author often wonders as the ideas and images flow onto the page how much control he or she has over the literary imagination while it is at work. At one point, Harriet Beecher Stowe told a close friend that she was not the real author of the book.

"Who was?" the astounded friend asked.

"God," Mrs. Stowe replied.[3]

Another aspect of her view of *Uncle Tom's Cabin* is even more surprising. Mrs. Stowe was disappointed when Southerners reacted to the novel with rage and dismissal. She apparently thought that she had presented many slave owners in a positive light—and hoped the book would inspire some sort of emancipation movement in the region. In the closing pages of the novel, George Shelby, the son of the original master, travels to Louisiana in an attempt to buy Tom's freedom, but he arrives too late. Tom is dead. Shelby returns to Kentucky and frees all his slaves.[4]

The central fact of *Uncle Tom's Cabin* was the way it aroused intense sympathy for slaves—and rage at slave owners. At least as important, *Uncle Tom's Cabin* had huge appeal to the chief readers of novels in the nineteenth century: women. Both reactions are visible in a letter to the author from a woman who had just finished the novel.

> I sat up last night long after one o'clock, reading and finishing Uncle Tom's Cabin. I could not leave it any more than I could have left a dying child; nor could I restrain an almost hysterical sobbing for an

hour after I laid my head upon the pillow. I thought I was a thorough-
going Abolitionist but your book awakened in me so strong a feeling
of indignation and compassion, that I seem never to have had any
feeling on this subject until now . . . This storm of feeling has been
burning, raging like a fire in my bones all the livelong night.[5]

.   .   .

Uncle Tom was by no means the only new influence on the public mind of
the 1850s. A handsome Swiss-born scientist named Louis Agassiz played a
large role in the way educated people discussed slavery. Agassiz had come
to America in 1846, after winning fame as a scholar of natural history in
Europe. Among his more startling discoveries was the existence of the Ice
Age. His series of lectures, "The Plan of Creation as Shown in the Animal
Kingdom," created a sensation in Boston. As many as five thousand people
showed up to hear him speak, and he had to give each lecture twice to satisfy his enthralled admirers. Soon the newcomer was named head of the
Lawrence Scientific School at Harvard, created specifically for him.[6]

In America, Agassiz developed a new scientific passion: anthropology.
He leaped into it with the same enthusiasm and self-confidence that had enabled him to churn out an astonishing amount of research on the history of
the fish and animal kingdoms. He was galvanized by a Philadelphia scientist,
Samuel George Morton, who had spent decades collecting and analyzing
human skulls. The key to understanding human abilities, as Morton (and
soon Agassiz) saw it, was cranial capacity. He saw humanity not as a unified
entity, but as a collection of races. In descending order, these were: Cau-
casian, Mongolian, Malay, Native American, and Negro. At the top of this
not-very-scientific heap were the German, English, and Anglo-Americans,
who had the largest cranial capacity. Negroes had the smallest. Not surpris-
ingly, some members of the latter race were, Agassiz concluded, "the lowest
grade of humanity."

Morton's skull collection was totally haphazard. As science it was virtually meaningless. But Agassiz, charging into the new field, swallowed his
conclusions in one spectacular gulp, and he used his fame to publicize them

across the nation. Stopping in Philadelphia at a hotel staffed by African Americans, he told of his reaction in these appalling words: "As much as I feel pity for this degraded and degenerate race, as much as their fate fills me with compassion . . . it is impossible to repress the feeling that they are not of the same blood as us. Seeing their . . . fat lips and grimacing teeth, the wool on their heads, their bent knees, their elongated hands . . . I could not turn my eyes from their faces in order to tell them to keep their distance."[7]

Agassiz soon concluded that "the philanthropists"—his name for abolitionists—and the defenders of slavery were both wrong. The abolitionists shared his reaction to negritude. They would never let their daughters marry a black man nor would they consider for an instant marrying a black woman. But the slave owners of the South were wrong when they tried to deny that a slave had any right to liberty. Agassiz did not seem to realize that his (pseudo) scientific opinions about the Negroes' intelligence made emancipation seem foolish and even dangerous.

Agassiz was soon telling his Harvard students and eager audiences in Boston that whites and Negroes were two distinct species. He journeyed to Charleston, South Carolina, to tell an assemblage of the city's best people the same thing. "The brain of a Negro is that of the imperfect brain of a seven months infant in the womb of a white," he said. It was the first of many Agassiz lectures in Charleston. He was as popular there as he was in Boston.[8]

Southerners were soon using Agassiz and colleagues who shared his views as proof that Negro slavery did not violate Jefferson's Declaration of Independence. When the founder wrote that all men were created equal, scientifically the statement did not include Negroes. In fact, Agassiz maintained that the whole history of the slave trade and the development of slavery in the New World was a gigantic mistake. The white and black races were never meant to interact in such an intimate and proximate existence.

Agassiz strenuously denounced all forms of interracial marriage and predicted mulattoes were doomed to swift extinction because racial intermixing violated the divine plan. At another point he declared that, scientifically speaking, sexual intercourse between blacks and whites was the equivalent of incest.

For Agassiz, Mexico was a living, breathing example of what racial mixing produced—a country in which the entire population suffered from massive mental instability and physical inferiority. "Can you devise a scheme to rescue the Spaniards of Mexico from their degradation?" he asked a Boston friend, Samuel Gridley Howe. Agassiz said America should remember what amalgamating the races did to this southern neighbor. Social equality between whites and blacks was "a natural impossibility, flowing from the very character of the Negro race." At the same time, Agassiz placated his Bostonian supporters by reiterating that he nevertheless believed that blacks should be free.

This pro forma statement did not prevent southern audiences from inviting him to speak again and again. Echoes of his theories resounded in southern newspapers. In 1856, the *Charleston Mercury* dismissed abolitionist attacks by editorializing: "The moral justification of the South lies in facts against which fanaticism and cant are both powerless. . . . The Negro is inferior to the White Man by nature and by destiny . . . he can never be his equal until the laws of God are abrogated."[9]

In 1859, an Englishman named Charles Darwin published a book, *On The Origin of the Species*, which maintained that the human race had evolved over millions of years but somehow retained, in spite of its many differences, a biological unity that made them a single species. Agassiz and his followers heaped scorn on this idea.

·   ·   ·

Yet another strand in bolstering the southern mindset about slavery was the reappraisal of the emancipation of Britain's West Indian blacks. In the 1830s and 1840s, Theodore Weld and others had journeyed to the islands and reported that all was peaceful and prosperous. By the 1850s, it was apparent that the impact of emancipation on the West Indies was an economic disaster.

Most of the ex-slaves had refused to resume toiling on the sugar plantations. They preferred to cultivate small plots on which they raised enough food to feed their families. Sugar production plummeted, leaving Brazil,

Cuba, and southern states such as Louisiana the uncontested rulers of this hugely profitable market.

In desperation, British officials approached the U.S. government, hoping it would cooperate in a campaign to hire free American blacks to work on the islands' plantations. They got a cold reception from federal spokesmen, many of whom were Southerners. They suspected that Britain was embarked on a policy of ruining slavery in other countries so they could emerge as the world's chief economic power, growing cotton and sugar and coffee in their vast Far East colony, India.[10]

The American government asked the U.S. consul in Jamaica, Robert Monroe Harrison, to give them a report on conditions on that island since emancipation. His reply was devastating. The price of land in Jamaica had declined by at least 50 percent. Some big plantations, which used to produce thousands of pounds in profits for their owners, were now worth about 10 percent of their pre-emancipation value. "England has ruined her own colonies," Harrison concluded, "and like an unchaste female seeks to put other countries, where slavery exists, in a similar state."

Harrison and other Southerners saw the international pressure that Britain put on Brazil and Cuba, and their attempt to bribe Texas into antislavery, as part of their devious plan. It had nothing to do with benevolence or human rights. They pointed to Britain's horrendous conduct toward oppressed Ireland, where the Parliament did next to nothing while a famine caused by the failure of the potato crop killed over a million hapless Celts.

The British tried importing thousands of East Indian "hill coolies" into Jamaica. They arrived in a state of near collapse after a voyage of 131 days. They, too, proved to be unproductive workers and were soon another clog on the islands' ruined economy.[11]

In 1856 the New Orleans *Picayune,* one of the South's leading papers, ran a long report from a correspondent who had just visited Kingston, Jamaica. "The impressions which, on a personal view, the dilapidation of Jamaica, has made upon me are of the most sad and somber character," he wrote. "This city, which once counted eighty thousand prosperous inhabitants, who resided more in a great accumulation of beautiful gardens than in densely built squares, now contains, we are told, only about forty thousand . . . people, composed in great measure, to use the expression of an English gentleman resident here, of poverty-crippled Negroes."

The white population was "rapidly disappearing." A large number of the better houses were now "abandoned ruins, with creepers and small bushes clinging to their crumbling walls." The wharves and storehouses were "sinking and going to decay, telling . . . of the abandonment of the fields and fertile vales of the interior."

"The colored population" was a study in contrasts. The young men looked "hale, well-fed and joyous." The young girls, mostly good looking, "sail along with the gait of a Juno and the simper of a Venus." But the middle-aged of both sexes "seem everywhere sad and joyless, and the old are images of haggard want and despair."

During a stroll around Kingston, the reporter found himself in the coolie section of the city. Here poverty was far worse than in the black neighborhoods. Everywhere beggars beseeched him in broken English for a few pennies to save them from starvation. The only prosperous people he saw were several dozen Chinese, who were running successful businesses. "The elements of society here are in rapid dissolution," the reporter said, in a harsh closing sentence. "Social insignificance and impotence is [sic] fast closing around the island."[12]

After eyewitness reports like this one in their newspapers, more than a few Southerners were not surprised when the *London Times* reported that slave emancipation in the West Indies was a colossal failure that had annihilated millions of pounds of capital and reduced blacks to a degradation lower than they had known as slaves. The *Times* urged English abolitionists to visit the West Indies and see with their own eyes what their fanaticism had wrought. Virtually every major paper in the South carried the story.[13]

·   ·   ·

In Washington, DC, politicians still sought a solution that would satisfy the South's demand to take their slaves into the western territories. The South continued to trumpet this demand as a constitutional right, never mentioning that other motivation, the fear of a slave insurrection as the density of the black population continued to grow. Senator Stephen A. Douglas of Illinois decided the answer lay in an idea that Lewis Cass, the Democrat who had run for president against Zachary Taylor in 1848, had proposed. Cass had called it "squatter sovereignty." The voters of each new state would decide whether they tolerated or rejected slavery.

Douglas had emerged as a leader in the passage of the Compromise of 1850. Only five feet tall, when he spoke in the Senate he became a verbal tornado with a voice that seemed to belong to a man ten times his size. Often he worked himself into a near frenzy, stripping off his coat, his vest, his shirt, and finally his undershirt, as he made his thunderous points. Before long he had earned the nickname "the Little Giant."

Douglas decided that the South would be mollified if they were allowed to bring slaves into one of the two new western states that he had in mind, Kansas and Nebraska. Blocking this idea was the 1819–1820 Missouri Compromise, which barred slavery from territories north of the 36-30 line of latitude. The senator's oratorical skills persuaded Congress to repeal the compromise, with the tacit understanding that Missouri slave owners would people Kansas and antislavery Iowans would do likewise for Nebraska. Douglas concocted a new slogan for his proposal, Popular Sovereignty.

The senator persuaded President Franklin Pierce that the proposal was the answer to achieving a peaceful solution to slavery. Pierce helped whip Democratic congressman and senators into line. On May 25, 1854, the Kansas-Nebraska Act passed with comfortable majorities in both houses, making the Missouri Compromise history.[14]

For New Englanders, the date almost coincided with the day that runaway slave Anthony Burns was led through the outrage-filled streets of Boston to the ship that would return him to Virginia. The coincidence produced something very close to hysteria in the Bay State. The frenzy multiplied when the Yankees learned that a Missouri senator was boasting that slave owners from his state were pouring into Kansas, staking out claims and virtually declaring a victory for southern pride and principles. Soon there was a New England response. An "Emigrant Aid Company" organized groups of antislavery pioneers and sent them to Kansas, armed with new breechloading Sharps rifles.

. . .

Among those who joined this throng of New England crusaders were John Brown and his four sons. Brown was descended from Puritans who had arrived in America not long after the Mayflower. In 1805, his father, Owen, had moved his growing family to Hudson, Ohio, just south of Cleveland in the Western Reserve, land that Connecticut had purchased for its rapidly growing population. The elder Brown combined farming with a tannery, and with land speculation in which he lost a great deal of money.

In this small community, John Brown acquired the strict, severe Calvinist faith of the seventeenth century, virtually undiluted by later fads and fancies. He followed his father's example and started a tannery near Hudson. But it did not prosper, nor did any of his other businesses. He plunged into ventures such as wool merchandising that ended with everyone angry and/ or disappointed with him, including his chief partner. His manic-depressive mind was constantly attracted to large schemes. But his inability to deal with details, or to get along with business associates, invariably led to disaster. At times, fear of failure made him a near-crook. He took out three different mortgages on one piece of property without informing his lenders.

When things went wrong, the anger bred in John Brown's soul by his harsh jeremiad-drenched faith exploded. In a dispute over some land in Ohio, he had holed up in a cabin with several of his sons and declared he would kill anyone who set foot on his property. He finally surrendered without a fight. As his failures and embarrassments multiplied, he began sinking into depressions, expressing "a strong wish to die."[15]

Brown was uniquely susceptible to the angry words exchanged in Congress and in newspapers between North and South over abolitionist petitions, the annexation of Texas, the admission of California, and the Fugitive Slave Act. From an early age he had sympathized with both free and enslaved blacks and tried to help them. In Ohio, his house had been a stop on the Underground Railroad. Soon he was a total believer in the evil designs of The Slave Power. Striking a blow against slavery became his last hope of ending his disappointing life in triumph.

Kansas offered John Brown an opportunity to make his commitment more than a war of words. His view of the conflict is apparent in a letter he wrote to John Brown Jr. in August 1854, only a few months after Congress had passed the Kansas-Nebraska Act. He asked if his son was thinking of going to Kansas or Nebraska, "with a view to help defeat Satan and his legions." As Brown and his sons and their fellow abolitionists saw it, Kansas was proof of The Slave Power's insatiable appetite for virgin land. The annexation of the immense prairies of Texas had not satisfied them, because they were constantly consuming productive soil, thanks to the careless way they raised cotton and the supposedly shiftless character of slave labor. These Slave Power critics knew nothing about the way the South was rapidly learning the science of soil rejuvenation and making huge profits from its chief crops, cotton, sugar, and indigo.[16]

By May 1855, Brown and his sons were in Kansas, settled near the abolitionist town of Osawatomie. They had staked out good claims to fertile land and begun growing crops. The last part of their trip took them through Missouri, where hostile inhabitants refused to sell them food or even give them water. In a letter to his father, Salmon Brown wrote: "We saw some of the curses of slavery and they are many. . . . The boys have their feelings well worked up so that I think they will fight."

The Browns minced words with no one. When a band of armed Missourians rode up to their settlement, the Browns told them, "We are free state, and more than that, we are abolitionists." When the proslavery Kansas settlers convened a legislature and wrote a series of laws making it a crime to speak out against slavery, John Brown Jr. told one of them that he did not think any person had a right to own a slave in Kansas. If anyone tried to arrest him for violating the new laws, he would "surely kill him so help me God."[17]

Their obsession with violence led the Browns to ignore attempts by moderate settlers to work out a compromise with the proslavery newcomers.

The moderates were "free soil" men, and they soon spelled out what that meant. They wanted to bar not only slaves but free Negroes from Kansas, a la the Wilmot Proviso. When John Brown Jr. freed two slaves from a nearby farm, the other members of his militia group, the Pottawatomie Rifle Company, were so angry that they voted to dismiss him as their captain.

John Brown Sr. was enraged by the antiblack attitude of the moderates and denounced them in a violent speech at a public meeting in Osawatomie in April 1856. He declared he was ready to see the country "drenched in blood" before he agreed to their view of black Americans. He considered them "his brothers and equals."

Both sides held elections and claimed majority support. Each group had its share of wild men. There was a rash of killings, some of them personal arguments that had nothing to do with slavery.

Anger mounted on both sides. The proslavery men struck first, after a proslavery sheriff was shot while sitting in his tent. About 750 Missourians, Alabamians, and South Carolinians stormed into Lawrence, Kansas's largest antislavery town, and wrecked the place. They burned and looted houses of the antislavery leaders, blew up the Free State Hotel, and smashed up two antislavery newspaper offices. They did not kill anyone, largely because the most outspoken antislavery men had fled in advance of their arrival.[18]

The Browns lived twenty-five miles from Lawrence. By the time they arrived with their thirty-four-man rifle company, the attackers had departed. John Brown was infuriated by the sight of the ruined hotel and other houses. "Something is going to be done now," he declared.

The following night, Brown, his four sons, and two other followers dragged five unarmed men out of their cabins along Pottawatomie Creek, known to be a proslavery stronghold. Brown ordered his sons to execute them before the horrified eyes of their wives and children, using two-edged cavalry swords that all but amputated arms and legs and heads. Perhaps most appalling were the murders of James P. Doyle and his two oldest sons, while Doyle's wife, Mahala, pleaded frantically for their lives and four other bewildered Doyle children watched the butchery. The Doyles were immigrants from Tennessee who had come to Kansas seeking a better life. They had no interest in owning slaves.

The goal of this slaughter, John Brown said, was "to strike terror into the hearts of the proslavery people." Its immediate effect was terror in the souls of his sons. Back in their camp, Owen collapsed in hysterical fits of weeping. "There shall be no more such work," he sobbed. John Brown Jr., who had already shown signs of mental instability, wandered in a daze, babbling. Jason, who was seriously mentally ill most of the time and had not accompanied the killers, shouted in his father's face that it was "an uncalled for wicked act." Brown grimly replied that he would let "God be my judge."[19]

CHAPTER 18

The Real Uncle Tom
and the Unknown South
He Helped Create

Readers of *Uncle Tom's Cabin* had no idea that there was a real Uncle Tom. His name was Josiah Henson. He was born a slave in Maryland in 1789. Harriet Beecher Stowe admitted more than once that his story was part of the inspiration for her novel. But she never adequately explained why her fictional Uncle Tom was so different from the real one.[1]

The difference was and is profound. The real Tom should prompt modern readers to reevaluate slavery's impact on American blacks. The traditional story runs something like this: Slavery was a degrading, humiliating, demoralizing experience. Any black man or woman who endured it was reduced to subhuman status. Therefore they and their descendants, even when emancipated, would have to be treated like children, at best, or creatures from an alien planet at worst. Before and after the Civil War, this idea played no small part in poisoning the idea of black equality in the American public mind, North and South.

Mrs. Stowe never spent any serious time in the South. Almost everything she knew about the slave system was acquired from reading Theodore Weld's *Slavery As It Is*, from conversations with abolitionist friends, and from visits to nearby plantations during the ten years she and her husband spent in Cincinnati, across the Ohio River from Kentucky.

During her visits to plantations in Kentucky, Mrs. Stowe saw blacks doing a remarkable variety of things. Often a black managed an entire plantation as the overseer. Others were blacksmiths, shoemakers, or tailors. But this, Mrs. Stowe believed, was only true of Kentucky, a border state. Elsewhere, especially on the Deep South's cotton plantations, slaves remained subhuman automatons.

To inspire outrage and pity, Mrs. Stowe portrayed her fictional Uncle Tom as an impossible mixture of competence and servility. She mentioned almost casually that he ran his master's plantation. But she never gave readers a glimpse of him at work. Instead she spent pages describing Tom as so kind-hearted that he verges on being a pathetic yes-man who rarely challenged his master's decisions.

Josiah Henson gives us a different picture of slavery in his autobiography, which was published in 1849. Henson left no doubt that the system could be brutal. His father got into a fistfight with an overseer who tried to molest his wife. He was given a hundred lashes and one of his ears was amputated. After that, the elder Henson became a morose sullen ghost of his previously cheerful self. A few years later, the master was drowned crossing a river on horseback and his slaves were sold by his heirs. Josiah and his mother were separated until she persuaded her new master to buy her son too.

These experiences did not break Henson's spirit. When he was still in his teens, his new master, Isaac Riley, began calling him "a smart fellow." His fellow slaves predicted he would do "great things" when he became a man. Soon he was vowing to "out-hoe, out-reap, out-husk, out-dance, out-everything every competitor." He did not hesitate to compete with white men as well as fellow slaves. He had a low opinion of the farm's sloppy, careless overseer. When he caught the man defrauding the master, Henson reported him.

Isaac Riley fired the thief, and Henson asked for a chance to oversee the farm. He was soon raising "more than double the crops, with more cheerful and willing labor, than was ever seen on the estate before." Not only did he superintend the day-to-day work, he brought the harvested wheat and to-bacco to market and bargained skillfully to bring home astonishing profits.[2]

The fictional Uncle Tom admired his incompetent master, even after he sold him south. "Set him 'longside of other masrs—who's had the treatment and the livin' I've had?" he told his wife. The real Uncle Tom had no such high opinion of Isaac Riley. He was "coarse and vulgar in his habits, unprin-cipled and cruel in his general deportment." Riley sometimes cursed Hen-son for not getting a better price for a crop, and yet boasted to friends about his new overseer's skill at the marketing table. "He was quite incompetent to handle the business himself," Henson added.

Riley was always short of money, thanks to his bad habits. He gave his slaves a minimum diet of cornmeal and salt herring. Henson secretly sup-plemented their allowances with selections from "the superior crops I was raising." He soothed his conscience by reminding himself that he was saving Riley a "large salary" for a white overseer.

At the age of twenty-two, Henson married "a very well-taught girl, be-longing to a neighboring family." By this time he had become a devout Christian, thanks to the influence of his mother and a white man named McKinney, who was a part-time preacher to local slaves. Henson's religion helped him put up with Riley. Henson considered it his duty to be "faith-ful to him in the position in which he placed me." For many years he made enough money to finance Riley's dissolute lifestyle.

Riley became involved in a lawsuit with his brother-in-law over some jointly owned property. This blunder created a scene that was the opposite of the slave servility so often pictured in *Uncle Tom's Cabin*. Stumbling into Henson's cabin well after midnight, a drunken Riley fell on his knees before the fire and moaned, "O Sie [Josiah] I'm ruined, ruined!"

"How so, Master?" asked Henson.

"They've got a judgment against me and in less than two weeks every nigger I've got will be put up and sold."

Riley began to curse his brother-in-law, who had won the lawsuit. Frantically, he threw his arms around Henson. "You can do it, Sie. Won't you help me? Won't you?"

Henson asked what he was talking about. Riley said he wanted Henson to take the farm's slaves to his brother Amos's plantation in Kentucky. There they would be safe from seizure and his brother would give Riley enough money for their services for him to survive in Maryland. Henson agreed to take the eighteen slaves (including his wife) beyond the reach of the Maryland court. He plotted a route, bought a wagon, and stocked it with food. They rode overland to Wheeling, West Virginia, where Henson sold the wagon, bought a boat, and sailed down the Ohio River to Cincinnati. There they encountered several free blacks, who urged them to head for Canada. Henson refused to double-cross his master.[3]

By mid-April 1825, they reached Amos Riley's Kentucky plantation. It was a large operation, with over a hundred slaves. Amos Riley, too, made Josiah Henson his overseer, and he successfully managed this much bigger business. A friendly Methodist clergyman gave Henson lessons in the art of preaching and urged him to seek his freedom. Henson persuaded Amos Riley to let him return to Maryland to visit Isaac Riley and black friends on nearby plantations. He had earned enough money from preaching in black churches in his Kentucky neighborhood to negotiate with Isaac Riley for his freedom. They agreed on $450, and Henson gave him $350 and a note for the balance.

Back in Kentucky, Henson learned from Amos Riley that he would have to raise another $650 to be a free man. Henson quietly planned and executed an escape to Ohio with his wife and four children. In a few weeks he was safe in Canada. There he started a sawmill that was soon selling thousands of feet of black walnut lumber in Boston and New York. He persuaded the Canadian government to let him start a manual-labor school to teach escaped slaves skills that would increase their earning power.

With help from affluent Canadian and American friends, Henson sailed to England to raise money for his school and to display the timber from his sawmill. He exhibited the gleaming wood at the 1851 London World's Fair.

With a mixture of pride and ruefulness, he noted that "among all the exhibitors from every nation in Europe, from Asia and America and the Isles of the Sea, there was not a single black man but myself."

Toward the end of this visit to England, the Archbishop of Canterbury invited Henson to his palace and chatted with him for about ninety minutes. The prelate was amazed to learn that Henson had spent most of his life as a slave. "Will you tell me, sir, how you learned our language so well?" he asked.

Henson said he had always listened closely to the way white people talked and learned to imitate those who spoke most correctly. The contrast between this extraordinary black man's conversation and Uncle Tom's crude dialect is final proof of how different the real Tom was from his fictional counterpart.[4]

. . .

Josiah Henson was not some sort of mysterious exception to the rule in the slave world of the South. There were black men like him in almost every southern state. In South Carolina, William Ellison's master (perhaps also his father) apprenticed him to a cotton gin maker. Ellison swiftly learned this technology and soon had enough money from repairing gins to purchase his freedom and then the freedom of his wife and children. By 1860, he owned a thousand acres of land and sixty-three slaves. He was one of the richest planters in the state.

We have seen that George Washington appointed slave overseers at Mount Vernon in the 1790s. By the 1850s, black overseers were far more common than most Northerners of that era—and most Americans of the twenty-first century—have realized. Some historians estimate that blacks predominated in that position on roughly 70 percent of the plantations with a hundred or more slaves. On smaller plantations, the overseer was almost always black.[5]

The importance of these black men can be glimpsed in a cry of distress from a Louisiana planter when his slave overseer died. "I have lost poor Leven, one of the most faithful blacks that ever lived. He was truth and honesty and without a fault that I ever discovered. He has overseen the plantation nearly three years, and has done better at it than any white man had ever done before."[6]

Managing plantations was by no means the only goal to which a black man might aspire in the Deep South, in spite of being a slave. Twenty-seven percent of the adult male slaves in the city of Charleston were skilled artisans such as blacksmiths, carpenters, and coopers. They operated as virtually free men. A slave carpenter or shoemaker would and could advertise his services, negotiate his own contracts, receive and pay money, and even live in his own house. His slave status required him to pay a percentage of his income to his owner. Otherwise he was a relatively free man.

Slave artisans frequently made enough money to buy their freedom. In the 1850s, with cotton soaring on the commodity exchanges, the price of a slave was high, perhaps $1,700 for a blacksmith. That a black artisan could earn this much money and pay his own living expenses and a portion to his owner is impressive. His slave status was in many ways more an artificial legality that a daily reality.

Skilled slaves were equally common on the plantations. About 25 percent of the bondsmen had jobs that required expertise. They ranged from overseers to artisans to teamsters and gardeners. The idea that all slaves were menial workers is false. Even some women slaves held jobs as seamstresses and nurses for the master's children.[7]

The South's 260,000 free blacks had an even more impressive net worth. They owned property worth $25,000,000. About one in every hundred owned slaves. Even more surprising to modern readers is the number of slaves who worked in factories, displaying a gamut of industrial skills. The papers of David Ross, who operated the Oxford Ironworks in Campbell County, Virginia, one of the largest factories in the nation, reveal that the business was staffed and run entirely by slaves. A black man named Abram was responsible for the highly technical and demanding day-to-day management of the blast furnace. The furnace keepers, Abram's chief assistants, had to know precisely how much charcoal and limestone to put into the furnace when it was in blast. All the other skilled workers—blacksmiths, potters, hammer men, miners—were slaves.

David Ross was proud of the many workers who had mastered more than one skill. His blacksmiths could double as potters and were adept at repairing or rebuilding the machinery of the forges, furnaces, or mills. Of manager Abram, Ross wrote that he "supports an unblemished character, for his integrity, good understanding, and talents." Like Josiah Henson, Abram had revealed these gifts virtually from his infancy, and still retained them in spite of his "gray hairs."

Once a white overseer of a nearby Ross farm complained that the owner had compared him unfavorably to Abram. Ross replied the man must be mistaken. "It is hard to compare a farmer with an ironmaster." If Abram were a free man, Ross said, he would earn twice as much as the overseer, whether he was working in the North, South, or West.[8]

. . .

As the profitability of cotton culture grew in the 1850s, money became an ingredient in raising productivity on many plantations. Owners frequently paid between $40 and $110 a year to experienced slaves for doing a good job. Slaves were also permitted to grow fruit and vegetables in their gardens, and sell the produce. One industrious field hand made $309 in a single year selling peaches and apples on the side. In modern money that sum would be about $5,000.

In tobacco farming, where a high degree of skill was necessary, planters frequently paid slaves as much as $300 a year to guarantee a good performance. Rice cultivation required equal amounts of savvy. The plantations were divided into dozens of small watery plots surrounded by dikes. One traveler visited a rice farmer in Georgia and found a slave engineer who received "considerably higher wages" (in the form of presents) than the white overseer for his skill in building and maintaining the dikes.[9]

On cotton plantations, the "gang" system required another group of leaders, who functioned as assistant overseers, somewhat like foremen in a factory or sergeants in an army. Before his gang went to work, the leader had to measure out their tasks for the day—no small job in fields that were often shaped irregularly. With a boy helper and the aid of a five-foot measuring rod, the leader would set stakes that usually covered about forty acres. Once his gang went to work, he watched them closely to make sure they were not "overstrained." If he saw they were seriously tiring, he had the authority to call a halt to the day's work. The next day he would order part of his gang to finish the previous day's assignment, while the rest moved on to another section of the field.[10]

Some planters, to increase productivity, entered into profit-sharing arrangements with their slaves. One Alabama owner permitted his bondsmen to keep two thirds of the profits of the plantation, setting aside a third for his private use. From the slaves' share came the cost of clothing and food for him and his family, the taxes for the farm, and medical bills. "What clear money you make shall be divided equally amongst you in a fair proportion agreeable to the services rendered by each hand," the contract stated. "Those that earn most shall have most."[11]

These startling facts have come to light in the last three or four decades, thanks to in-depth research by a new generation of historians, who are trying to get beyond the myths perpetrated by abolitionist critics and southern defenders of slavery.

· · ·

Perhaps the most startling fact these statistic-minded scholars have uncovered is the South's breathtaking wealth. In the 1850s, the fifteen slave states were by far the most prosperous section of the nation. Southern farms, many of them slave-managed, were between 35 and 50 percent more profitable than comparable farms in the free North and Midwest. In 1860, the South, if considered as a separate country, would have ranked as the fourth-richest nation in the world. Southern whites had a higher per capita income than citizens of France, Germany, or Denmark.

Instead of the pleasure-wallowing wastrels portrayed by the abolitionists in their assaults on The Slave Power, most southern planters were hardworking businessmen who studied the latest techniques in scientific farming and did their best to keep their slaves contented in spite of the restrictions and confinements of the system.

A man who owned fifty slaves and managed them well with the help of a good overseer could clear $7,500 a year—the equivalent of $250,000 today. This was sixty times the average white American's per capita income, North or South, in the 1850s. The black slave overseer might get a bonus of $50 or $60 and a new suit at the end of the year, but he continued to live in a humble cabin in the slave quarters, starkly different from the master's "Big House."[12]

Inevitably, this inequality bred resentment in black Americans. They were being cheated out of a fair share of the profits. Historians estimate the average field worker was underpaid by three or four thousand modern dollars annually. Overall, the South's slaves would have earned $84 million each year, if they had been given a fair share of the profits they were making for the owners.[13]

Perhaps most remarkable is how much the South's four million slaves were worth as property: $3 billion. That sum exceeded the North's investment in railroads and factories. This figure does not include the value of the land that the South's farmers owned, worth at least another $3 billion. If we study the income of those men who owned twenty slaves or more and qualified as "planters"—some 46,274 individuals—the picture is even more astonishing. These men owned half of all the slaves, which means their net worth was at least $1.5 billion. Put another way, a mere 0.58 of the South's population composed 70 percent of the richest people in the United States in 1860.

On a per capita basis, the four wealthiest states in the Union were South Carolina, Mississippi, Louisiana, and Georgia. In the top twelve were only two northern states, Connecticut and Rhode Island. These newly discovered facts demolish the standard abolitionist assumption that the North was the dynamic section of the country and the slave-encumbered South was mired in backwardness and poverty.[14]

In the past, black men and women have been given very little credit for the South's remarkable wealth. It is time to revise that mindset. The slaves participated in the system, not as mere automatons, but as achievers, frequently mastering the technology of the South's agriculture as well as the psychology of leadership. A substantial number of black men and women did not succumb to the worst tendencies of the system. Their industrious lives within the unjust institution of slavery were frequently a triumph of the human spirit over adversity that should no longer be overlooked.

·   ·   ·

Among the many ironies of this new information about the South's wealth is the almost total ignorance about it that prevailed in both sections in the 1850s. The classic example is an 1857 book by a North Carolinian, Hinton Rowan Helper, *The Impending Crisis in the South.* Helper claimed to draw on statistics from the 1850 census to prove that the South was far poorer and less economically developed than the North. Helper said he spoke for "the Plain Folk of the Old South" who were in the grip of the wealthy minority of slave owners. The *New York Tribune,* eager to prove that slavery was an economic as well as a moral plague, gave it an eight-column review, making the author famous.[15]

·   ·   ·

The new facts about the economic success of southern slavery lead to an interesting and possibly significant conclusion: slavery was evolving. Overall it remained a deplorable institution. But American freedom, sometimes disguised as business enterprise, was constantly seeping into the system. Would it have continued to move toward more and more freedom? Many planters did not like slavery but were baffled by the problem of how to eliminate it. Haunted by the specters of Haiti and Nat Turner, they did not think the black and white races could live in peace if both were free. This was a view that was shared by almost everyone in the North as well as the South. In most northern states, blacks could not vote, serve on juries, or obtain decent jobs. They lived a segregated way of life in housing, schools, and even churches.

It seems inevitable that, sooner rather than later, southern masters would have had to confront American slavery's greatest failure: its lack of freedom, not only for gifted leaders like Josiah Henson and skilled artisans and factory managers like David Ross's Abram, but for the children and grandchildren of these men. Slaves with above-average intelligence and abilities would find it harder and harder to tolerate a system that did not reward them adequately and that condemned their descendants to the caprices of being sold to settle a dead master's estate or of paying the debts of a dissolute living owner. More and more individuals like the Louisiana planter who mourned the death of his black overseer might have become ready to risk emancipation rather than to live with such gross injustice on a day-to-day basis.

Alas, the momentum of the multiple diseases of the public mind, North and South, would prove too strong for this fragile hope to acquire substance. The myths of The Slave Power and genetic black inferiority twisted in this deadly wind while the South's unspoken fear of a race war was visible night after night in the slave patrols that continued to ride the shrouded southern roads. As the 1850s lurched toward a close, a perfect storm of deadly emotions was poised to engulf the United States of America.

What the nation desperately needed was a leader who would confront these aberrations with a voice of sanity and moderation. This savior was on the scene, but before he could speak with the needed political power, John Brown and his wealthy secret backers triggered an explosion of hatred and fear that shattered all hope of a peaceful solution.

CHAPTER 19

Free Soil for
Free (White) Men

"I have no prejudice against the Southern people. They are just what we would be in their situation. If slavery did not now exist amongst them, they would not now introduce it. . . . I surely will not blame them [Southerners] for not doing what I should not know how to do myself. If all earthly power were given to me, I should not know what to do, as to the existing institution [slavery]. . . . When they [Southerners] remind us of their constitutional rights, I acknowledge them, not grudgingly, but fully and fairly, and I would give them any legislation for the reclaiming of their fugitives which should not, in their stringency, be more likely to carry a free man into slavery. . . . But all this, to my judgment furnishes no more excuse for permitting slavery to go into our . . . free territory than it would for reviving the African slave trade by law."[1]

Abraham Lincoln spoke these enormously important words in Peoria, Illinois, not long after the passage of the Kansas-Nebraska Act. They simultaneously declared his disagreement with the abolitionists' gospel of hate and vituperation and his commitment to preventing slavery from becoming legal in any new states formed from the western territories. This stance seemed to him a political compromise that would preserve the Union and put slavery on the path to eventual elimination. From a distance of 150 years, we can see its seeming reasonableness—and its potentially fatal flaw. The refusal to permit Southerners to take slaves into the territories not only insulted and infuriated them, it also meant that they were left to confront the growing density of their slave population, which was rapidly approaching four million—almost 40 percent of the whites' numbers.

·   ·   ·

The quarrel over the extension of slavery had moved the issue to the center of the political debate in a new and dangerous way. The Whig Party collapsed as it became apparent that there was no longer any agreement between northern and southern members. Another political party, the Know-Nothings, had a brief ascent. As their name suggests, they operated as a semisecret society. When asked about the party's inner workings, a member was supposed to respond, "I know nothing."

The Know-Nothings were devoted to arousing the nation to the supposed menace of the recent flood of mostly Catholic German and Irish immigrants. For a few years they seized a large share of the northern public mind, electing governors and congressmen. But the Know-Nothings crumbled when it became apparent that they could not agree on slavery, no matter how much they all hated the "Popish" newcomers.

Out of the wreckage of the Whigs and Know-Nothings rose a new political party, the Republicans. The name was an ironic revival of Thomas Jefferson's 1790s party, which had opposed the supposedly aristocratic, potentially tyrannical Federalists, followers of George Washington and John Adams. The name Republican still had some of its old populist aura, even though most of the Jeffersonian Republicans' political descendants were now members of the only national party left somewhat united, the Democrats.

The Republicans concocted a slogan: "Free Soil for Free Men." This banner helped them attract the small Free Soil Party, which had begun as a protest movement against compromises backed by both Whigs and Democrats.

The slogan also echoed the demand of the Kansas antislavery settlers—a state without blacks, either enslaved or free. By not explicitly saying "free white men," the Republicans managed to attract abolitionist-leaning voters in the Midwest and New England who were committed to opposing the mythical machinations of The Slave Power.

Ex-Whig Abraham Lincoln joined the Republicans warily at first, but soon found himself a convinced convert. The party's opposition to the extension of slavery made it a congenial political home for the prairie lawyer, who detested the peculiar institution. It also supported other Whig policies Lincoln liked, such as the creation of a transcontinental railroad. Unfortunately, the new party's appeal to Southerners was close to zero, and southern Democrats reinforced this disadvantage by nicknaming them "Black Republicans."[2]

.   .   .

In the U.S. Senate, the furor over Kansas had raised tempers to a white-hot level. A new antislavery champion had risen there: Senator Charles Sumner of Massachusetts. Six feet two and as handsome as he was arrogant, he made no secret of his contempt for the South and things southern. In mid-May 1856, when South Carolina's aging Senator Andrew P. Butler tried to defend the South's right to take slaves into Kansas, Sumner replied with a political and personal denunciation that matched in dark ferocity anything produced by Cotton Mather and other New England preachers of the seventeenth century.

Sumner described Butler as a man who had chosen a mistress who was ugly to others, but was "always lovely to him—I mean the harlot, slavery." Butler had a speech impediment, which caused him to speak haltingly, especially when excited. Sumner sneered at the way the senator "with incoherent phrases, discharged the loose expectoration of his speech" on the people of Kansas. "He cannot open his mouth but out there flies a blunder." Sumner proceeded to climax this performance by imitating Butler for several minutes.

If the Southerners had asked northern fellow senators to disown this abuse, Sumner's congressional career might have been over. But southern anger was by this time as difficult to control as abolitionist moral superiority. Three days later, South Carolina Congressman Preston Brooks, a cousin of Senator Butler, strolled into the Senate and smashed Sumner over the head with a gutta-percha cane until it broke. The beating inflicted near-fatal injuries that left Sumner an invalid for the next four years.

Northern outrage was universal. In the South, Brooks was inundated with congratulations and replacement canes. The story of the attack was flashed around the nation by telegraph and supposedly made John Brown decide to slaughter those unarmed Southerners on Pottawatomie Creek. Brown needed no such inspiration for those crimes.[3]

•   •   •

The atmosphere of escalating hatred was reflected in the nation's newspapers. James Gordon Bennett, editor of the country's largest paper, the *New York Herald*, blamed the abolitionists for the turmoil, and wrote editorials denouncing the Reverend Henry Ward Beecher and other clergymen for "their scandalous political sermons." Bennett was equally savage toward his fellow newspapermen. He called Horace Greeley, editor of the antislavery *New York Tribune*, "a nigger worshipper" and "Massa Greeley."

The *Tribune*'s leader returned the compliment in kind, calling Bennett and the *Herald* a collection of "nigger drivers." That repulsive word, now banned from civilized usage, was in circulation everywhere.

Both papers, along with many other dailies in New York and other cities, practiced a tradition that makes today's editors and reporters wince to recall. The reporters saw themselves as entitled to embellish stories with imaginary facts and quotations. The custom was known as "faking it." Although James Gordon Bennett insisted his paper was independent of any and all politicians and attacked members of both parties, he seldom questioned the facts in a story, as long as it made lively reading. Greeley's antislavery *Tribune* was equally careless.

The champion in the faking game was the *New York Sun*. At one point the paper stood the metropolis on its ear by announcing the discovery of new planets and stars, supposedly reported from the *Edinburgh Journal of*

Science. A new telescope had revealed these wonders; it was so powerful that astronomers could see the moon as clearly as if it were a hundred yards away. The stories continued for several days, while the *Sun's* circulation soared to record heights. Only after a reporter told a drinking friend that the whole thing was a hoax did the *Sun* admit it had made up the story to divert the public mind from "that bitter apple of discord, slavery."

The daily circulation of Greeley's *Tribune* did not come close to matching Bennett's *Herald*. But the *Weekly Tribune* had over 200,000 readers nationwide, making it the most influential paper in the nation. It was read throughout the Yankee Midwest, where Theodore Weld and his followers had left a legacy of antislavery sentiments. It was commonly said that the *Tribune* was second only to the Bible all through the West.

Greeley infuriated Bennett by sending reporters into the South to describe the worst aspects of slavery. One vivid story portrayed a dialogue between a slave and a would-be buyer at a slave auction. A male slave was trying to persuade the white man to buy him, his wife, and two children.

"Look at me, Masr. Am prime rice planter; sho you won't find a better man den me . . . Do carpenter work too, a little. I be good servent, Masr. Molly, my wife, too . . . Fus rate rice hand. Mos' as good as me. Stan' out, Molly, let the gen'lemu see."

Molly stepped out and her husband praised her. "Good arm, dat, mas'r. She do a heap of work mo. Let good Mas'er see your teeth. All reg'lar." He ordered his seven-year-old son, Israel, to step out and "show the gen'lman how spry you be."

Next he displayed his three-year-old daughter, Vandy. "Make prime girl by and by. Better buy us, Mas'er. We fus'rate bargain."

The story closed with the reporter's acid words, "The benevolent gentleman . . . bought someone else."

Along with stories that had the ring of probable truth in them, such as this one, the *Tribune* subscribed totally to the myth of The Slave Power: It pictured southern plantations as nothing less than "Negro harems." It claimed there was scarcely one southern president who "has failed to leave . . . mulatto children." Southerners regularly hired blacks from slave owners "for purposes of prostitution." In a typical southern city, every night "ebony hued divinities" strolled to "the office of a colonel on one street, a doctor in another, a lawyer in another." Such obsessive dissipation redoubled the average Southerners scorn of daily labor. The South had fewer religious people and fewer churches than the North. In every conceivable way, the region was a thousand years behind the North in respect to civilization. It was a barrier to America's progress in every imaginable way, morally, economically, politically.[4]

Soon it became dangerous to read the *Tribune* publicly in the South. The *Herald*, on the other hand, was read everywhere below the Mason-Dixon Line. A reporter for the *Springfield Republican*, one of the many lesser papers that followed the *Tribune's* Slave Power lead, claimed to be amused by the way the *Herald* was "devoured at its earliest arrival here . . . and what is worse, to see the simplicity of these southern fellows, who seem to pin their whole faith in it."

·   ·   ·

In this atmosphere, the Republicans held their first national convention in Philadelphia. They bypassed Abraham Lincoln and a far more outspoken antislavery politician, Senator William Seward of New York. The party nominated John C. Fremont, an army officer who had won fame as an explorer of the West and had been a leader in the conquest of California during the War with Mexico. He was married to the daughter of former senator Thomas Hart Benton of Missouri, one of the chief proponents of Manifest Destiny. The choice underscored the new party's uneasiness about the abolitionists in their ranks. They wanted a standard-bearer who had little or no connection to these unpopular radicals.

The Democrats met a few weeks later and declined to renominate Franklin Pierce for a second term—the first time a sitting president suffered such a humiliation. They also declined to support Senator Stephen A. Douglas. The after-shocks of the Kansas-Nebraska Act had decimated northern Democrats in the 1854 congressional elections. The nominee was James Buchanan, who had been ambassador to Britain since 1853, leaving him unstained, in theory, by the sectional hatred raging in Kansas.

The election went to Buchanan, who polled 1,838,569 votes. The political unknown Fremont won 1,345, 264 ballots, almost all from nonslaveholding states. Ex-President Millard Fillmore, backed by remnants of the Know-Nothings and Whigs, won 874,354—evidence that a hefty portion of the electorate was confused and uncertain about the direction in which the United States should move. Buchanan was the first president since 1828 to win an election without carrying a majority of free states along with the slave states.

As the possibility of a purely sectional party explicitly hostile to slavery acquired flesh in the North, not a few politicians in many parts of the South began talking disunion. There were panicky rumors of slave insurrections. Whites feared that blacks who could read the newspapers or who overheard their worried masters' conversations at dinner tables would see the possibility of freedom on the horizon and grow rebellious. Thomas Jefferson's nightmare was still alive in the southern public mind.[5]

. . .

On December 2, 1856, a month after Buchanan's election, lame duck President Franklin Pierce sent his last message to Congress. It featured a furious attack on the agitators who had ruined his first and now only term—the abolitionists. He saw the presidential election as a repudiation of their doctrines, and he characterized them as people who threatened the "liberty, peace and greatness of the Republic" by organizing "mere geographical parties" and "marshalling in hostile array the different sections of the country." He declared "schemes of this nature" could not be popular in any part of America if they were not "disguised" and encouraged "by an excited state of the public mind."

Under the shelter of America's liberty, some individuals were "pretending to seek only to prevent the spread of the institution of slavery," Pierce continued. In reality they were "inflamed with the desire to change the domestic institutions of existing states." To accomplish this, they were devoting themselves to "the odious task . . . of calumniating with indiscriminate invective not only the citizens of the particular states with whose laws they find fault, but all others of their fellow citizens throughout the country who do not participate with them in their assaults upon the Constitution."

The abolitionists' object, Pierce insisted, was nothing less than "revolutionary." They knew their attempt to change the relative condition of the white and the black races in the slave holding states could only be accomplished "through burning cities and ravaged fields and slaughtered populations . . . all that is most terrible in [a] civil and servile war."[6]

·   ·   ·

Like most statements of outgoing presidents, this warning was largely ignored. One of the few readers who found it significant was far away from Washington, DC, on the plains of Texas. After three years as West Point's superintendent, Lieutenant Colonel Robert E. Lee had become second in command of a cavalry regiment, responsible for keeping peace between Indians and settlers in the wild country north of San Antonio. He missed his family at "dear Arlington." As Christmas 1856 approached, he wrote a wistful letter to his wife. "Though absent, my heart will be in the midst of you."

Colonel Lee welcomed James Buchanan's election as president. "I hope he will be able to extinguish fanaticism north and south, cultivate love for the country and the Union, and restore harmony between the different sections," he wrote. Not long after he mailed this letter, a package of newspapers arrived from his wife. In one of them was a copy of President Pierce's message to Congress. Lee was stirred by his former commander in chief's words. In another letter to his wife, he said the warning of a possible "Civil & Servile" war was "truthfully and faithfully expressed."

Lee was no believer in slavery as a positive good. "In this enlightened age, there are few . . . but what will acknowledge that slavery as an institution is a moral & political evil in any country." But he thought the blacks were "immeasurably better off here than in Africa, morally, socially and physically." The Colonel admitted he did not expect slavery to disappear soon. "How long their subjugation may be necessary is known and ordered by a wise Merciful Providence . . . Although the Abolitionist must know this & must see he has neither the right or power of operating except by moral means and suasion. . . . If he means well to the slave, he must not create angry feelings in the Master. . . . Still I fear he will persevere in his evil course. Is it not strange that the descendants of those pilgrim fathers who crossed the Atlantic to preserve their own freedom, have always proved themselves intolerant of the spiritual liberty of others?"[7]

. . .

Elsewhere in the nation, John Brown, that personification of a Puritan, if not a Pilgrim father (the Pilgrims were gentle, peace-loving souls—almost total opposites of the fierce, violent Puritans), was pursuing an ever more grandiose desire to attack and destroy slavery. Kansas had become pacified by Mississippi-born John A. Geary, a tough-minded territorial governor handpicked by President Pierce. Geary had disbanded armies on both sides and ordered guerilla troublemakers to leave the state. Brown had spent his final months in Kansas hiding out in the brush as a wanted man. Roaming squads of U.S. cavalry had a warrant for his arrest for the Pottawatomie murders.

Brown and his sons sensed their militant style was welcomed by neither side and prepared to depart. As a farewell gesture, they launched a raid into Missouri. They liberated eleven slaves, shot dead a slave owner who tried to resist them, stole horses and other property, and headed for Canada. With an effrontery that testified to the influence of the abolitionist campaign against The Slave Power, they travelled in daylight and Brown paused to give a speech in Cleveland, Ohio. They were confident that they were surrounded by Southern-hating allies who would manhandle any federal marshal foolish enough to pursue them.[8]

Returning from Canada to Tabor, Iowa, a town with a strong antislavery majority, Brown decided it was time to go east and tap into some of the money and guns that various emigrant aid societies had been sending to Kansas. He was especially stirred by news that an old friend, New York millionaire Gerrit Smith, had pledged ten thousand dollars to raise a thousand men to make sure Kansas became a free state.

Smith had rescued Brown and his family from destitution after the multiple failures of his business career. He had offered them land in New Elba, north of Lake Placid, where the millionaire had founded a colony for indigent free blacks. Smith had inherited a fortune from his father, a partner of John Jacob Astor. The son devoted himself to a bewildering range of good causes and good works. At various times he was in favor of colonization, then of abolitionism, and he had been a vice president of the American Peace Society.

Timbucto, as blacks called the New Elba colony, was a disastrous geographical choice for African Americans. After living for generations in warm climates, they were physically and mentally unprepared to endure northern New York's brutally cold winters. They were even more unready to master the art and science of raising crops in the relatively unfertile soil. Nor were any of them adept at building houses. Within a year or two, most of the farms were abandoned. The Browns stayed, largely because they had no place else to go.

Smith evinced no interest in giving Brown a slice of his ten-thousand-dollar pledge, so the Captain headed for Boston, where the Massachusetts Kansas Committee reportedly was rolling in dollars. He found the committee operating from a small cluttered office in a garret peopled only by twenty-six-year-old Franklin Sanborn, the volunteer secretary. Nevertheless, Brown's hopes rose when Sanborn recognized him as "Brown of Osawatomie"—the title antislavery journalists in Kansas had given him.

Brown was soon convinced that God had led him to Sanborn. The young Harvard graduate ran a college preparatory school in Concord and knew all the famous names of that community—Ralph Waldo Emerson, Henry David Thoreau, Bronson Alcott. Sanborn listened with growing excitement as Brown told him that he needed twenty thousand dollars to buy guns and supplies for a hundred men to renew the armed struggle for Kansas. The territory was not by any means safe from the grasp of The Slave Power.

Revealing an unexpected ability to sell himself, Brown described his exploits in Kansas in heroic terms. In the "battle" of Black Jack, he and his followers had captured at gunpoint a squad of Missouri raiders. He omitted mentioning that a troop of U.S. cavalry had forced them to surrender the prisoners shortly afterward. He made his role sound even more heroic in his description of the struggle to defend the state's antislavery headquarters at Osawatomie. In fact, the abolitionists had been routed and the town burned.

Captain Brown did not say a word about the killings on Pottawatomie Creek. When Sanborn mentioned a rumor of murders there, Brown assured him he had had nothing to do with such a ghastly crime. Soon Sanborn was seeing Brown as "of the unmixed Puritan breed"—the sort of hero who had fought and won the American Revolution. George Washington and other Americans south of New England were missing in this view of the history of 1776.

Sanborn introduced Brown to other men who believed in armed resistance to The Slave Power. Theodore Parker was a minister whose views on Christianity and antislavery were so radical that he was barred from every church in Boston and preached to a congregation at the city's Music Hall. Samuel Gridley Howe was a medical reformer who had launched a noteworthy school for the deaf and blind. In his youth he had gone to Europe to help the Greeks win their independence from the tyrannical Turks. He and Parker headed a "vigilance committee" to protect escaped slaves from federal marshals. The two persuaded the Kansas Committee to give Brown two hundred Sharps rifles that they had shipped to Tabor, Iowa, to renew the war for Kansas.

Sanborn introduced Brown to George Luther Stearns, a wealthy businessman who had raised almost $80,000 for the Kansas Committee. Stearns was so impressed with Brown's fictitious version of his exploits in Kansas that he paid $1,300 for two hundred pistols from the Massachusetts Arms Company. Stearns and his wife gave a reception for the Kansas free soil fighter at their plush suburban mansion. In the course of the evening, Brown met William Lloyd Garrison, who told him that he disapproved of his policy of violent resistance to slavery. The two men exchanged conflicting quotes from the Bible; otherwise Brown concealed his contempt for all-talk-and-no-action Garrisonians.

Franklin Sanborn persuaded his Unitarian minister friend, Thomas Wentworth Higginson, to hurry from Worcester to meet Brown. Higginson was a direct-action man on a par with the Kansas hero. He had already been dismissed by one congregation for his violent antislavery rhetoric. Although he vowed to help his cash-short fellow crusader, no money was forthcoming.

By now John Brown was growing more than a little frustrated by this lack of follow-through from most of his Boston well-wishers. Nevertheless, he allowed Sanborn to escort him to Concord, where he met Henry Thoreau at the house of his parents. The two men conversed over dinner and Thoreau declared he had "much confidence in the man—he would do right." The following night Brown visited the Emersons and then spoke in the Concord Town Hall to a large turnout.

Brown denounced slavery, its defenders, and the U.S. government, but he insisted he was no lover of violence. The necessity for it was clearly the will of God. The Bible and the Declaration of Independence were the two most important documents in world history, and it was "better for a whole generation of men women and children should pass away by violent death than that a word of either be violated in this country." The applause for this macabre nonsense was fervent but donations were few. Emerson gave only a few dollars, Thoreau "a trifle."

This pattern persisted in almost every Massachusetts town in which Brown spoke. He seldom raised more than seventy or eighty dollars. Then came a flash of bad news from his son Jason, who was waiting for him in Iowa. A deputy U.S. marshal was on his way to Massachusetts with a warrant for his arrest for the Pottawatomie murders. Brown went into hiding in the home of Thomas B. Russell, an abolitionist who was a judge of the state's supreme court. Brooding about his lack of cash, Brown barricaded himself in a third-floor bedroom and declared he would fight any and all U.S. marshals to the death. He frightened Mrs. Russell by brandishing a long bowie knife and several pistols.

At the Russell dinner table, consuming generous portions of well-cooked beef and fowl, Brown talked about the vile food he had been forced to eat while hiding out in Kansas—"joints and toes of creatures that surely no human being ever tasted," Mrs. Russell recalled. He took pleasure in making his affluent hosts uncomfortable. Finally he read aloud to the shocked Russells a diatribe he intended to distribute all over Boston:

Old Browns Farewell: to the Plymouth Rocks, Bunker Hill Monu-
ments, Charter Oaks and Uncle Toms Cabbins ... He leaves the [New
England] States with a DEEP FEELING OF SADNESS: that after having
exhausted *his own small means*: and with his family and his BRAVE
MEN: suffered nakedness, hunger, cold, sickness (and some of them
imprisonment, with the most barbarous cruel treatment: *wounds and
death* ... after all this to sustain a cause for which every citizen of this
"Glorious Republic" is under equal moral obligation to do: for the
neglect of which he will be held accountable by God ... he cannot
secure, amidst all the wealth, luxury and extravagance of this 'Heaven
exalted' people; even the necessary supplies of the common soldier.
HOW ARE THE MIGHTY FALLEN.

Brown sent copies of this rant to George Stearns and Theodore Parker. Mrs.
Stearns became almost hysterical and urged her husband to bankrupt himself if necessary to get Brown the money he needed. Stearns pledged seven
thousand dollars for "the defense of Kansas," which Brown was free to use
as he saw fit. But no actual cash materialized.

. . .

In his private journal, Ralph Waldo Emerson expressed awe and near-worship
of John Brown after meeting him in Concord. It was fresh evidence of the
way the Fugitive Slave Act of 1850 and its enforcement in Massachusetts
had tilted The Sage of Concord toward abolitionist extremism. The federal
government was "treason," Emerson now declared, and for a while preached
that California's vigilante justice was the best solution to the uproars created
by attempts to capture runaway slaves. With every man armed with a knife
and revolver, "perfect peace reigned" he claimed, betraying a total ignorance
of the Golden State.[9]

John Brown's religion of violence was even more appealing. Emerson saw
him as part of nature's law. He spoke of Brown as a sheep herder from Ohio,
ignoring the fact that he had failed in this venture, as he had in all his other
forays into earning a living. The Sage saw Brown as a man with a unique gift

for making friends with his horse or his mule. He was equally friendly with the deer that wandered onto his Ohio farm. "He stands for Truth," Emerson said. "And Truth & Nature help him . . . irresistibly."

Henry David Thoreau had also been transformed by the Fugitive Slave Act. After the runaway Anthony Burns had been returned to Virginia, Thoreau publicly burned copies of the Act and the Constitution. "My thoughts are murder to the State and involuntarily go plotting against her," Thoreau said. This was several dozen steps beyond the anti–tax-paying civil disobedience he had preached during his opposition to the Mexican War.

The more the two Concord philosophers discussed John Brown, the more convinced they became that he was a reincarnation of Oliver Cromwell. Even the New Englanders of 1776 had repudiated this infamous tyrant. After he defeated the royal army in the British civil war of the seventeenth century, Cromwell had beheaded King Charles I, dismissed Parliament, and ruled as a dictator for three decades. Cromwell was the bogeyman that New Englanders and others summoned when George Washington began acquiring an outsize reputation as the leader of the Revolution.

There was also the matter of Cromwell's bloodsoaked invasion of Ireland, during which he slaughtered whole populations of towns that resisted his army. Like John Brown, Cromwell claimed that the murders had God's approval. Henry Thoreau was soon saying that Brown's denunciations of slavery were "like the speeches of Cromwell." Brown's Kansas soldiers, including the murderers of the unarmed men on Pottawatomie Creek, were "a perfect Cromwellian troop." Franklin Sanborn and others who were part of the Concord world echoed this bizarre canonization.[10]

· · ·

When John Brown reached Tabor, Iowa, in August 1857, he had only $25 in his pocket. He was expecting to find most if not all of the $7,000 that George Stearns had promised him available to help him muster another troop of Cromwellian followers. Instead the local agent for the Massachusetts Kansas Committee gave him $110 and said he had no idea where or when more money was likely to appear.

The nation had been struck by a financial panic. The stock market had plunged and banks were collapsing. Thousands of men were marching in northern cities with banners reading: "Hunger is a Sharp Thorn" and "We Want Work." An oblivious Brown fired infuriated letters at Stearns and other Boston backers, claiming he needed $1,000 immediately for "secret service and no questions asked."[11]

Events in Kansas made this demand seem dubious or worse to Stearns, who was struggling to avert bankruptcy. Another Southern-born territorial governor, appointed by President Buchanan, was continuing the evenhanded policies of his predecessor. Fighting between proslavery and antislavery settlers had dwindled to the vanishing point. Elections to a territorial legislature were held, and free-state voters won overwhelmingly. Peace of sorts seemed to dawn on the military front, though Kansas would soon provide more political shocks.

John Brown had lost interest in this minor war. As his depression caused by the failure of his fundraising campaign lessened, his manic faith in his destiny resumed its grip on his unstable mind. Over the next year and a half, Brown would reveal to Stearns, Sanborn, and four other Boston backers a far more ambitious plan. With their help he would assault The Slave Power in the proud state where it had been spawned—Virginia.

CHAPTER 20

The Whole World Is Watching

In Illinois, Abraham Lincoln decided to challenge a weakened Stephen A. Douglas when he announced his candidacy for another term in the U.S. Senate. Like other midwestern states, Illinois had a split personality. Its southern counties had been settled by Kentuckians and Missourians, its northern tier by New Englanders. Douglas was popular in the southern counties and disliked in the northern ones. But Douglas had also had the courage to repudiate a southern attempt to seize control of Kansas, giving him statewide appeal.

Kansas proslavery settlers had gathered in the town of Lecompton and cooked up a constitution, which they proclaimed as the law of the land. President Buchanan, remembering that he was elected by mostly southern votes, recognized it. "Kansas," he announced, "was as much a slave state as Georgia or South Carolina." After investigating the rigged election that supposedly approved the constitution, Senator Douglas condemned it as an unethical grab for power and called for new elections to determine Kansas's status. The antislavery voters had won by a huge margin.

A furious Buchanan had declared war on Douglas inside the Democratic Party. Postmasters, marshals, and land agents appointed on the Senator's say-so were dismissed in wholesale lots. When Douglas began his run for reelection, Buchanan fielded a third candidate, and he ordered Democratic newspapers and politicians to oppose the Little Giant in every possible way.[1]

·   ·   ·

The president had already used his long years in Washington to bring the Supreme Court into the quarrel about slavery in what he hoped was a decisive way. The court had been inclined to let stand a case brought by Dred Scott, a Missouri slave who was suing for his freedom because he had resided in Illinois, a free state, for several years with his master, an army doctor, before returning to Missouri. The state supreme court had rejected his appeal, because he had supposedly returned to Missouri voluntarily. Buchanan persuaded one of the associate justices, an old friend, to pressure the U.S. Supreme Court to hear the case.

Chief Justice Roger Brooke Taney wrote the majority opinion, which declared that Scott must remain a slave. Congress had no power to interfere with slavery in the territories, Taney argued, because the Missouri Compromise was unconstitutional. A slave was property and was never intended to be anything else. The "enslaved African race" was not included in the Declaration of Independence's assertion that all men were created equal. Negroes were not regarded as citizens in the Constitution. The Maryland-born Taney sought to settle the dispute over slavery, once and for all.

Instead, the chief justice ignited another tremendous uproar. The decision made thousands of Northerners wonder if William Lloyd Garrison was right when he repeatedly burned the Constitution in public. *New York Tribune* editor Horace Greeley wondered why six million Southerners had more influence on the court than sixteen million Northerners. Since a majority of the court's justices were Southerners like Taney, the myth of The Slave Power got yet another boost.[2]

·   ·   ·

In this atmosphere, Lincoln's speech accepting the Republican nomination for Douglas's U.S. Senate seat was one of the boldest of his life. When he read it to the state party's leaders, they urged him not to deliver it. He went ahead, thrusting himself into the central issue confronting the nation. "We are now far into the fifth year since a policy was initiated . . . with the confident promise of putting an end to slavery agitation," he said. Instead of ceasing, the agitation has "constantly augmented." He was now convinced that "only a major crisis would end it."

Then came words that reverberated around the nation. "A house divided against itself cannot stand. I believe this government cannot endure, permanently half slave and half free. I do not expect the Union to be dissolved—I do not expect the house to fall—but I do expect that it will cease to be divided. It will become all one thing—or all the other. Either the opponents of slavery will arrest the further spread of it, and place it where the public mind shall rest in the belief that it is in the course of ultimate extinction, or its advocates will push it forward, till it shall become alike lawful in all the states, old as well as new, North as well as South."

Many people would seize on these words to claim that Lincoln foresaw—or even helped to start—the Civil War. Later generations would use it to justify the war's million dead. But Lincoln was not talking about a crisis he believed was imminent. He thought his solution, confining slavery to the southern states, might take a long time to eliminate the evil institution. In some notes he made during his contest with Senator Douglas, which he never used in his speeches, Lincoln wrote: "I have not allowed myself to forget that the abolition of the slave trade by Great Britain was agitated a hundred years before it was a final success."

Another thing worth remembering: Lincoln was keenly aware that he had a rival for the leadership of the Republican Party, Senator William Seward of New York. In 1856 Seward had made a speech, describing the tension between North and South as an "irrepressible conflict" that would only be decided by a "higher law." This brinksmanship thrilled the abolitionist wing of the new party. The House Divided speech showed Lincoln, too, could play the scare tactics game. Like Seward, who immediately began denying that he favored a civil war, Lincoln rapidly backed away from his confrontational words.[3]

Even after the Dred Scott decision and President Buchanan's interference in Kansas, Lincoln remained convinced that the Founding Fathers' intention to eliminate slavery was still at work, in a slow but inexorable progress. Lincoln insisted in the debates about slavery at the Constitutional Convention and in the first sessions of Congress, "You will not find a single man saying that slavery is a good thing." Why? "The framers believed that the Constitution would outlast slavery" if the peculiar institution were isolated in the states where it was legal.

Lincoln did not succumb to the paranoid version of The Slave Power that was gripping so many minds in New England and the Yankee Midwest. He only said that people were understandably wondering if there was a conspiracy, after Dred Scott and Buchanan's attempt to wangle a slave state label for Kansas. Lincoln felt Democratic Party explanations were in order to prevent the darkest, most worrisome conclusion. But he continued to hope that gradualism combined with compensated emancipation would take a steady toll on the evil institution. In 1859, he told another friend he was "quite sure it [slavery] would not outlast the century." Lincoln did not—and could not—know that John Brown was looming on the horizon.[4]

. . .

Lincoln and Douglas met in seven debates during which Lincoln did not hide his antipathy to slavery. "If slavery is not wrong," he said, "nothing is wrong. I cannot remember when I did not so think and feel." But he was up against a tough opponent who had a rare ability to read the temper of the public mind of 1858. Douglas claimed he was indifferent to whether slavery was voted up or down in any territory or new state. He saw himself as an advocate of American freedom, even when there were times that free men made choices that disturbed other free men. This was a policy a lot of Americans preferred to unnerving ultimatums.[5]

In his speeches, Douglas repeatedly accused Lincoln of seeking equality between the two races, and even "amalgamation"—a word that scientists like Harvard's Louis Agassiz had made frightening as well as reprehensible. Lincoln was aware that Illinois was a divided state, and his reply to this accusation should be understood in the context of his struggle to win the election. At one point he remarked that there was no need for him to campaign at all in northern Illinois, which backed him before he said a word, and no point in even visiting the southern counties, so firmly were they committed to the Democratic candidate. The election was decided in the mixed population of the central counties, where Douglas's approach had a potentially fatal impact on Lincoln's candidacy.

On the platform in these counties, Lincoln firmly and even vehemently denied he had anything like racial equality or amalgamation in mind. "I will say that I am not, nor ever have been in favor of bringing about in any way the social and political equality of the white and black races." Nor did he favor making blacks voters or jurors, or qualifying them to hold office. "There is a physical difference between the white and black races which I believe will for ever forbid the two races living together on terms of social or political equality," he said, sounding like a reincarnation of John C. Calhoun.[6]

These words were not far from Thomas Jefferson's racist doubts about black and white equality and the improbability of peaceful proximity. Lincoln too favored colonization as the only practical solution, even though by 1858 it was evident that American blacks all but unanimously rejected it. With 500,000 free blacks and 4,000,000 enslaved, the American Colonization Society was sending only a few hundred blacks to Liberia each year. The *New York Herald* called the society "an old fogy affair."

· · ·

The outcome of Lincoln's contest with Douglas showed that the Democrat's racist attacks had hit home. The Little Giant carried seventeen out of twenty-five legislative districts in central Illinois. Lincoln's attempt to make the Kansas-Nebraska Act a proslavery policy faltered when Douglas pointed to his opposition to the Lecompton Constitution. Those central districts gave Douglas the margin of victory in the Illinois legislature, which chose

U.S. senators in accordance with the Constitution. Not until the twentieth century were senators elected by popular vote.

Lincoln assumed his defeat ended his political career. He spoke of being ready to "serve in the ranks" to help Republicans win an eventual victory and keep the territories free of slavery. But many Republicans who had listened to his speeches or read excerpts from them in the newspapers had other ideas. Some of them began backing him for president in 1860.[7]

·   ·   ·

On October 21, 1857, Colonel Robert E. Lee, now commander of the Second Cavalry Regiment in Texas, received dismaying news. His father-in-law, George Washington Parke Custis, had died. Lee's two oldest sons, Custis and Rooney, were both on duty in the army. (As sons will, before and since, they had ignored their father's advice and chosen military careers.) His third son, Robert Jr., was away at boarding school and was too young (fourteen) to deal with the crisis. Mary Custis Lee was a semi-invalid, crippled by arthritis. Colonel Lee requested leave and rushed to Arlington.

There he found little to comfort him. The old house was a decaying wreck with a leaky roof and bushes and weeds growing on its once stately lawns. His father-in-law's will had freed the 196 slaves he owned on three plantations, in imitation of George Washington's example, and left Arlington to Mary Custis Lee during her lifetime. After her death, the colonel's son Custis Lee would inherit it. Grandfather Custis left the two other plantations to Rooney and Robert Jr. He also bequeathed $10,000 (the equivalent of perhaps $200,000 in twenty-first-century money) to each of the Lees' four daughters. He had borrowed against Arlington and he wished these debts—about $10,000—repaid as soon as possible.

The will directed that the slaves should be freed within the next five years, or sooner if the bequests were made and the debts were paid. If Lee wanted to sell some of the land to raise money, he was free to do so. But the colonel was reluctant to choose this solution. On his small army salary, he was unlikely to have anything to leave his children. Their grandfather's legacies were their only hope of acquiring a decent inheritance. Lee decided, pending approval of the courts, to make Arlington profitable first, pay the debts and the legacies, and then begin freeing the slaves. His wife, Mary, agreed that this was the best course.[8]

Both Lees were revealing a psychological flaw of southern slave owners—a reluctance, amounting to an inability, to understand the deep desire for freedom that was in the soul of almost every slave. They thought that Arlington's sixty-three slaves, who had not been called upon for much labor in the years preceding their master's death, would agree to work—and work hard—to turn the plantation into a profitable enterprise.

The opposite rapidly proved to be the case. The slaves were sullen, uncooperative, and often defiant. Some told Colonel Lee they considered themselves free and accused him of bad faith in detaining them. Lee had no experience in dealing with slaves, and he fell back on the routines he had learned in his decades in the U.S. Army. Orders were to be obeyed. Disobedience merited punishment.

This policy led to several run-ins with recalcitrant slaves that came close to violence. Mrs. Lee told a friend, "The attitude and bad conduct of these slaves . . . has wounded me sorely." She was probably talking about Arlington's house servants, who had seemed devoted to her. For many years, Mary Custis Lee had been a promoter of colonization. She set up a Sunday school at Arlington in which she and her daughters taught the slaves to read and write, and she urged them to consider Liberia as a possible homeland when they became free. In her diary she hoped that they could "carry the light of Christianity to that dark heathen country." She saw this as an attempt to do something "for the benefit of those so entirely dependent upon one's will and pleasure."

Colonel Lee began hiring out some of slaves who refused to labor productively at Arlington to neighboring plantations, where overseers used to obedience would make them work, or else. This created another problem—almost all Arlington's people belonged to three large families, and they protested at seeing their relationships disrupted, even when they were told it was a temporary arrangement.

Arlington's proximity to Washington, DC, added yet another problem. Abolitionists were numerous in the capital, and they often made forays into Virginia and Maryland, pretending to be peddlers or travelers. They would talk to slaves, and if they sensed discontent they would urge them to run away. The Lee family discovered two of these activists conversing with Arlington's slaves soon after Mr. Custis's death.[9]

These uninvited visitors would have had no trouble getting the Arlington's slaves to tell them that they were being denied their freedom. The slaves even concocted a touching story, in which the ailing Mr. Custis had summoned them to his bedside and told them they would be free when he died.

In 1859, three slaves made a dash for freedom—Wesley Norris, his sister Mary, and a cousin, George Parks. They were caught in Maryland on their way to the free state of Pennsylvania and were returned to Arlington. Lee hired them out to plantations in eastern Virginia, where a successful second escape would be difficult.

Several days later, two letters appeared in the *New York Tribune*. Both accused Colonel Lee of ordering his overseer to strip the slaves and whip them on their return to Arlington. When the overseer refused to whip the young woman, the letter writer claimed, "Mr. Lee himself administered the thirty nine lashes to her."

Lee's only response to these stories was a letter to his son Custis: "The N.Y. Tribune has attacked me for my treatment of your grandfather's slaves. I shall not reply. He has left me an unpleasant legacy." Generations of historians have dismissed these letters as abolitionist propaganda. But a recent Lee biographer has found evidence that convinced her they may be substantially true.

In 1866, Wesley Norris published a letter in a Baltimore newspaper, reiterating that he had been whipped. This version omitted the story of Lee personally lashing Norris's sister, Mary. Norris cited the name of the constable and other details, including how much money Colonel Lee paid the lawman. These additional facts have convinced Lee's biographer that Norris's letter was not an abolitionist creation and the previous letters were substantially true.[10]

Contradicting this conclusion is a vehement letter that Lee wrote to a friend in 1866, calling the charge slander. "There is not a word of truth in it. No servant, soldier or citizen that was ever employed by me can with truth charge me of bad treatment."[11]

.   .   .

During his twenty-six months at Arlington, Colonel Lee was a harassed and unhappy man. He was both master and overseer, constantly involved in disputes with the slaves, with planting and harvesting corn and other crops, and with crucial repairs to the Arlington mansion and the slave quarters. Mrs. Lee's arthritis continued to worsen, and it was soon evident that she would be crippled for life.

In the midst of these travails the colonel received a summons to the White House, where President Buchanan ordered him to leave immediately for Harpers Ferry to put down some sort of insurrection in or near the federal arsenal there.

In his confrontation with John Brown, Colonel Lee kept his emotions under tight control, as every combat leader is trained to do. As we have seen, Lee was present when Brown was interviewed by Virginia's Governor Henry Wise and other politicians. The colonel heard the intruder's distortions of his mission and his warning that slavery was a problem that the South had better solve soon. The next day Lee supervised the transfer of Brown and his surviving men to Charlestown, Virginia, the county seat, where they would stand trial.

Lee looked through the papers that Lieutenant J. E. B. Stuart had seized at Brown's headquarters on the Kennedy farm. With typical inattention to details, Brown had left behind a carpetbag containing four hundred letters, compromising his Boston backers, Gerrit Smith, and many other people. Lee decided that any conclusions about this evidence were beyond his authority and forwarded the documents to Washington, DC, without comment.

At nine o'clock on the night Lee hoped to leave Harpers Ferry, he received a message that raiders had descended from the nearby mountains and had massacred a family in Pleasant Valley, Maryland, a village about five miles away. The colonel and Lieutenant Stuart rushed there with twenty-five marines but found the town peaceful. Colonel Lee returned to the Ferry, finished his official report on Brown's capture, and left on the 1:15 a.m. train.

The report virtually dismissed John Brown and his grandiose scheme. "The result," Lee wrote, "proves the plan was the attempt of a fanatic or a madman." Lee was probably playing down Brown's attack, hoping to calm jittery civilians. He was much too intelligent not to recognize the significance of this murderous foray, especially since the seized letters revealed that it had been financed by wealthy northern backers.[12]

The colonel would soon learn that Pleasant Valley's panic was spreading through Maryland, Virginia, and the rest of the South. Everywhere seldom-summoned militias were hastily ordered to start drilling. A college in Richmond organized a group of "minutemen," invoking the heroes of 1776. One of the nation's leading Republican newspapers, the *New York Times,* was soon reporting that Virginians were "almost insane with terror as their telegraph lines hummed with exaggerated and frantic alarms."[13]

Anyone who said a word against slavery in the South in the weeks after John Brown's foray was threatened with expletive-thick violence. Northerners, especially New Englanders, were regarded with special hostility and suspicion. One man in Pulaski County, Virginia, was hanged from a tree until he was close to death for no apparent reason beyond his Yankee accent. The *Times* called for calm in both South and North and condemned the abolitionists as people "who do not love the slave as much as they hate the white."[14]

The *Richmond Enquirer* cited a story in the *New York Herald,* a paper it praised for "its open, fearless and powerful denunciations of the fanatics . . . of the North." The *Herald* warned "another insurrection is in preparation, more bloody and extensive than the first." In support of this alarm bell, the *Enquirer* quoted the abolitionist *Washington Era,* the first publisher of *Uncle*

Tom's Cabin. The paper claimed that Brown's aborted upheaval would soon be "extended to other southern states, where the black population are more numerous in proportion to the whites"—a good summary of Brown's overall plan. It would be hard to suggest more explosive words. They aroused the South's worst fear—a race war.[15]

Robert E. Lee's friend and Arlington neighbor, Constance Gary Harrison, had a typical southern woman's reaction to John Brown. Harpers Ferry was far away from Fairfax County. She belonged to a family that was among the first in Virginia to emancipate their slaves. "There seemed to be no especial reason to share the apprehension of an uprising by the blacks" she wrote, years later. "In the daytime it seemed impossible to associate suspicion with those familiar black or tawny faces that surrounded us . . . What subtle influence would transform them into tigers thirsting for our blood? The idea was preposterous. But when evening came again . . . rusty bolts were drawn and rusty firearms loaded . . . Peace . . . had flown from the borders of Virginia."[16]

·   ·   ·

In the North, abolitionists seized on the stories about the South's panic and claimed that the much-touted courage of the slave-owning cavaliers was a myth. One of the first to speak out was the British-born journalist, James Redpath, an early booster of John Brown. In the *Boston Atlas*, he declared that Brown had first exposed the South's spinelessness in Kansas. Harpers Ferry demonstrated that the typical slave owner was "only a cowardly braggart, after all." Proof was the "daily accounts" of the South's "shrinking and quaking."

A posse of policemen, Redpath sneered, should have been able to capture or kill Brown and his men in ten minutes. Instead, "fifteen states had trembled for fifteen days" and "they are not done quaking yet. I am very much afraid *diapers* will be needed before the trial of Old Brown shall be finished." All in all, Redpath concluded, "As a demonstration of the South's cowardice John Brown's exploit is a brilliant success."[17]

Again, it would be difficult to write anything that was more likely to arouse southern men to fury. Redpath was already hard at work on a biography of

Brown, full of the same insults to Southerners, which would be a best seller in 1860.

William Lloyd Garrison called Brown's raid "misguided, wild and apparently insane." But it was "well intended." While the father of abolitionism remained opposed to "war and bloodshed even in the best of causes," he nonetheless hoped that no one "who glories in the Revolutionary struggle of 1776 denies the right of the slaves to imitate the example of our fathers." As usual, Garrison blended his pacifism with hopes of violence by ignoring the bloodshed and death that permeated the Revolutionary War. His hatred of white Southerners and his indifference to the horrors of a race war remained impenetrable.[18]

.   .   .

Republican politicians, including Abraham Lincoln, were especially vehement in their denunciations of John Brown, showing their sensitivity to the political danger of abolitionists in their crowded tent. Presidential candidate Lincoln went out of his way to say Brown was "no Republican." Democrats and their newspapers did their utmost to use Brown to prove that the Republicans should not be trusted with national power.

The *New York Herald* headlined the raid "THE ABOLITION OUTBREAK IN VIRGINIA" and said it was "the first act in the great drama of national disruption plotted by that demagogue, William H. Seward." To substantiate this smear, editor James Gordon Bennett ran a copy of Seward's 1856 Irrepressible Conflict speech, as if he had given it yesterday. In this rancid atmosphere, it is easy to see why President Buchanan's claim that Brown exemplified a disease in the public mind had little or no impact.[19]

.   .   .

When Brown's trial for murder and treason began, this negative public attitude underwent a slow but ultimately momentous change. The terrorist of Harpers Ferry portrayed himself as a man inspired by God. He resisted his lawyers' attempts to have the court declare him insane. Though he had recovered from his superficial wounds, Brown claimed that he was too weak to stand or sit. He lay on the floor on an improvised bed, an image of help-less suffering. For Brown, the trial was a stage on which he performed for the entire nation. He was achieving his wish to die and simultaneously ful-filling his lifelong hunger for fame, after so many failures.

It took the jury only forty-five minutes to find Brown guilty of treason against the state of Virginia, conspiring and advising with slaves to rebel, and murder in the first degree. Still prone on his pallet, Brown showed no emotion as he heard these words. His lawyers asked for an arrest of judg-ment, a formality that had no hope of success. The judge said he would rule on the motion the following day. He had to preside at the trial of one of Brown's confederates that afternoon.

The next day, Brown was brought to the courtroom when darkness was falling. This time he walked the short distance from the jail, displaying what a *New York Tribune* reporter called "considerable pain." He sat down beside his lawyers, and the judge dismissed the arrest of judgment plea. He asked Brown if he had anything to say before he pronounced the sentence. After a moment's silence Brown rose to his feet. Overhead, glowing gas lamps gave his face what the same reporter called "an almost deathly pallor."

I have, may it please the court, a few words to say.

In the first place, I deny everything but what I have all along admit-ted, of a design on my part to free slaves. I intended certainly to have made a clean thing of that matter, as I did last winter when I went into Missouri, and there took slaves without the snapping of a gun on either side, moving them through the country and finally leaving them in Canada. I designed to have done the same thing on a larger scale. This was all I intended. I never did intend murder, or treason, or destruction of property, or to excite slaves to rebellion or to make insurrection.

I have another objection, and that is that it is unjust that I should suffer such a penalty. Had I interfered in the manner in which I admit, and which I admit has been fairly proved—for I admire the truth-fulness and candor of the greater portion of the witnesses who have testified in this case—had I so interfered in behalf of the rich, the powerful, the intelligent, the so called great, or on behalf of any of their friends, either father, mother, brother, sister, wife or children, or any of that class, and suffered and sacrificed what I have for this inter-ference, it would have been all right; every man in this court would have deemed it an act worthy of reward rather than punishment.

The Court acknowledges, too, as I suppose, the validity of the law of God. I see a book kissed, which I suppose to be the Bible, or at least the New Testament, which teaches me that whatsoever I would that men should do to me, I should do even so to them. It teaches me, further, to remember them that are in bonds as bound with them. I endeavored to act up to that instruction. I am yet too young to un-derstand that God is any respecter of persons. I believe that to have interfered as I have done, as I have always freely admitted I have done, on behalf of His despised poor, I did no wrong, but right. Now, if it is deemed necessary that I should forfeit my life for the furtherance of the ends of justice, and mingle my blood further with the blood of millions in this slave country whose rights are disregarded as wicked, cruel and unjust enactments, I say let it be done.[20]

These words would have a huge impact on thousands of people in the North. They testify to John Brown's genuine sympathy for the slave. But they were intertwined with egregious evasions and lies. As Brown's maps and correspondence proved, he had planned a huge slave insurrection. That was why he had seized the federal arsenal with its thousands of guns and had brought with him hundreds of pikes. Even the minor claim of freeing slaves in Missouri without so much as snapping a gun was untrue. Brown or one of his sons had killed a slave owner in a shootout.

The second paragraph was an appeal to hatred of the rich and successful, which demagogues have been using since ancient Greece and Rome. The closing paragraph was an interpretation of the Bible that was beyond the recognition of any serious reader of that book. Shortly after Brown's capture, he was visited by a Catholic priest, who asked him how he could claim that the Bible countenanced his claim of divine sanction for a slave insurrection.

The priest quoted verses from St. Paul, in which the apostle urged slaves to be obedient to their masters. Brown exploded into fury and replied that if the Bible said such a thing, the book was worthless trash.

The judge condemned Brown to hang. He met his fate with unflinching courage, convinced that his sacrifice was part of God's providential plan. During the two weeks while Charlestown prepared for his execution, he received hundreds of letters. He answered them with the same conviction of his innocence before his God.

One letter Brown did not answer came from Mahala Doyle, the widow and mother of three of the men he had murdered in Kansas. She told him she felt "gratified to hear that you were stopped in your fiendish career at Harpers Ferry, with the loss of your two sons." She hoped he would appreciate her grief when Brown "arrested my husband and two boys, and took them out in the yard and shot them dead in my hearing." The crime was especially unforgiveable because they had never owned a slave "or expected to own one." She only wished that her surviving son could be at Charlestown to tie the rope around Brown's neck.[21]

． ● ●

While Brown was on trial, wealthy Virginia slave owner Edmund Ruffin was hard at work on a very different task. He had rushed to Harpers Ferry and joined his friend, Governor Henry Wise, in interviewing Brown on the day he was captured. Ruffin had persuaded Wise to give him a sizeable number of Brown's pikes. He saw these weapons as convincing proof that Virginia should secede as soon as possible.

With a fanatic's energy, Ruffin distributed the pikes to key people throughout the South. Every state governor received one. With each pike was a letter from Ruffin asking if the recipient appreciated what Brown's wealthy abolitionist backers had given him to arm the slaves. Could the South stay in the same country with people who could complacently look forward to seeing these weapons thrust into the bodies of helpless women and children?

Ruffin was fanatical on the subject of secession. Otherwise he was a very intelligent man. He had studied how Southerners should and could farm their bountiful acres more scientifically, adding chemicals to prevent the soil from becoming depleted. If more farmers took his advice, the South's annual income, already far superior to the North's, would continue to grow. Among plantation owners he was already famous. Governors would pay attention to a letter from him. When it was reinforced with one of Brown's pikes, Ruffin's message would not be forgotten anytime soon.[22]

.   .   .

John Brown's courtroom performance had a huge impact on newspaper readers in the North. Above all it captured the passionate sympathy and admiration of the group that would win John Brown widespread vindication in New England and the Midwest—the thinkers and writers of Concord. Henry David Thoreau led the way. He was transfixed by Brown's attack on Harpers Ferry. He all but babbled in his journal: Brown was Jesus. He was a Puritan who had died in Cromwell's army. Above all he was a Transcendentalist—with Emersonian faith in the power of the individual soul to ignore churches and sacred texts and achieve its own brand of salvation.

Thoreau announced that he would give a lecture on his hero. The local Republican Party and Concord's antislavery committee begged him not to speak. He ignored them and denounced the "hypocritical and diabolical" American government. He compared Brown to a meteor that had plunged into the complacent America of 1859. The Pottawatomie butcher was "the bravest and humanest man in the country."

Thoreau aroused the more cautious and realistic Emerson. The Sage abandoned all inclinations to find a peaceful solution to slavery. He described John Brown as "that new saint, than whom none purer or more brave was ever led by love of men into conflict and death. . . . the new saint who would make the gallows as glorious as the cross."[23]

Those last words swiftly acquired the status of Emerson's paean to Concord Bridge, in which he had said the militiamen of 1775 "fired the shot heard round the world." James Redpath dedicated his bestselling biography of Brown to Emerson, Thoreau, and Wendell Phillips, whom he called "Defenders of the Faithful who when the mob shouted Madman said Saint."[24]

· · ·

Less glorious and far less transcendental was the behavior of John Brown's backers, the six men who had sent him money and encouragement. Their letters, seized in Brown's carpetbag, began appearing in several leading newspapers. The *New York Herald* called for the arrest and prosecution of Gerrit Smith as an accessory to Brown's crime. The paper claimed that the carpetbag contained an uncashed check for $100 from Smith. It seemed likely that similar punishment would be demanded for the other five.

While the imprisoned Brown calmly awaited death, panic and cowardice characterized his backers. Gerrit Smith had never been stable—two of his brothers were incarcerated in a New York state mental hospital. He began reeling toward a similar destination.

Smith babbled to friends and family that he had been responsible for the bloodshed at Harpers Ferry. He talked of going to Charlestown and joining Brown in his prison cell. One of his close friends, Edwin Morton, who lived with him and knew in intimate detail Smith's role in Brown's plot, decamped for England. Smith grew more and more incoherent, and his family decided he might be safer in the asylum for the insane at Utica.

After John Brown's execution eliminated him as a witness in a treason trial, Smith emerged from the asylum and spent the rest of his life denying that he had ever talked to Brown about a slave insurrection. The millionaire backed up his lies with threats of lawsuits for defamation, which caused accusers to retreat. This after-the-fact behavior arouses suspicion that Smith's breakdown was designed to keep federal marshals at bay.[25]

In Boston, Franklin Sanborn rushed to consult John Albion Andrew, one of the best attorneys in the city (and a passionate abolitionist). Andrew advised him to head for Canada. Samuel Gridley Howe, the storied liberator of Greece, fled in the same direction, as did wealthy George Stearns. They stayed there until John Brown was executed.

In mid-November, Howe published an hysterical denial in a Boston paper, claiming that the event "at Harpers Ferry was unforeseen and unexpected by me." He found it hard to reconcile the assault with John Brown's "characteristic prudence, and his reluctance to shed blood or excite servile insurrection." The Reverend Thomas Wentworth Higginson, another member of the Secret Six, as Brown's backers were now being called, sent him a blazing reproach: "Is there no such thing as honor among confederates?"[26]

Higginson dared federal authorities to arrest him. He was ready to defend himself and go to prison if necessary. Meanwhile he joined a plot to liberate Brown from his Charlestown prison cell. Nothing came of it but a lot of frantic letter writing and pleas for money from the plotters.

The only other member of the group who stood his ground was the Reverend Theodore Parker. He wrote a public letter declaring that he had always approved of slave insurrections. But he was in Rome, Italy, dying of tuberculosis, and had little to fear from federal warrants.

Frederick Douglass was not one of John Brown's backers, but Brown had invited him to join the raid and had spelled out all the details only a few weeks before the doomed venture. Douglass's name was in several letters in Brown's abandoned carpetbag. As a black man, he had good reason to fear that with race prejudice virulent in the North as well as the South, the Buchanan administration might fasten on him as a collaborator or even instigator. The former slave decided he might be safer in England and headed for the nearest ship.[27]

· · ·

On December 2, 1859, the day of John Brown's execution, tension ran high in Charlestown. Governor Henry A. Wise took no chances. He had been bombarded with hundreds of letters threatening or vowing that Brown would be rescued. Wise requested the return of Colonel Lee and a contingent of federal troops to guard the approaches to the city. Around the execution site he arrayed hundreds of Virginia militiamen.

Among the men in uniform was a contingent from the Virginia Military Academy under the command of Thomas Jackson, one of the West Pointers who had distinguished himself in Mexico. In the militia's ranks wearing a borrowed uniform was a well-known actor, John Wilkes Booth, who had a passion for politics and sided with the South's view of the quarrel. Colonel Lee, sticking to his public statement that Brown was an irrelevant fanatic, told friends he was bored with "the Harpers Ferry War" and would welcome a return to Texas, where he might accomplish something fighting Comanches.[28]

Elsewhere, church bells rang in dozens of New England cities and in the Yankee portion of the Midwest. It was the culmination of a campaign to turn Brown into a hero-saint. In the weeks before the hanging, there were huge meetings in Boston and other cities, at which orators held forth on Brown's courage and self-sacrifice. At one conclave, Ralph Waldo Emerson again compared him to Jesus Christ. At Natick, Massachusetts, Henry C. Wright, a Garrisonian abolitionist who had abandoned pacifism, declared that Christ, who had failed to end slavery in America in spite of three decades of prayers and appeals in His name, was a "dead failure" compared to John Brown, who would be "a power far more efficient." The similarity of these frantic theological somersaults to the public frenzy that gripped Massachusetts during the witch trials of 1692 is striking.[29]

In many meeting places, a large reproduction of John Brown's speech to the judge was displayed like a banner. Some people followed William Lloyd Garrison's example, disapproving of John Brown's tactics but praising the prospect of "slave insurrections everywhere." In Cleveland, Ohio, speakers admitted that Brown had mistaken "the method, the time and the place" for his attack. But it was now clear that slavery could only be subdued by giving it "war to the knife, with the knife to the hilt."

A passion for a violent solution to slavery was sweeping the abolitionist citizens of the nation. No one stoked the conflagration better than John Brown. As he left his prison cell for the trip to the gallows, he handed his jailer a note. *I John Brown am now quite certain that the crimes of this guilty land: will never be purged away, but with Blood.* A reporter who was expert in the art of faking it wrote in the *New York Tribune* that Brown paused on the way to the gallows to kiss a baby in the arms of a grieving black woman. It was one more lie in the campaign to elevate him to spurious sainthood. A painting would later memorialize this nonevent.[30]

. . .

When Congress reconvened in late December 1859, a Senate committee headed by Senator James M. Mason of Virginia opened a probe of the

Harpers Ferry raid. Mason was a grandson of George Mason, who had been a passionate foe of the slave trade at the Constitutional Convention. Three decades of abolitionist abuse had turned the descendant into a disciple of John C. Calhoun. The committee summoned numerous witnesses, including Colonel Lee, who was asked only a few perfunctory questions about the final assault on Brown and his surviving defenders.

The committee sent a federal marshal to Massachusetts with a warrant for Franklin Sanborn, but he eluded him. The next day Sanborn got a writ from the state Supreme Court declaring that the committee had no authority in the Bay State. The politicians also summoned Samuel Gridley Howe and George Stearns, who had returned from Canada. After conferring with attorney John Albion Andrew, who was running for governor of Massachusetts, they decided to testify. Andrew had concluded the politicians had a strange lack of desire to find out anything significant.

Both Howe and Gridley swore to tell the truth, and then lied steadily about their relationship with John Brown. Stearns solemnly assured the senators, "I never supposed he contemplated anything like what occurred at Harpers Ferry." Having it both ways, Stearns added, "I should have disapproved of it [Brown's raid] if I had known of it. But I have since changed my opinion."[31]

Why did Chairman Mason let these men get away with perjury? Probably for the same reason that he did not summon the defiant Thomas Wentworth Higginson. The atmosphere in Congress and in Washington, DC, was already so tense that the committee feared an outbreak of violence. Almost every member of both houses of Congress was carrying a gun. In the crowded galleries, there were undoubtedly more weapons. John Brown's fanaticism seemed to be in charge, North and South.

CHAPTER 21

An Ex-President Tries
to Save the Union

Six months after John Brown's execution, Abraham Lincoln was nominated for president by the Republican Party. Brown was indirectly responsible for disposing of his chief opponent, Senator William Seward. The senator had been in Europe when Brown seized Harpers Ferry. On Seward's return to America, he was dismayed to find voters blaming him for the reckless foray.

The *New York Herald*'s attack on Seward on the day the Harpers Ferry story broke convinced Democrats they could drive Seward out of politics. He was up for reelection in the Senate as well as running for president. The Democrats followed up the *Herald*'s blast with a pamphlet, *The Rise and Progress of the Bloody Outbreak at Harpers Ferry*, which accused Seward and Republicans in general of creating—and in some cases justifying—Brown.

Southern newspapers, almost all Democratic, quickly took up the cry, pointing as evidence to the way so many Republican editors and politicians were frantically backing away from Brown. The *Herald* continued its assault, claiming that a Brown accomplice had visited Seward in 1858 and told him exactly what Brown planned to do at Harpers Ferry. Seward vehemently denied any connection to Brown and called Harpers Ferry an act of rebellion and treason. He even said Brown's execution was "necessary and just." Trapped by his need to retain his abolitionist supporters, Seward also called Brown's fate "pitiable." These statements did not do him much good with northern voters who dreaded a civil war. Lincoln, on the other hand, had made several statements deploring abolitionists and their tactics. With no taint of radicalism about him, he easily won the nomination in Chicago.[1]

· · ·

The drama in the nominating stage of the 1860 election was all on the Democratic side. Their success in linking Republicans with John Brown made it a near certainty that the new party would win no votes in the South and would lose quite a few in the North. This meant that the Democrats were the nation's only hope of electing a president who could hold the two seething sections of the nation together.

Their convention met in Charleston, South Carolina, on April 23, 1860. In the aura of the John Brown–stirred hysteria gripping the nation, sensible men should have urged another site. The city and the state were still the headquarters for secessionist thinking, even though their patron saint, John Calhoun, had been dead for almost ten years. Everyone knew the leading candidate, Stephen Douglas, was still locked in a ferocious feud with President James Buchanan over Kansas. Maneuvering in the background was Senator Jefferson Davis of Mississippi, who had a convoluted scheme to make a proslavery man president.

In the foreground stood the chairman of the convention, balding Caleb Cushing of Massachusetts, as oily—and brilliant—a character as ever slithered through American politics. His chief claim to fame (or better, power) was engineering the presidential nomination of fellow New Englander Franklin Pierce for president in 1852. Ostensibly, Cushing went to Charleston in search of a compromise. But he was already on record as believing that the separation of North and South was inevitable.

Cushing did nothing to block or dissuade Jefferson Davis, who demanded a "black code" for the federal government that would legalize slavery in all the territories. The chairman may have been covertly involved in Davis's plan to break up the convention and create a third party, which would produce a winner without an electoral vote majority. That event would throw the final decision into Congress in a repetition of 1824, which had enabled John Quincy Adams to become president. Davis was hoping to wangle Senator Joseph Lane of Oregon, a pro-Southerner like Buchanan, into the White House.

Other Southerners trumped Davis with a demand that the party's plank include a declaration that slavery was "right." When Stephen Douglas and his mostly northern backers demurred, fifty-one delegates from the eight cotton states walked out. In 1948, hard-core segregationists would take a similar walk; the party's leaders simply declared them ex-Democrats and resumed the convention without them, nominating President Harry S Truman for another term. Cushing refused to rule that the walkouts had left the party. To win the nomination, Douglas would still have to win two thirds of the total number of delegates, rather than two-thirds of the delegates who remained.

After dozens of ballots, Douglas was still far short of the necessary figure. The infuriated northern Democrats—a clear majority—abandoned Charleston for Baltimore, where they reconvened. The cotton-state delegates followed them, triggering a wild battle about who should and who would not be seated. This led to another walkout—this time by 110 southern delegates. Douglas's backers then named him the party's "official" nominee.[2]

The Democracy, as Andrew Jackson had called it, was no longer a party. It was a mélange of anger and ideology cartwheeling toward dissolution. The southern delegates convened a rump convention over which Cushing, showing his convictions (or lack of them), presided. They nominated Kentuckian John C. Breckinridge for president and Senator Lane for vice president. Breckinridge was already vice president under Buchanan. Their platform was proslavery in every imaginable respect. It now seems likely that secessionists, with the help of the pliable Cushing, were in control of this breakaway group from the start.[3]

Despairing moderates from the North and South nominated a third ticket, whose platform consisted of little more than a call to obey the Constitution. They named former Whig Senator John Bell of Tennessee and Edward Everett of Massachusetts as their candidates. Everett was a famous orator and former governor and senator, who often attacked abolitionists as a menace to the Union.

The election was vigorously conducted, with parades and bonfires and speeches. The Bell-Everett parades featured a huge bell, which was clanged to warn people that the Union was in mortal danger. Douglas was the only candidate who campaigned in the South as well as the North, exhausting himself with day after day of speeches in his roaring over-the-top style.[4]

On November 6, Abraham Lincoln won the election with a clear majority in the electoral college. He carried every northern state except New Jersey, but he got only a handful of votes in the South, probably from nostalgic ex-Whigs. His three opponents polled almost a million more votes, a clear signal that the Republicans were by no means a majority party. The Democrats still controlled both houses of Congress. Lincoln would have to work with them to implement any policy. But in the South, where John Brown had reignited Thomas Jefferson's nightmare of a race war, the Republican victory only deepened the panic.[5]

· · ·

In Port Gibson, Mississippi, two days after Lincoln's election, an orator declared that a "black Republican" president meant that the South was on its way to "the bloody scenes on St. Domingo, the destruction of the white race, and the relapsing into barbarism of the black race." He was joined by a chorus of speakers and writers in other states. In New Orleans, the pastor of the First Presbyterian Church predicted a repetition of the horrors that "converted St. Domingo into a howling waste." The sermon was published and sold 100,000 copies. An editorial in the Montgomery, Alabama, *Advertiser* declared that government by abolitionists could have only one horrific outcome: "Look at St. Domingo."[6]

In South Carolina, huge rallies led by marching bands and thousands of men waving palmetto leaves called for secession from a government run by the "bigoted blackguards of the New England states." Andrew Pickens Calhoun, son of the famous senator, predicted that Lincoln's antislavery rhetoric would invite a repetition of Santo Domingo. On December 20, 1860, little more than six weeks after Lincoln's election, a Charleston convention voted to secede, 169 to 0. In another forty days, state after state from the Deep South joined the procession—Mississippi, Florida, Alabama, Georgia, Louisiana, and Texas.[7]

In some states, such as Alabama and Georgia, the decision was far from unanimous. But there was little doubt that a majority of the voters backed secession. The only state to put the decision to a ballot was Texas, where secession won by 3 to 1. Senator Judah Benjamin of Louisiana, one of the first Jewish-Americans to win high office, described the Deep South's mood as a "wild torrent of passion . . . a revolution of the most intense character."[8]

Joy was the prevailing emotion in celebrations after the conventions voted. No one seemed to worry about a war. There was an almost universal opinion that the Yankees were cowards who would flee at the first glimpse of a southern bayonet. If any bloodshed occurred, it would not be enough to fill "a lady's thimble," according to one South Carolinian. On February 8, delegates from the seceded states met in Montgomery, Alabama, and declared that they were the Confederate States of America. The following day they elected Jefferson Davis as their president. Next came a constitution, which provided no federal supreme court and declared that their congress could never pass a law "denying or impairing the right of property in Negro slaves."[9]

. . .

In Texas, Colonel Robert E. Lee was stunned and dismayed by the swiftness of the Union's collapse. He was even more dismayed when friends began resigning from the U.S. Army to join the army of the new confederacy. Kentuckian Albert Sidney Johnson, another West Pointer who had won distinction in the Mexican War, had been in command in distant San Francisco. He had tried to stay neutral, but someone in the Buchanan administration abruptly removed him. It may have been a Democrat who wanted him to join the new confederacy. Virginian Joseph Johnston, a West Point classmate and close friend of Lee, struggled to stay neutral as chaos swirled around him in Washington, DC, where he was serving as the army's quartermaster general.[10]

Lee still hoped that the politicians could find a formula to lure the seceded states back into the Union. He deplored the extremists on both sides and trusted there was "wisdom and patriotism enough" somewhere to rescue the situation. "I cannot anticipate so great a calamity to the nation as the dissolution of the Union," he told a niece in one of his many letters. At the same time he admitted he sympathized with his fellow Southerners. He resented "the aggressions of the North, their denial of equal rights of our citizens to the common territories of the commonwealth."

Lee approved President Buchanan's December message to Congress, in which he blamed the looming disaster on a disease in the public mind and urged the legislators to pass an "explanatory amendment" to the Constitution, affirming the right of property in slaves and an obligation to protect this right in the territories. "The propositions of the president are eminently right and just," Lee told his oldest son, Custis. The lame-duck president's message was as totally ignored as the departing tirade of his Democratic predecessor, Franklin Pierce.[11]

Colonel Lee's temper visibly rose when some cotton-state politicians uttered threats against Virginia and other border states because they had not joined the march to secession. Even more disturbing was the discovery that several politicians from these seceded states wanted to know why Lee had not resigned his commission and joined the Confederate army. He exploded into uncharacteristic rage that left his fellow soldiers stunned and amazed. They were even more amazed by Lee's reaction when they heard the news that Texas had seceded. "I shall never forget [Lee's] look of astonishment . . . his lips trembled and his eyes [were] full of tears," one friend later recalled.[12]

During these weeks, the colonel read Edward Everett's *The Life of George Washington*, a somewhat sketchy but admiring portrait. "How his spirit would be grieved to see the wreck of his mighty labors," Lee wrote in another letter. He refused to believe that his contemporaries would "destroy the work of [Washington's] noble deeds." Personally, he was ready to sacrifice "everything but honor" to save the Union. He had no doubt whatsoever that secession was treason. The Constitution had declared the union "perpetual" in its preamble.

Over the crackling telegraph came news that stirred hope. Virginia had gone to the polls and elected a convention to consider secession. By a two to one margin, they had chosen delegates opposed to rupturing the Union. On February 4, 1861, came a new surprise. Colonel Lee was relieved of command of the Second Cavalry and ordered to report to Washington, DC, by March 1. As Lee departed, one of his younger officers asked, "Colonel, do you intend to go South or remain North?"

"I shall never bear arms against the Union," Lee replied. "But it may be necessary for me to carry a musket in defense of my native state." He was apparently thinking of the threats Virginia had received from the cotton-states firebrands.[13]

Already it was obvious that many people were concerned about Colonel Lee's role in the looming conflict. He probably suspected his summons to Washington had not a little to do with this large fact. At the beginning of the year, General Winfield Scott had sent a pamphlet to Texas advising his officers on how to deal with the crisis. He had ordered it shown to Lee's commander, General David Twigs, and then to Colonel Lee.

The officer who delivered the document remarked good humoredly, "Ah! I know General Scott fully believes that God Almighty had to spit on his hands to make Bob Lee." In Virginia, an Arlington neighbor put the issue more explicitly: "For some the question of 'What will Colonel Lee do?' was second only in interest to 'What will Virginia do?'"[14]

.   .   .

In Massachusetts, John Albion Andrew, the man who had helped the Secret Six escape prosecution for backing John Brown, had just been elected governor. He had only one thing on his mind: war. He wrote fiery letters to other New England governors, telling them that southern society would have to be totally reorganized to remove their slave-owning mindset. "We must conquer the South," he declared. "To do this we must bring the Northern [public] mind to a comprehension of this necessity."

Andrew decided to visit Washington to assess the situation there. He met with Charles Francis Adams, son of Old Man Eloquent. Adams was recoiling from the prospect of a civil war, but he feared the South was going to start one. He told Andrew that there was a good chance Southerners would seize the capital and prevent Lincoln's inauguration. Adams introduced Andrews to Virginia Senator James M. Mason, who had headed the committee that investigated John Brown. Perhaps recalling Andrew's role in advising John Brown's backers, Mason told the governor that the South would never rejoin a Union in which Massachusetts, led by people like him, was a member.

Andrew retreated to the company of Republicans such as Senator Charles Sumner. He had recovered from his beating and was back in Congress, more South-hating than ever. On Christmas Eve, Andrew joined a Republican congressional conference, which concluded that the nation's future depended on preserving the integrity of the Union—and destroying The Slave Power—"though it cost a million lives." No one realized these words were a prophecy.[15]

.   .   .

Another Virginian watched the rush to secession with mind and heart at least as troubled as Colonel Lee's. In Sherwood Forest, his plantation in Charles City County on the lower James River, seventy-one-year-old ex-president John Tyler told a friend, "We have fallen on evil times. . . . Madness rules the hour and statesmanship . . . gives place to a miserable demagogism." Unlike Lee, Tyler had been living in Virginia since he left the White House in 1845. In these fifteen years, he had seen the state's slave population continue to grow. In his home country, blacks now outnumbered whites more than two to one.

This mounting imbalance was the root of the national crisis, as Tyler saw it. Virginia, he told his friend in the same letter, "will never consent to have her blacks cribbed and confined within proscribed and specified limits— and thus be involved in all the consequences of a war of the races in some 20 or 30 years. She must have expansion . . . But no more slave states has apparently become the shibboleth of Northern political faith."

Few people, North or South, have so succinctly stated the hidden heart of the crisis between the two sections. No more slave states meant James Madison's idea of diffusion as a step to the eventual elimination of slavery had become impossible as a way to calm the South's fears.[16]

What to do? As an ex-president, Tyler's devotion to the Union remained intense. He decided to risk his health—and his political reputation—by proposing a solution to the crisis. On December 14, 1860, he issued a call for a peace convention composed of delegates from twelve border states, six slave and six free. These states, he explained to his old friend Caleb Cushing, were the ones most interested in keeping the peace. "If they cannot come to an understanding, then the political union is gone."[17]

Over the next few weeks, Tyler's idea acquired weight as other proposals for compromise were voted down in Congress. Arkansas and Missouri had also elected for their conventions a majority of delegates opposed to secession. North Carolina and Tennessee voters rejected calling a convention, so strong was their Union sentiment.

In the North a surprising Tyler ally emerged—Senator William Seward. He had abandoned the irrepressible conflict and higher-law side of his persona and become an apostle of a peaceful solution. "Every thought we think," he told president-elect Lincoln, "should be conciliatory." A dubious Lincoln went along, but his reply, if John Tyler had read it, would have instantly terminated the peace convention. Lincoln told Seward that conciliation must not include a compromise "which assists or permits" the extension of slavery. Free soil for free (white) men was still the linchpin of the Republican Party.

Meanwhile, the politicians in Richmond turned John Tyler's brainchild into a grotesque abortion. The legislature issued a call for a peace convention of delegates from *all* the states still in the Union. Tyler instantly saw that this idea would produce nothing but bedlam. With seven southern states in secession, the North would have a majority on every question. Tyler rushed a plea for his original idea to the *Richmond Enquirer*, which he bolstered with a searing description of what a race war would do to the nation.

Virginia's legislature stuck to its call for all the states to send delegates. Tyler agreed to become one of Virginia's five spokesmen and was soon in Washington, DC, with his wife, Julia. She was delighted to be returning to the scene of her first-lady triumphs. But Tyler grew more and more discouraged as Texas and Louisiana joined the cotton states in secession, and Arkansas, Tennessee, and Virginia warned President Buchanan that they would secede if the Federal government attempted to "coerce" the departed states. The nadir was a meeting with Buchanan in the White House at which the exhausted president whined that the South had rewarded all his efforts on their behalf with base ingratitude. Their seizure of federal forts along their seacoast had made him look inept and impotent.[18]

Things only got worse when the peace convention met in a hall next to Willard's Hotel on February 4, 1861. There was no shortage of political skill and experience in the conclave. Among the 132 delegates were 6 former presidential cabinet members, 19 former governors, 14 ex-senators, and 50 ex-congressman. But almost all these men were near Tyler's age, and many were in precarious health. The newspapers dubbed them "the Old Gentleman's Convention." Tyler was elected president. One reporter said he was an apt choice, calling him "a tottering ashen ruin."[19]

There was some truth to those harsh words. Tyler's health was not good; he suffered from a debilitating stomach disorder that caused severe indigestion and an almost continuous pain in his abdomen. Nonetheless, he opened the proceedings with a rousing speech, calling on everyone to join him in achieving "a triumph over party." The convention immediately began failing to obey this noble injunction. The sessions were marred by bickering, irrelevant speech making and not a little sectional hostility.

Several times Tyler lost all control of the proceedings and sat helplessly while delegates shouted insults at each other. The problem was the one he had foreseen: too many delegates from too many states. Spokesmen from New York and Massachusetts had no interest in a compromise. They simply reiterated the Republican Party's resistance to any extension of slavery, anywhere.

A private letter from Julia Tyler on February 13 gives a glimpse of how the hopes of both Tylers were sinking. She deplored the way New York and

Massachusetts were trying to "defeat this patriotic effort at pacification." The only consolation was the belief that even if the convention failed, Virginia would "have sustained her reputation" as a national leader. The Old Dominion would be able to "retire with dignity" and "join without loss of time her more southern sisters."[20]

. . .

When President-elect Abraham Lincoln arrived in Washington, DC, for his inauguration, ex-President John Tyler arranged a meeting with him. He brought along a delegation from the peace convention. A Virginia member, James A. Seddon, ignored Lincoln's attempts at cordiality and dared him to explain why he had backed a murderer like John Brown and a mischief maker like William Lloyd Garrison, whose writings were spread through the South to inspire slave insurrections.

Lincoln's cordiality vanished. "Mr. Seddon," he said. "I will not suffer such a statement to go unchallenged, because it is not true. A gentleman of your intelligence should not make such assertions."

A wealthy New York delegate, William E. Dodge, warned Lincoln that it was "for you to say whether the whole nation shall be plunged into bankruptcy . . . and the grass shall grow in the streets of our commercial cities."

Lincoln's voice remained cold. He told Dodge that his question seemed to ignore the fact that he was about to take an oath to preserve and defend the Constitution. "Not the Constitution as I would like it, but as it *is*."

Even more dismaying to Tyler, Lincoln insisted that he would not consider the Constitution preserved and defended until it was "enforced and obeyed in every part of every one of the United States."[21]

The meeting resolved John Tyler's growing doubts about the value of the peace convention. The ex-president changed from a unionist to a secessionist who stubbornly clung to a hope for ultimate peace. As he now saw it, Virginia's best choice was departure from the Union. If she did it with the aplomb of a leader, there was a good chance that she would bring the rest of the slave border states—Maryland, Kentucky, Tennessee, Missouri, and Delaware—with her. Possibly even some free border states such as Pennsylvania would follow her lead. That would create a southern confederacy strong enough to discourage any northern attempt to resolve the crisis with bayonets. Once force was removed as an option, perhaps negotiation could achieve peace without bloodshed or permanent disunion.

This imaginary, improbable balance of power was the ironic remnant of John Tyler's hopes for his peace conference. He watched, more or less passively, as the delegates, after additional days and nights of wrangling, produced a proposal for a constitutional amendment that would allow slavery to be extended to the Pacific coast along the 36'30 line of the old Missouri Compromise. South of the line any state could vote to legalize slavery if her citizens wanted it. The idea was not much different from proposals already presented and rejected by the Republican-dominated Congress.

Tyler dutifully sent this message up to Capitol Hill, where it was ignored by both Democrats and Republicans. The ex-president returned to Virginia and on February 28 gave a speech on the steps of Richmond's Exchange Hotel, calling for immediate secession. To his consternation, nothing happened. The convention delegates and the voters who had sent them were still heavily pro-Union and were waiting to hear what President Lincoln had to say at his inauguration on March 4.[22]

Nine months later a weary ex-President Tyler died gazing into his wife's eyes, after a massive heart attack. His last words were: "Perhaps it is best."[23]

CHAPTER 22

The Anguish of Robert E. Lee

In the nine days Abraham Lincoln spent at the Willard Hotel before he took his oath of office, he faced pressure from two directions. The abolitionists, led by Senator Charles Sumner, exhorted him to concede nothing. They were ready, even eager for war. "I am in morals, not politics," Sumner liked to say. Senator Benjamin Wade of Ohio talked freely of the need for some "bloodletting." He kept a sawed-off shotgun in his desk on the Senate floor to make sure no Southerner gave him a Sumner-style beating. The conciliators, led by William Seward, now included Charles Francis Adams. "On which side would Lincoln be allied, that, north and south, was the question," wrote his son, Charles Francis Adams Jr.

The younger Adams had written an article, "The Reign of King Cotton," which he had just published in *The Atlantic Monthly*, New England's favorite magazine. In it he demonstrated that if war could be avoided, global economics would diminish cotton's imperial power—and with it the South's secessionist arrogance. Adams argued that India was rapidly overtaking the South in the production of cotton, at far less cost per bale. Not yet developed, but certain to appear in the near future, would be cotton plantations in British colonies in Africa, such as Egypt. A surplus of cotton would cause a drop in the price, making the South's plantations, burdened by their four million slaves, a losing proposition. The postwar price of cotton did in fact plunge by 50 percent, but the reasons were far more complex than young Adams foresaw. His argument might have convinced thoughtful men. But they were pathetically few in the swelling frenzy that confronted President-elect Lincoln.[1]

.   .   .

On the day before the inauguration, Congressman A. R. Boteler of Virginia, whose district included Harpers Ferry, appeared without warning at the door of Lincoln's hotel room, begging for a chance to talk to him. Lincoln was soon listening to a very agitated man. Congress was about to adjourn. But before it departed, Representative Benjamin Stanton of Ohio, an aggressive abolitionist, was determined to pass a force bill that would authorize (and hopefully encourage) Lincoln to call out all the regular and militia soldiers in the nation if the crisis worsened. Boteler had warned Stanton that the bill would inspire Virginia's secession. Stanton said the bill was going to pass, whether Boteler and the rest of Virginia liked it or not.

Lincoln reminded Boteler that he was not yet president. But he had some friends in Congress. He would see what might be done. That night at ten p.m., Stanton brought the force bill to the floor of the House. Elihu Washburne of Illinois, a Lincoln friend, promptly rose and made a motion to adjourn. It failed. But two other Republicans repeated the proposal. On the third try the House got the message and voted to end their session by a vote of 77 to 60, leaving the force bill in limbo. The experience convinced Congressman Boteler that Lincoln was not one of the "bloody-minded extremists," like Stanton, who were eager to "let slip the dogs of war."[2]

.   .   .

The next day, the streets of Washington, DC, were jammed with an estimated 25,000 strangers. Many of them had been forced to spend the previous night on porches and sidewalks; the city's hotels and rooming houses

were overwhelmed. Toward the end of the morning, army riflemen took covert possession of roofs along Pennsylvania Avenue; General Winfield Scott
was taking no chances on a last minute assassination attempt.

The capital had been buzzing for a week about a rumored plot to kill
the president-elect in Baltimore. Lincoln's friends had persuaded him to slip
through the hostile city in disguise, a decision he soon regretted. It enabled
critics in Democratic newspapers to ridicule him as a coward.

President Buchanan escorted Lincoln from the Willard Hotel and they
rode down Pennsylvania Avenue smiling and waving to the crowd. Lincoln was fashionably dressed in a brand new stovepipe hat, a black suit, and
gleaming black boots. He carried a gold-headed ebony cane. Ned Baker,
the equally well-dressed Republican senator from Oregon, who was an old
friend from Lincoln's days as a Whig congressman, stepped to the podium
before the east portico of the capitol and said, "Fellow citizens, I introduce
to you Abraham Lincoln, the President Elect of the United States."

Lincoln's words had been carefully chosen—and rechosen—in the preceding week. He had come to Washington keenly aware that most southern
states had not only seceded but were seizing federal forts, mints, and ar-
senals within their borders. The closing lines of his first draft had warned
the South not to assault the federal government. "I cannot shrink from the
defense of it. With you, not with me, lies the solemn question, shall it be
peace or a sword?" William Seward, soon to be Lincoln's secretary of state,
had warned him that this was "too warlike" and persuaded him to make an
important change.

Most of the address was a careful mixture of Lincoln's resolve to reclaim
federal property and a promise not to interfere in any way with the institution of slavery. He also promised to remain faithful to the federal government's responsibility to return runaway slaves to their masters. But he
insisted that the federal Union was "perpetual" and secession was a violation of that historical and legal fact. "Secession," he said, "is the essence of
anarchy."

He moved beyond these words to a plea for reconciliation. "Physically
speaking, we cannot separate. We cannot remove our respective sections

from each other nor build an impassable wall between them." Even more important, he urged the South to remember that "this country belongs to the people who inhabit it. . . . Why should there not be a patient confidence in the ultimate justice of the people? . . . Nothing valuable can be lost by taking time [to] think calmly and well upon this whole subject." He called on everyone to rely on "Him who has never yet forsaken this favored land."

Then came the soaring words Seward had persuaded Lincoln to use as his closing lines: "We are not enemies but friends. We must not be enemies. Though passion may have strained, it must not break our bonds of affection. The mystic chords of memory, stretching from every battlefield and patriot grave to every living heart and hearthstone over this broad land, will yet swell the chorus of the Union, when again touched, as surely they will be, by the better angels of our nature."[3]

.   .   .

In Virginia, well over half the delegates to the state convention in Richmond heard a hope of peace in Lincoln's words.

Not even a two-day-long pro-secession oration by ex-President Tyler on March 13 changed their minds. They ignored his call to make Virginia's "proud crest" [her flag] lead "the great procession of states" who were determined to defend their liberties, "peaceably if they can, forcibly if they must."[4]

That same day Colonel Robert E. Lee attended a reception at the White House for seventy-eight high-ranking military officers. It was the only time he met President Lincoln. There is no record of any conversation between them. But there is a strong likelihood that Lincoln gave him more than a passing glance. Already, General Winfield Scott was telling people that Lee was worth "fifty thousand soldiers" to the Union army, if war came. A few days later, at Scott's recommendation, Lincoln promoted Lee to full colonel in command of the First Regiment of the U.S. Cavalry, one of the most coveted appointments in the U.S. Army. On March 28, Lee accepted the promotion without the slightest trace of hesitation.[5]

Not long after he returned from Texas, Colonel Lee had spent three hours with General Scott in his office. The visit did not go unnoticed among the government's insiders. Lee probably learned that Scott had advised Lincoln to withdraw the garrison from Fort Sumter in Charleston's harbor—one of the two federal forts in the South still in the government's possession. (The other was Fort Pickens, in Florida.) Scott was trying to outmaneuver the hotheads in South Carolina, who were eager to start a war. The general also told Lee that he was prepared to use force—or at least the threat of force— to end the secession of the cotton states.

Scott was relying on his memory of President Andrew Jackson's success in 1833, when he responded to South Carolina's attempt to secede by summoning a hundred thousand volunteers. Charleston's boasters and strutters had crumpled without anyone firing a shot. Scott also probably told Lee that he himself was too old to take the field, and that he would appoint someone to act as his second in command. There was little doubt who that someone would be.

The name of the game, as Scott and the political conciliators saw it, was finding a way to keep Virginia and the other border states in the Union. Without them, the cotton states would be a minority, some of which might start talking peace. Lee's acceptance of his colonel's commission from President Lincoln suggested he was ready to cooperate with this solution. It was certainly evidence that he considered Lincoln his legally elected commander in chief.

Another sign of the colonel's thinking was his reaction to a message from L. P. Walker, the Confederate secretary of war, offering him a brigadier's commission in the secessionists' army. Lee did not even bother to reply. Eight days later, on April 3, the Virginia convention voted down another secession resolution, 90 to 45.[6]

.   .   .

Elsewhere the omens for peace became embroiled in the contest between the abolitionists and the conciliators swirling around Lincoln. South Carolina was demanding the surrender of Fort Sumter. They had come very close to seizing the fort in the last days of Buchanan's term. John Tyler had talked them out of it. The demoralized president was so grateful that he had abandoned protocol and called on Tyler and his wife in their hotel room to thank them personally. On March 15, Lincoln had asked his cabinet what they thought he should do about Sumter. Five out of the seven members recommended evacuation. The combination of General Scott and Secretary Seward had been persuasive. Without consulting Lincoln, Seward had even told Confederate commissioners who had come to Washington to negotiate relations between the two governments that the fort would be evacuated. Lincoln had refused to meet with these diplomats. He had made it clear in his inaugural address that he still considered the seceded states part of the Union.

Only one cabinet member, Postmaster General Montgomery Blair, a spokesman for a border state, Maryland, urged an attempt to keep Fort Sumter. Blair argued that surrender of the fort would discourage southern unionists. He even said giving up the fort would be tantamount to giving up the Union. Like General Scott, Blair was remembering Andrew Jackson's triumph in 1833, from a different angle of vision. His stand ignited the combative side of Lincoln's character that he had largely concealed in his inaugural address.

The president was also being bombarded by angry taunts from northern newspapers. "HAVE WE A GOVERNMENT?" one headline screeched. The administration, the New York Times growled, "must have a policy of action." Its publisher, Henry Raymond, was one of the founders of the Republican Party. Lincoln invited Raymond to visit him in the White House. The president told the newsman that most of his time since his inauguration had been consumed by office seekers. "I am like a man so busy in letting rooms at one end of his house, that he can't stop to put out the fire that is burning in the other." The New York Herald concluded: "The Lincoln administration is cowardly mean and vicious."

The president decided to act. Major Anderson, the commander of Fort Sumter, had reported that he would run out of food by April 15. Lincoln sent a courier to the governor of South Carolina, informing him that the federal government planned to resupply the Sumter garrison "with provisions only." There would be no attempt "to throw in men, arms or ammunition" unless the South Carolina government resisted the process.

The governor telegraphed the message to Confederate President Jefferson Davis in Montgomery. Davis asked his secretary of state, Robert Toombs, to advise him. Toombs replied: "The firing on that fort will inaugurate a civil war greater than any the world has yet seen . . . Mr. President, at this time it is suicide, murder and you will lose us every friend in the North."[7]

Others disagreed. Virginian Roger Pryor told Davis that he would never persuade the Old Dominion to join them if he did not "strike a blow!" Edmund Ruffin, the distributor of John Brown's pikes, was even more vehement on this point.

President Davis decided on gunfire and telegraphed Brigadier General Pierre G. T. Beauregard, the commander in Charleston, permitting him to choose the time. On April 11, Beauregard tried to persuade Major Anderson to surrender peacefully. Anderson, a fellow West Pointer, replied that he was "cordially uniting with you in the desire to avoid the effusion of blood." He offered to surrender the fort on April 15, when his supplies ran out. That was not the kind of surrender Beauregard—and Davis—wanted. Within minutes, Anderson was told that the Confederate batteries in Charleston would open fire within the hour.

The man who pulled the lanyard of the first gun was Edmund Ruffin—a veritable admission that it was an extremist act. For the next thirty-three hours, cannon and mortars hurled tons of metal at the old fort at the mouth of the harbor. The fort's gunners replied often enough to satisfy their honor as soldiers and then surrendered. In Washington, DC, President Lincoln issued a proclamation, summoning 75,000 militia to "suppress combinations" too powerful for the government to confront with ordinary means.[8]

Across the North, passion exploded everywhere. Huge rallies proclaimed a readiness for war. Watching 50,000 people surge into Union Square at Broadway and Fourteenth Street in New York City, book publisher William Appleton said, "We shall crush out this rebellion as an elephant would trample on a mouse."

In Boston the rallies were even more immense. Governor Andrew welcomed the war. Within three days he had three regiments on the way to

Washington, DC. Gerrit Smith said he was ready to finance a regiment of Negro troops and would send his only son, Greene Smith, into battle without pay. Wendell Philips, the most ferocious of New England's antislavery orators, said he was no longer a disunionist. William Lloyd Garrison, burner of the Constitution and another apostle of northern secession, said similar things. For forty years, New England had sulked and defied the federal government in two wars, mocked President Jefferson's embargo, and conferred in Hartford on terms of disunion. At last they could combine patriotism with their hatred of the South.[9]

Less visible—and far more crucial—was the reaction of the border states. The Virginia Convention went into secret session and took a vote. A narrow majority—60 to 53—still resisted secession. But it was more and more obvious that the unionists were losing ground. Kentucky's governor called the president's request for troops "wicked." The governor of Missouri said it was "diabolical." Both refused to send a man. Tennessee's governor said similar things, as did the governors of North Carolina and Arkansas. Maryland said nothing but also made no attempt to summon her soldiers. Nor did Delaware. Spokesmen such as John Bell of Tennessee, who had campaigned for the presidency as a unionist, called for a "united South" and accused Lincoln of declaring war.

.   .   .

At Arlington, Colonel Robert E. Lee's hopes sank as he watched passion replace reason across the South and the North. On April 17, a soldier leaped from a lathered horse with a message from General Scott. He wanted to see Colonel Lee in his office. The envelope also contained a letter from a cousin, John Lee, asking him to talk with Francis P. Blair. Colonel Lee had become friendly with Blair during a tour of duty in St. Louis, Missouri.

Even without that connection, the Colonel would have recognized Blair's name, as would anyone who worked for the federal government in the previous three decades. Blair was a mover and shaker of awesome dimensions. Under President Jackson, he had edited the *Congressional Globe*, the paper that everyone faintly interested in politics read to find out what the White

House was thinking. The *Globe* had been the mouthpiece of the Democratic Party for a decade.

When Senator Douglas repealed the Missouri Compromise in 1854, Blair became a Republican with undiminished political influence. He chaired the 1856 and 1860 Republican Conventions, where he was instrumental in Lincoln's nomination. Postmaster General Montgomery Blair was his son—and we can be sure that when he urged Fort Sumter's resupply, Lincoln considered the advice as coming from his father.

On April 18, 1861, Colonel Lee rode across the long bridge that linked Virginia to Washington, DC, and tied his horse in front of Montgomery Blair's house on Pennsylvania Avenue, opposite the building containing the State War and Navy Departments. It was an appropriate setting for one of the most crucial conversations in American history.

Waiting for him was balding seventy-year-old Francis Preston Blair. There is no record of the exact words, but we know that Blair, after the usual courtesies, grew solemn and told Lee that he had been authorized by President Lincoln to offer him command of the northern army that would assemble when the 75,000 volunteers reached Washington.

Here was a moment when history's direction hung on the loyalties and beliefs and emotions of a single man. If Robert E. Lee had accepted this offer, there is at least a possibility that Virginia would have refused to secede. Even if she seceded, Lee's prestige as a soldier, and his links through his father and his wife to George Washington, would have had an enormous impact on the legitimacy of the South's resistance. Northern newspapers would have trumpeted the significance of his decision. Divisive doubts would have been implanted in the souls of thousands of wavering southern unionists, especially in Virginia. The duration of the war—its very nature—might have changed.

As Robert E. Lee sat there trying to absorb this astounding offer, what did he think and feel? What did he remember? Almost certainly his first thought was John Brown. That madman's rant about the sin of slavery and the blood that was required to wash it away, the pikes he had been prepared to put into the hands of slaves, weapons that might have been thrust into the bodies of Lee's daughters and wife, the letters in Brown's carpetbag linking him to wealthy northern backers. Could General Lee invade Virginia or any other southern state at the head of an army composed of men who believed John Brown was as divine as Jesus Christ? How would the orders of a southern-born general, a slave owner thanks to his wife, restrain such men?

Next perhaps came the memory of the way the abolitionists had smeared him in their newspapers in 1859—accused him of stripping a young black woman and personally lashing her. Did he want to fight for a government that had been elected, in part at least, by these fanatics? What would prevent them from smearing him all over again if he lost a battle or even a skirmish? The thought of their righteous arrogance filled him with loathing.

Finally might have come that now distant but still terrible memory of the way Nat Turner and his army of maddened black men had slaughtered men, women, and children only a few miles from Fortress Monroe. Would that happen again if his northern army routed the South's soldiers? Would there be times—even for a few hours—when slaves ran wild that way?

No, No, No. That was the word that whispered in Robert E. Lee's soul. He could never undertake such a task. He could not dismiss his anger at the way the abolitionists had reviled southern white men for so long. In sad, careful phrases, Colonel Lee thanked Francis Preston Blair and President Lincoln for this remarkable offer of command. But he could not accept it. He "could not take part in an invasion of the southern states."

Blair refused to let him leave. They talked for another hour, with Blair trying to convince Lee of how much he could achieve as the army's commander. The politician portrayed himself as a sympathetic fellow Southerner. But he could not change Lee's mind. History, coinciding with so many personal memories, was simply too strong.

Lee finally escaped by promising to discuss the offer with General Scott. In his office, it did not take more than a glance for Lee to see that Scott was aware of what Blair had offered, and was hoping—even desperately hoping—that Lee had accepted. There was no need for small talk. Lee immediately told him what had been said, and his answer. "Lee," the general said. "You have made the greatest mistake of your life. But I feared it would be so."

Scott also could not let him go. He revealed his secret hope. An overwhelming federal force, with Lee as its leader, would intimidate the South into talking peace, without any need for a bloody offensive. Sadly, painfully, Lee demurred. He was sure that an invasion of Virginia would be necessary—and it was something he could not and would not lead.

Scott sighed and asked Lee if he intended to resign. For a moment Lee was mute. This was the decision that he had tried not to think about for weeks. It would mean the repudiation of thirty-four years of his life. He had hoped to keep his commission until Virginia voted to secede. But Scott reminded him that an officer could not remain on active duty after he turned down an assignment. "You should resign at once," Scott said. "Your present attitude is equivocal."[10]

Those words were a sad farewell from someone Lee admired more than any other man in his life, even his father. For a full minute the two men stood there, hands clasped, too moved to say a word. Then Lee turned and strode out of Scott's office, and out of the U.S. War Department, forever.

That night back in Arlington, Lee learned that Virginia militia, led by ex-Governor Henry Wise, had seized the arsenal at Harpers Ferry. The Virginia Convention had been in secret session since April 16. Three days later, on April 19, the historic date on which gunfire at Lexington had begun the American Revolution, newspapers reported that the convention had voted for secession.

For another two days, Lee could not bring himself to resign. One of Arlington's slaves later recalled watching him walk up and down the mansion's porch, trying to make up his mind. "He didn't cahr [care] to go," the black man said. Lee's daughter Agnes said that Arlington "felt as if there was a death in it." They were watching a man whose heart was with the South while his head remained loyal to the North. There were so many ties forbidding that letter of resignation: Arlington itself, with its memorabilia of Washington and Mary Custis Lee's link to Mount Vernon; his father's legacy as the general who smashed the Whiskey Rebellion; his West Point oath committing him to Duty, Honor, Country.

Finally, Lee wrote a one-line letter of resignation and showed it to his wife. "Mary," he said. "Your husband is no longer an officer in the U.S. Army." The letter went to Simon Cameron, the Secretary of War. With it Lee attached a note to General Scott. He begged his mentor and friend to understand his agonized struggle to decide whether "to separate myself from a service to which I have devoted all the best years of my life."[11]

Forty percent of the West Point graduates from Virginia did not agree with Lee. They remained loyal to the Union. So did many members of the Lee family. Lee knew that his oldest son, Custis, disagreed with him. In one of the many letters he wrote to relatives, Lee asked his wife to tell Custis that he was free to make up his own mind. "If I have done wrong, let him do better." Mary Custis voiced strong unionist sentiments almost to the day Lee resigned. Their son Rooney followed his father's lead, but he made no secret of his opinion that the southern people had "lost their senses."[12]

Ultimately, there seems to be little doubt that the primary disease of the northern public mind—abolitionism—and the primary disease of the southern public mind—fear of a race war—made Robert E. Lee a reluctant secessionist.

CHAPTER 23

The End of Illusions

Lee's resignation was a shock to many people. His cousin, Orton Williams, who was on General Scott's staff, reported that the whole army was "in a stir over it." Simon Cameron, the Secretary of War, wrote in a memorandum much later that Lee should have been arrested before he left General Scott's office. President Lincoln felt embarrassed. He knew the story of his offer to Lee would become public knowledge.

Three days later, former Colonel Lee departed by train for Richmond with Judge John Robertson, an advisor to Virginia's governor, John Letcher. Lee had met several of Robertson's associates in front of Christ Church in Alexandria, when he attended services there on the day after he resigned. Lee's daughter Agnes, watching the men converse, had no doubts about their topic. Her father's face showed "a mortal struggle, much more terrible than any known to the din of battle." The men were telling Lee that Governor Letcher had invited him to Richmond to discuss Virginia's military needs and plans. Their conversation closed with Lee agreeing to meet Robertson in Alexandria for the trip.[1]

Agnes was not the only spectator of this conversation in front of Christ Church. Virtually the entire congregation watched from a discreet distance. The local paper had just published an editorial, urging the governor to consider Colonel Lee for a high post. "There is no man who would command more of the confidence of the people of Virginia than this distinguished officer," the editor wrote. An acquaintance who saw Lee on the train said he was "the noblest looking man I had ever gazed upon—handsome beyond all men I had ever seen." Unquestionably, Lee had the look of a leader. Just short of six feet tall, at fifty-four he still emanated physical vitality. His dark hair had only a few streaks of grey; his trim mustache was entirely black. At two stations on the trip to Richmond, Lee was forced to go to the rear platform of the train to acknowledge crowds of people calling his name and cheering when he appeared. Obviously many Virginians had been hoping—even relying—on his help as the crisis with the North grew more ominous.[2]

At Richmond, Lee went directly to the capitol, where Governor Letcher awaited him. A baldheaded, bottle-nosed lawyer, Letcher had been a cautious unionist until Lincoln called for troops after Fort Sumter's bombardment. The governor probably told Lee that the vice president of the Confederacy, Alexander Stephens of Georgia, had just arrived in Richmond to negotiate an alliance with Virginia. Letcher was a busy man and did not waste words. Would General Lee accept an appointment as "commander of the military and naval forces of Virginia, with the rank of major general?" he asked. The governor added that his advisory council had already recommended Lee for the post.

When Lee said yes, Governor Letcher sent his acceptance to the Virginia convention, which was still in session. The delegates approved the appointment unanimously. Former Colonel Robert E. Lee was now a major general in the army of a seceded state.[3]

·   ·   ·

Meanwhile, the first blood in the war had been spilled in an unlikely place: Baltimore. The Sixth Massachusetts Regiment arrived there on April 19. It was one of the three regiments that Bay State Governor John Andrew had rushed to the capital to help fight the war he so eagerly welcomed. There was no direct rail service to Washington, DC; Baltimore had banned soot-spewing steam engines from its streets. There were five stations at which trains arrived from the west and north. The Bay State soldiers were on a Philadelphia, Wilmington & Baltimore Railroad train, which arrived at the President Street station. Their cars were to be towed by horses through the city to the Camden Street station, where a Baltimore & Ohio engine would haul them to Washington.

The soldiers arrived fearing the worst. Baltimore was known as "Mob City," with a tradition of civic unrest that went back to the War of 1812. Worsening matters was Maryland's hostility to the Republican Party. Lincoln had received only 3.6 percent of the vote in Baltimore and 2.6 percent in the state. On the previous day, over five hundred Pennsylvania militia had arrived at the Bolton Street Station and they were immediately confronted by an angry mob. They endured volleys of bottles, stones, and epithets as they marched through the city to the Mount Clare Station to embark on another line to Washington, DC.

Local police made little or no attempt to control the mob; they frequently laughed at the volunteers' discomfiture. The Keystone State's soldiers headed for Washington with several of their number painfully wounded by flying stones.

When the Massachusetts soldiers arrived at the President Street station, the pro-secessionist mob was far more organized. They had stockpiled rocks and bricks along the line of the march. Some people carried pistols. The mere mention of the word Massachusetts further inflamed everyone. These were the abolitionist Yankees who had started this war.

Fearing the worst, the commander of the Sixth Massachusetts distributed twenty rounds of ammunition to his men and authorized them to fire at anyone they saw aiming a gun at them. Again, Baltimore's police chief made no attempt to control the gathering crowd. From all sides catcalls and insults rained on the marching men. Then came the bricks, stones—and gunshots. The soldiers fired back, killing a sniper who toppled from a second floor window into the street. A Massachusetts soldier was hit by a brick and fell into the gutter, where the mob beat him to death. His name was Luther C. Ladd; he is considered the first casualty of the war.

The regiment reached Washington with four men dead and seventeen wounded. Behind them on Baltimore's bloody streets lay twelve dead civilians and an uncounted number of wounded. Southern newspapers called it "the Baltimore Massacre."[4]

The mayor and the police chief persuaded Maryland's governor to let them destroy the railroad bridges that connected Baltimore to Philadelphia and Harrisburg, severing the two chief train routes to Washington, DC. The governor declared Maryland's "neutrality" in the war. President Lincoln reacted with executive ferocity. He ordered the U.S. Army to arrest secessionist leaders, including the mayor and police chief, and incarcerate them in Fort McHenry. When lawyers for one of the prisoners demanded his freedom on a writ of habeas corpus, Supreme Court Chief Justice Roger Brooke Taney heard the case and ordered his release. The president refused to obey the order. He said that his reading of the Constitution entitled him to jail anyone who assailed the federal government verbally or physically while it was fighting a war.

Lincoln also ordered federal marshals to raid telegraph offices in every northern state and seize copies of all messages sent and received in the previous twelve months. The goal was detection of conspiracies against the government. The president also commandeered millions of dollars in the U.S. Treasury without any authorization or knowledge of Congress (it was not in session) and secretly sent huge amounts by special messengers to industrialists with orders for guns and uniforms and equipment for the embryo Union army. Many of the five hundred Pennsylvanians had arrived without weapons or uniforms.[5]

· · ·

The ruined Baltimore bridges did not prevent thousands of additional volunteers from reaching Washington, DC, by more circuitous routes. Soon the capital was safe from southern attack. Many of the arriving regiments sang a new marching song as they entered the city. Based on a traditional camp meeting melody, it had been introduced by a Massachusetts regiment departing from Boston and won instant popularity among New England soldiers.

> *John Brown's body lies a-mouldering in the grave*
> *John Brown's body lies a-mouldering in the grave*
> *His soul's marching on!*

Regiments from other states added their own often irreverent words to the basic text. One of the favorites was, "We will hang Jeff Davis from a sour apple tree." A Chicago version had a mocking verse:

> *He captured Harpers Ferry with his nineteen men so few*
> *And frightened old Virginny till she trembled thru and thru*
> *They hung him for a traitor, themselves the traitor crew*
> *But his soul is marching on.*

Later in the year, Julia Ward Howe, wife of one of John Brown's secret backers, converted the song into a fiery hymn, which began:

> *Mine eyes have seen the glory of the coming of the Lord*
> *He is trampling out the vintage where the grapes of wrath are stored.*

The Battle Hymn of the Republic helped transform the war into a holy crusade for many soldiers.

The South soon responded with its own song.

> *I wish I was in the land of cotton*
> *Old Times they are not forgotten*
> *Look away! Look away! Look away! Dixie Land!*

Originally a minstrel tune, popular in vaudeville theaters, Dixie radiated love of the South. The Confederate government soon made it a war song.

Southern men the thunders mutter!
Northern flags in South winds flutter
To arms! To arms! To arms, in Dixie[6]

·   ·   ·

On May 23, by a four-to-one margin, Virginia voters approved the convention's decision to secede. The Old Dominion was now part of the Confederacy, and General Scott decided it was time to seize the high ground on the Virginia side of the Potomac, including the Lee estate at Arlington. He ordered the town of Alexandria occupied as well. Rebel troops were stationed there and the Confederate flag flew from several poles.

The operation went smoothly. Engineers and infantry poured over the bridges across the Potomac at two a.m. on May 24 and began building trenches and forts around Arlington and elsewhere along the river. A U.S. Navy sloop of war preceded a transport carrying a regiment of Union soldiers to Alexandria. The sloop gave the small Confederate garrison an hour to evacuate the town. The rebels departed with only a few random potshots that the Union men ignored.

The regiment, under the command of Colonel Elmer C. Ellsworth, soon disembarked. They were wearing bright red uniforms; the imaginative Ellsworth had copied the style from French colonial troops. Born in New York State, Ellsworth had moved to Illinois to practice law and had become friendly with Abraham Lincoln; for a time he had worked in his Springfield office.

Colonel Ellsworth ordered the Alexandria railroad station occupied and headed for the telegraph office with a small escort. On the way, he noticed a Confederate flag flying on the roof of the Marshall House Inn. Irked, Ellsworth charged into the hostelry and up the stairs to the roof, where he found a ladder and quickly cut down the flag.

As the colonel and his escort descended the stairs, James W. Jackson, the owner of the inn, stepped from the shadows on the first floor landing and killed Ellsworth with a point blank shotgun blast to his chest. Ellsworth's

escorts instantly dispatched the assassin with bullets and bayonets. Scream-
ing hysterically, Jackson's wife flung herself on her husband's bleeding
corpse. If it was not war, it was a gruesome imitation of it.

A grief-stricken President Lincoln ordered Ellsworth's body carried to
the White House, where it lay in state in the East Room. Flags were lowered
to half mast and church bells tolled. The president gazed at the corpse and
murmured: "My boy, my boy! Was it necessary that this sacrifice be made?"
Thousands came to view the fallen hero, and northern newspapers claimed
his murder was proof of the South's bloody intentions. It was a graphic summary of the hatred inflaming so many on both sides.[7]

. . .

A far more influential symptom of the growing appetite for war emanated
from the *New York Tribune*. For more than a decade Editor Horace Greeley
had been a critic of the South and slavery. But after Fort Sumter, Greeley
was horrified by the oncoming bloodshed and tried to become a voice of
compromise. His managing editor, handsome, forty-one-year-old Charles
Dana, had a very different view of the conflict.

New Hampshire born, Dana's poverty had forced him to drop out of Harvard after a single year. But he managed to hobnob with New England's elite
at an experimental commune called Brook Farm and absorbed their attitude of moral superiority toward the rest of America—especially Southerners. He became an early convert to their belief in The Slave Power. At one
point he shared a lecture platform with William Lloyd Garrison.

At Dana's urging, on June 26, 1861, the *Tribune* proclaimed:

THE NATION'S WAR CRY

Forward to Richmond! Forward to Richmond!

The Rebel Congress must not be allowed to meet there on the
20th of July!

BY THAT DATE THE PLACE MUST BE HELD BY THE NA-
TIONAL ARMY![8]

Along with persuading Virginia to join the Confederacy, Vice President Alexander Stephens had proposed that Richmond become the capital. The Virginia legislature accepted the offer and President Jefferson Davis and the rest of the government began moving from Montgomery, Alabama, with visibly eager haste. It was more evidence of the importance of Virginia to the southern cause.

Dana's instinct to strike at this target was unquestionably sound—if one had no compunction about starting the war and were confident that the southern cavaliers were all bluster and no courage. Hadn't their reaction to John Brown proved that?

Dana had already demonstrated his abolitionist credentials at the *Tribune* with another headline. Starting in January 1861, while Greeley was out of town on a lecture tour, the *Tribune* began running a banner on its front page, above the daily stories: "No compromise! No concessions to traitors! The constitution as it is!" Greeley objected to this provocation, but Dana ignored him. When the editor in chief returned to New York, relations between the two men began to deteriorate.

Greeley still hoped desperately for peace. President Lincoln now had 30,000 troops in Washington, DC. But it was an army in name only; almost all were untrained men wielding a wild variety of weapons from squirrel guns to Sharps rifles. Another 200,000 men were assembling at training centers elsewhere in the nation. The president described this gathering host as "the greatest army in the history of the world."

Greeley went along with Dana's "Forward to Richmond" banner at first because he imagined that when this overwhelming force assembled in and around the capital, the South would come to its senses and negotiate a settlement. He too remembered the way South Carolina had collapsed when President Jackson confronted her 1833 secession with the threat of a massive invasion.

· · ·

Dana ran the "Forward to Richmond" banner day after day. Other Republican papers, notably the influential *Chicago Tribune*, took up this war cry.

Soon an estimated one hundred papers were running the slogan or paraphrasing it on their editorial pages. On July 4, Congress assembled in Washington, DC, and many Republicans, notably Senators Charles Sumner of Massachusetts, Ben Wade of Ohio, and Zachariah Chandler of Michigan, began saying the same or similar things. They were convinced that the corrupt slave owners lacked the courage to meet virtuous free men in open battle. A determined assault would smash their rebellion overnight.

President Lincoln went before Congress and defended his use of executive authority since he took office by saying the South had left him no choice but to "call out the war power of the government." The president asked for $400 million to raise an army of 400,000 men to guarantee that the contest would be "short and decisive." Applause swept the overwhelmingly Republican legislature.[9]

.   .   .

In Richmond, Major General Robert E. Lee had become President Jefferson Davis's military advisor. The two men were old if not close friends from West Point days and the War with Mexico. When Virginia joined the Confederacy and Davis arrived in Richmond, Lee expected and even hoped that he would be assigned to a field command. But Davis valued his advice too highly to let him leave his inner circle.

Lee had never returned to Arlington after his April 23 trip to Richmond. He had immediately gone to work mobilizing an army to defend Virginia, a state the size of all New England. He did not share the Republican illusion that the conflict would be a brief struggle. On April 30, he told Mary Custis Lee that "the war may last ten years." He issued similar warnings to the civilians in Richmond. They were "on the threshold of a long and bloody war."

Lee's strategy was defensive. Virginia had neither the resources nor the justification for attacking the North. He vetoed a reckless proposal to rush Virginia troops to rebellious Baltimore. In another letter to his wife, Lee deplored the bombast that filled southern newspapers about the South's ability to whip the effete abolitionists.

At one point, an influential man talked his way into Lee's office with his five-year-old son. The boy gave Lee a Bible and his father asked, "What is General Lee going to do to General Scott?"

"He is going to beat him out of his breeches," the boy piped. It was an obviously rehearsed remark.

"My dear little boy," Lee said. "You should not use such expressions. War is a serious matter and General Scott is a great and good soldier." Lee's eyes were on the father as he said these words.[10]

• • •

Lee's first task was fortifying Virginia's rivers to bar federal warships from threatening cities and towns with their guns. He emplaced heavy artillery found in the Norfolk Navy Yard at key points. Next he had to worry about the Harpers Ferry arsenal, seized by Virginia militia even before the state seceded. He put fellow West Pointer Thomas Jackson in charge and had no further worries about that troublesome site.

Lee appointed other West Pointers to take command of the Virginia militia. Soon Joseph Johnston, Richard S. Ewell, and other soon-to-famous professional soldiers were beginning the task of disciplining and training an army. Its size grew rapidly as Lee pondered how many fronts he had to defend. The civilians had originally estimated that 15,000 men would be more than enough. Lee raised that figure to 51,000 and urged every man to be enlisted for the duration of the war.

The civilians in Richmond, influenced by the overconfidence of their newspapers, envisioned a short war and voted for one-year enlistments. Lee acquiesced without protest. But he refused to enlist anyone younger than eighteen years of age. Sixteen- and seventeen-year-olds were sent home. Lee added a comment that the civilians ignored. "I fear we shall need them . . . before this war closes."

Lee soon had an army gathered around Manassas, a railroad junction about twenty miles from Washington. Another army defended the western counties in what is now the state of West Virginia. A third army, commanded by Joseph Johnston, was positioned between them at the head of the Shenandoah Valley, ready to assist either army or defend this vital area of the state.

Lee had no difficulty raising men. Nor did recruiters in other Confederate states. Although only 6 percent of Southerners owned slaves, the people of the South lived in a society with immense numbers of blacks in their midst. Albert Gallatin Brown, a former governor of Mississippi, explained why these nonslaveholders were ready and even eager to fight. They assumed that the goal of the "Black Republicans" was the emancipation of the South's four million slaves. If that happened, "the Negro would intrude into [their] presence." Blacks would insist on living on terms "of perfect social equality . . . His son shall marry the white man's daughter and the white man's daughter his son." If the nonslaveholder rejected these terms, "then will commence a war of races such as marked the history of San Domingo."[11]

There it was again: Thomas Jefferson's nightmare.

· · ·

In Washington, DC, the *New York Tribune* arrived at the White House every day with ON TO RICHMOND above the day's news. President Lincoln began to feel the mounting political heat generated by Charles Dana's war cry. Letters poured in, and congressmen and senators wondered aloud what Lincoln was going to do with the army he was assembling.

Twenty miles away across the Potomac River, Brigadier General Pierre G. T. Beauregard, the man who had seized Fort Sumter, commanded the Confederate army around the rail junction at Manassas. A turgid creek named Bull Run (sometimes called a river) added a defensive barrier. Beauregard had issued an exhortation to Virginians: "A reckless and unprincipled tyrant has invaded your soil. Abraham Lincoln, regardless of all moral, legal and constitutional restraints, has thrown his Abolition hosts among you . . . All rules of civilized warfare are abandoned . . . Your honor and that of your wives and daughters are involved in this momentous contest."

Here was Thomas Jefferson's nightmare as a Confederate war cry. The General apparently thought there was no need to reiterate "Santo Domingo." Portraying the Union Army as would-be rapists said more than enough.

General Scott urged President Lincoln to avoid a war of conquest, which would leave "fifteen devastated provinces" in the reunited nation and would require an army in their midst "for generations." Instead, he proposed that they blockade southern ports and seize control of the Mississippi River to suffocate the rebellion. Newspapers dismissed the idea as an "Anaconda Plan" that would take years to succeed. The Republican voters of the North wanted action. The ninety-day volunteers would soon be going home.

Stocky Brigadier General Irvin McDowell, the West Pointer in command of the Washington, DC, army, joined General Scott in urging caution. As professional soldiers they viewed the ninety-day volunteers as worse than useless. McDowell warned he might defeat Beauregard's force but he did not have enough men to capture Richmond. President Lincoln, thinking politically as well as militarily, replied, "You are green, it is true. But they are green also." Lincoln hoped a shattering defeat might demolish the rebels' overconfidence and end the war without desolating the South.

McDowell drew up a promising battle plan. He would pretend a frontal assault on Beauregard's army and outflank him with a ten-thousand-man column that would overwhelm the Confederate left wing and throw the rebels into a panic. Crucial to the success of the plan was preventing the Confederate army in the Shenandoah Valley commanded by Brigadier General Johnson from reinforcing Beauregard. Another Union army, led by Brigadier General Robert Patterson, was assigned the task of attacking—or at least menacing—Johnston to keep him out of the battle. The president gave the plan his approval, and General Scott added a reluctant nod.

From the start, things went wrong. McDowell's army was supposed to march on July 8. That was two weeks before most of the ninety-day enlistments would expire. But a shortage of supply wagons delayed them for another eight days. By that time, the ninety-day men were thinking about home, and two of the regiments, who were among the first to respond to Lincoln's call, refused to march and headed for the railroad station.

Meanwhile, General Patterson, a sixty-nine-year-old veteran of the War of 1812, wildly overestimated the size of Johnston's army and declined to attack it. He stayed so far away that Johnston concluded he was free to rein-force Beauregard anytime he pleased.

Once McDowell marched from Washington, speed was essential. But his amateur soldiers, each carrying fifty pounds of equipment in the hot July sun, took three days to cover twenty miles. The Confederates repeatedly blocked the road with felled trees that had to be chopped up and dragged away. Another distraction was the way some soldiers wandered off to steal chickens and other edible animals from nearby farms, and in some cases loot the houses. They apparently felt slave owners could be abused with impunity. General McDowell issued a stern prohibition against this mis-conduct. Meanwhile, General Johnston was transferring his army to Beau-regard's command on a railroad that ran day and night.

On July 21, a scorchingly hot, sultry day, the battle began. So confident were the Republican politicians of a victory that they turned the clash into a spectator sport. Senators Wade of Ohio, Chandler of Michigan, Wilson of Massachusetts, Trumbull of Illinois, and Grimes of Iowa rushed from the capital, accompanied by a swarm of congressmen. Many brought along wives and/or lady friends in holiday crinoline gowns, while servants lugged picnic baskets and wine coolers and water jugs up a hill about two miles from the battlefield. It was going to be such rare sport, watching the cow-ardly slaveholders scamper for the horizon, or plead piteously for mercy if captured. John Brown was about to be avenged, justified, and glorified. The politicians might even have sung his song as the guns began to thunder.

In spite of the confusion and delays, General McDowell stuck to his bat-tle plan. General Beauregard had arrayed his army along the south bank of Bull Run, with nine out of ten brigades on his right flank, positioned to defend the railroad junction, which he assumed McDowell would make his prime objective. The conqueror of Fort Sumter had a plan of his own—a frontal assault on McDowell's left flank.

As the sun rose, Beauregard got a rude surprise. Starting at two a.m. Mc-Dowell had led his ten-thousand-man column on a six-mile march to an undefended ford across Bull Run and hurled his brigades at Beauregard's under-strength left flank. As rifles cracked and cannon boomed, the Confederate commander rushed two brigades to reinforce the lone brigade falling back before this onslaught. At first the Confederates gave ground grudgingly. But when they grasped McDowell's numerical advantage, panic sent several regiments fleeing to the rear.

On their hill, Republican senators and congressmen danced with glee. Those who had brought along spyglasses could see little but figures shrouded by clouds of gunsmoke. But messengers from the battlefield rushed to telegraph the good news to the White House. Exultant reporters did likewise to their waiting newspapers. If only John Brown were alive to see this fulfillment of his life's work!

The celebration was premature. Generals Beauregard and Johnston had joined the defenders of the collapsing flank with more reinforcements. For much of the afternoon, the two armies attacked and counterattacked on and around Henry House Hill. Mrs. Henry, a widow, had refused to leave her house. Before the day ended she would be killed by an exploding shell.[12]

Much of the fighting was uncoordinated. At one point when a Union brigade surged forward, out of the Confederate line burst a regiment of horsemen led by an officer wearing an exotic plumed hat. It was Jeb Stuart, the West Pointer who had tried to persuade John Brown to surrender at Harpers Ferry. His horsemen shattered the charging Union infantry, cutting men down by the dozen with their murderous sabers.

Another climactic moment made a hero of Thomas Jackson, the taciturn soldier whom Robert E. Lee had put in charge of Harpers Ferry. He led a fresh brigade from General Johnston's army onto Henry House Hill as a South Carolina brigade broke and ran for the rear. Their general pointed up the hill and shouted, "Rally behind the Virginians! There is Jackson standing like a stone wall!" Minutes later the general went down with a bullet in his heart. Jackson's brigade met the oncoming Union assault with astounding courage and discipline. Henceforth they were known as "the Stonewall Brigade" and their leader became the soon-legendary general, "Stonewall" Jackson.[13]

As the afternoon waned, the Union army began to falter. Men who had been marching and fighting since two a.m. reached the limit of their stamina. Nothing contributes more to battlefield panic than exhaustion. At first individuals, then whole companies, began stumbling out of the battle. At four p.m. the Confederates received crucial reinforcements. The last brigade from General Johnston's army debarked from their train and charged into the gunsmoke, shouting a bloodcurdling combination of a wail and a scream. It was the first appearance of another legend—the rebel yell—which would symbolize the South's defiance for the next four sanguinary years.

General Beauregard, sensing the shift in momentum, ordered the rest of his army to attack. McDowell's army collapsed. The ninety-day men were among the first to flee as images of homes and parents, neighbors and sweethearts, shredded their nervous systems. They ran for the fords across Bull Run and kept running for most of the next twenty miles to Washington. They streamed past the horrified, disbelieving abolitionist politicians on the hill behind the battlefield without giving them so much as a glance.

Some of the politicians rushed down to the road and exhorted them to stop. They called the running men cowards and swine and traitors. They begged them to remember the courage of John Brown. Some congressmen brandished pistols and threatened to shoot them. Not even the threat of sudden death slowed their pace.

It dawned on the civilians and their lady friends that they, too, were in danger. Mounting their horses and climbing into their buggies and gigs, they abandoned their picnic baskets and joined the thousands of fugitives on the road. As the soldiers ran, they threw away hats, coats, blankets, guns, canteens. The road began to resemble a scene from a nightmare.

The only glimpse of hope was a brigade commanded by an Ohio West Pointer named William Tecumseh Sherman. They retained their discipline and formed a rear guard that discouraged a Confederate pursuit. McDowell added fresh regiments from two brigades that had been guarding the opposite flank and had never entered the battle.

On the other side of Bull Run, hundreds of Union soldiers surrendered while the rest of their army fled. Beauregard's men looked at each other in amazement. Most of them were so exhausted by the heat of the day and the tension of the seesaw battle that they found it hard to believe they were victors. No one was more pleased than Confederate President Jefferson Davis.

Unable to stand the suspense, he had taken a train from Richmond and rushed from the Manassas station to the battlefield. Along the way he met retreating Confederate regiments in panicky disarray and stragglers who told him the battle was lost. But General Johnston soon gave him the good news.

The elated President urged a vigorous pursuit—perhaps even a capture of Washington, DC. But Generals Beauregard and Johnston both shook their heads. Their army was almost as disorganized as the fleeing unionists. Supplies and wagons to transport them were inadequate. Better to play it safe and let the newspapers shout the news of their glorious victory. Maybe it would convince the Yankees to accept a negotiated peace.[14]

Unmentioned in the praise that was soon pouring from the southern presses was the man whose strategy had made the victory possible. It was General Robert E. Lee who had positioned the two Confederate armies so that they were linked by a rail line and could come to each other's assistance if needed.

. . .

When the political spectators fleeing Bull Run reached Washington's night-shrouded streets, some rushed to the White House to tell the President what they had seen. By that time, Lincoln knew the worst. His day had been an emotional roller coaster. Well into the afternoon, telegrams from the battlefield were optimistic, almost triumphant. The president decided he could end the day with a ride in his carriage with his wife and sons—something of a daily custom. While he was gone, Secretary of State Seward appeared at the White House, looking almost as frantic as the retreating soldiers. He had heard reports, perhaps from one of the fleeing senators who rode a fast horse, that "the battle is lost."

When the president returned, his two secretaries, John Hay and John G. Nicolay, told him of Seward's visit. Lincoln rushed to army headquarters, where a clerk handed him a dispatch from a captain of the engineers: "The day is lost. Save Washington and the remnants of this army." Lincoln showed it to General Scott, who said it was too soon to lose hope. The president decided to summon his cabinet for an emergency session. Then came a telegram from General McDowell: his army had disintegrated into a "confused mob."[15]

For the rest of the night and much of the following day, the remnants of McDowell's shattered regiments reeled behind the forts that General Scott had constructed along the Potomac. Even more dismaying were wagons loaded with 1,154 wounded. Behind them on the battlefield they left 560 corpses. No one knew that Confederate losses almost equaled the Union's toll. For the next few days, Lincoln had to endure an avalanche of criticism from newspaper editors, blaming everyone and everything for the disaster. Even the picnicking senators and congressmen and their lady friends shared in the obloquy. One critic claimed that the politicians had been among the first to run and communicated their panic to the soldiers.

Unhappiest of these believers in John-Brown-fabricated illusions of easy victory was Congressman Alfred Ely of New York. He had not run fast enough and would spend the next six months in a Richmond prison.

Newspapers fanned the flames of war on both sides. James Gordon Bennett, while still damning Republicans at every opportunity, had committed the *New York Herald* to the defense of the Union. One of the paper's correspondents described how rebel artillery had taken special pleasure in blasting groups of Union wounded, and "rebel fiends in human shape" bayoneted helpless dying men. Other rampaging rebels had amputated heads from Union corpses and kicked them around the battlefield like footballs. The newsman claimed these and other sadistic acts revealed what Southerners meant by their "boasted chivalry." He was faking it, of course, hoping hatred would restore the North's shattered morale.

At the end of the week, President Lincoln received a letter from Horace Greeley, which began, "This is my seventh sleepless night." He told Lincoln that "the gloom in this city [New York] is funereal—for our dead at Bull Run were many and they lie unburied yet. On every brow sits sullen scorching black despair." Greeley did not care what the president did next, as long as it involved withdrawal from the war. Lincoln could disband the army, recognize the Southern Confederacy, or call for a national constitutional convention—the *Tribune* would support him. Greeley closed the letter, "Yours in the depth of bitterness." Whether the latter word was directed at himself, or Lincoln, or Charles Dana (whom he would soon dismiss) was unclear.[16]

Lincoln did not answer the erratic editor. Instead, the president requested and obtained from Congress the power to raise another 500,000 men. In Richmond, President Jefferson Davis asked the Confederate Congress to summon 400,000 men. Civil war—on a scale never foreseen or seldom imagined by anyone North or South—had begun.

CHAPTER 24

The Third Emancipation Proclamation

In the summer of 1862, the Union cause seemed to be going nowhere. Two victories in the west made a hitherto unknown general named Ulysses Grant the hero of the moment. But a Confederate army attacked his army at Shiloh, Tennessee, and came close to inflicting a catastrophic defeat. A staggering 23,741 men were killed, wounded, or missing, making it the bloodiest clash ever fought on American soil. In the east, General George McClellan, commanding an even larger Union army, was mired in mud and equally staggering casualties on the Yorktown Peninsula, still a long way from Richmond. Intimidated by General Robert E. Lee's aggressive tactics, McClellan would soon retreat to Washington with his demoralized battalions.

Horace Greeley sent President Lincoln a letter, which he published on the front page of the *New York Tribune* and titled "the Prayer of Twenty Millions." Claiming he spoke for the entire population of the North, Greeley told the president that he was "strangely and disastrously remiss in the discharge of your official and imperative duty." What was that duty? To do more to free the South's slaves. "We have fought wolves with the devices of sheep," Greeley cried. It was time to start fighting "slavery with liberty."[1]

Abraham Lincoln's reply was succinct and candid. "My paramount object in this struggle is to save the Union, and is not either to save or destroy slavery." If he could save the Union without freeing a single slave, he would do it. If he had to free all the slaves first, he would do that. The preservation of the Union was his *official* duty, as president. It did not in any way modify his "oft-expressed *personal* wish that all men everywhere should be free."[2]

Behind these words lay a political no-mans-land that Lincoln had been traversing for a year. Four border states with tens of thousands of slaves—Kentucky, Maryland, Missouri, and Delaware—had not seceded from the Union. Their politicians repeatedly warned Lincoln that any attack on slavery would turn their voters into Confederates, making the South too strong to defeat. Lincoln's native state was especially important. "To lose Kentucky," he told a friend, "is nearly the same as to lose the whole game."

Meanwhile, Lincoln refused to relinquish his search for a way to end the bloodshed by negotiation. The president invited politicians from these four border states to the White House and spent hours trying to persuade them to accept compensated emancipation to free their slaves. He told them that this policy would persuade other states with large numbers of Unionist voters such as North Carolina and Virginia to accept the same offer and quit the Confederacy. But the president got nowhere with these timid senators and congressmen. All of them hesitated to change what they called their "social arrangements." Thomas Jefferson's race war nightmare still infested their souls.[3]

Elsewhere, several Union generals had improvised emancipation programs on their own authority. General Benjamin F. Butler of Massachusetts, an ex-Democrat and canny lawyer, decided he had no obligation to return slaves who fled to his protection at Fortress Monroe, the seacoast bastion where Captain Robert E. Lee and his bride had encountered Nat Turner's rebellion in 1831. Butler reasoned that slaves of rebel Virginians were now "contraband of war" and their owners had no claim on them. This clever idea became unworkable when a Maryland runaway took shelter in the camp of an Ohio regiment. When the abolitionist-inclined Midwesterners refused to let his pursuers search their camp, a Maryland congressman warned the president that the state might soon abandon the Union.[4]

Elsewhere two other Union generals declared martial law and freed the blacks in states where they were in command. General John C. Fremont, the losing Republican candidate in 1856, applied this idea to Missouri, creating consternation in nearby slave-owning Kentucky. General David Hunter, from abolitionist-minded northern New York, issued a similar declaration for all slaves in South Carolina, Georgia, and Florida, even though he commanded only a few offshore islands and bits of their seacoasts.

Lincoln fired the defiant Fremont and declared Hunter's decree "altogether void." The president told abolitionist leaning Salmon Chase, the secretary of the Treasury, who favored Hunter's move, "No commanding general shall do such a thing, upon my responsibility, without consulting me." In the tradition of George Washington, he was determined to protect his presidential powers from cooption and trivialization.[5]

The abolitionists in Congress were infuriated. Since the war began, Senator Charles Sumner had been urging fellow senators to press upon Lincoln "the duty of emancipation." Senators Wade of Ohio and Chandler of Michigan boasted that they were often in the White House until midnight reminding Lincoln of this obligation. They had created a Committee on the Conduct of the War, which interrogated and rebuked generals such as McClellan who they thought insufficiently aggressive on the battlefield. They repeatedly expressed their contempt for West Pointers and their military science, which they considered synonymous with cowardice.[6]

·　　·　　·

Neither Horace Greeley nor Senator Sumner knew that a month before the editor hurled his rebuke at the president, Lincoln had summoned two of his cabinet members to the White House and read to them the draft of a proclamation freeing all the slaves in the seceded states. A week later, he read it to his entire cabinet. Some approved, others were dubious. Secretary of State William Seward warned the president that if he issued it now, it would be regarded as "the last shriek" of an exhausted government. It would be wiser to wait until he could announce it when it was backed by a "military success."

The words were scarcely out of Seward's mouth when news of another Union army catastrophe inflicted by General Robert E. Lee reached the White House—the Second Battle of Bull Run. A weary president decided Seward was right and put the proclamation away to hope for better days. That was why there was no mention of it in the president's response to Horace Greeley.[7]

Meanwhile, abolitionist attacks on Lincoln grew more ferocious. The Reverend Henry Ward Beecher declared that there was not a line in any of Lincoln's messages that might not have been written by the Czar of Russia, Emperor Louis Napoleon of France, or Jefferson Davis. "Lincoln would like to have God on his side but he must have Kentucky," sneered another abolitionist. Wendell Phillips called the president a mere "county court advocate" whose antislavery principles were invisible. Among the many abolitionists Lincoln disliked, Phillips was at the top of the list. "I don't see how God lets him live!" the president once exclaimed to a White House visitor after hearing about one of the Boston aristocrat's denunciations.[8]

.   .   .

Abraham Lincoln was not an overtly religious man. He never joined an established church. But he was a reader of the Bible from boyhood and came to believe that Americans were "an almost chosen people" whose rise held out "a great hope to all the people of the world." In his first inaugural address, that belief had been the source of his plea to the South to have a "patient confidence" in the eventual wisdom of the people and return to the Union, trusting in God's guidance.

When Jefferson Davis decided to fire on Fort Sumter and the war began, Lincoln's relationship with God entered a new dimension. To his friend Noah Brooks, a reporter for the *Sacramento Daily Union,* he confessed that he was "driven many times upon my knees by the overwhelming conviction that I had nowhere else to go." As the bloodshed multiplied and the corpses became a towering mountain in his anguished mind, Lincoln repeatedly turned to God, seeking strength to endure the seesaw struggle and wisdom to choose the right path through the slaughter.

Again and again, Lincoln told people he prayed not to get God on his side but to get his presidency on God's side. He urged people to make this the central theme of their prayers for him. To the end of his life, Congressman James F. Wilson of Iowa remembered the day a delegation of abolitionist clergymen admonished the president to take a more resolute stand on slavery. They warned him that if he did not "do right," the nation was doomed.

Lincoln's face, Wilson said, "came aglow like the face of a prophet." He rose to his full six feet four height and stretched out his arm. "My faith is greater than yours," he said. "I believe He will compel us to do right in order that He may do these things, not because we desire them, but because they accord with His plans for this nation."[9]

During a talk with two other antislavery clergymen, Lincoln urged them to understand that they were part of a movement, which meant they talked mostly to each other. As president, he heard opinions from many sorts of people throughout the nation and "it appears to me the great masses of the country care comparatively little about the Negro." He urged them to go home and try to bring more people to their views. They could say anything they pleased about him, if it would help, he added wryly.

Abruptly, he became serious. "When the hour comes for dealing with slavery," he said. "I trust I will be willing to do my duty, though it cost me my life."[10]

.   .   .

Not long after General Lee's victory at the Second Battle of Bull Run, he invaded the North, hoping to end the war. The Union army met him in a tremendous battle at Antietam, Maryland. On the eve of this clash, Lincoln made a solemn vow to God. If the Union army defeated Lee, he would issue the proclamation. After another bloodletting on a par with Shiloh, Lee retreated to Virginia. The president decided Antietam looked enough like a Union victory to publish the Emancipation Proclamation on September 22, 1862.

Still hoping for a negotiated peace, Lincoln announced he would wait until January 1, 1863, to make the proclamation official. The public reaction in the North was not encouraging. "While commendation in newspapers and by distinguished individuals is all that a vain man could wish," Lincoln wrote to Vice President Hannibal Hamlin, "the stocks have declined and troops come forward more slowly than ever."

Worse, the Republican Party took a drubbing in the November midterm elections. Kentucky was carried for the Union using totally desperate tactics. At each polling place, there were detachments of Union troops. When a Democrat arrived to vote, the officer in command warned him that he could not guarantee his safety on his return to his home. Most of the time, the man decided not to vote. Kentucky's fraudulently elected delegation enabled the Republicans to retain control of the House of Representatives. If the Democrats had won, they would have had the power to cut off funding for the war.[11]

The South's reaction to the proclamation was vitriol. "What shall we call him?" raged the *Richmond Enquirer*. "Coward, assassin, savage, murderer of women and babies? Or shall we consider them all as embodied in the word fiend, and call him Lincoln the Fiend?" The murderous language reinforced Lincoln's suspicion that doing his duty about slavery might cost him his life. It was also dolorous proof that Thomas Jefferson's dread of a race war continued to permeate the southern public mind.[12]

From abroad came better news. England was no longer tilting toward recognition of the Confederacy. The ruling class's favorite magazine, *Punch*, portrayed Lincoln in dozens of grotesque and uncomplimentary ways. But the preliminary proclamation had stirred a surge of approval among the middle and lower classes. This was doubly amazing because a shortage of southern cotton had put 500,000 men and women out of work in Britain's textile mills. The antislavery seed John Woolman had planted was flowering again to rescue his agonized country.[13]

As January 1 approached, Lincoln made another attempt at a negotiated peace. In his annual message to Congress, the president asked the lawmakers to consider a constitutional amendment that would guarantee compensated emancipation to any state, including those in rebellion, that would agree to abolish slavery gradually by 1900. He added a long, carefully reasoned argument in support of this idea, and closed it with one of his most effective phrases: "The dogmas of the quiet past are inadequate to the stormy present."

The abolitionists exploded in almost insane fury. William Lloyd Garrison declared, "The president is demented—or else a veritable Rip Van Winkle." His proposal "borders upon hopeless lunacy" and stirred thoughts of impeachment. Wendell Phillips said the president "had no mind whatever" and compared him to a tortoise. "He may be honest [but] nobody cares whether the tortoise is honest or not." As hatred-inflamed as ever, the abolitionists were blind to the way their rage poisoned Lincoln's peace proposal for the South.[14]

. . .

From our distance of a century and a half, there are two clauses in the proclamation that have become hugely important in our evolving comprehension of the Civil War. The first dealt directly with the fear of a race war. *And I hereby enjoin upon the people so declared to be free to abstain from all violence, unless in necessary self defence; and I recommend to them, in all cases when allowed, they labor faithfully for reasonable wages.* The slaves' response to this exhortation suggested that Thomas Jefferson's race war nightmare was created by the special circumstances of the struggle for freedom in Haiti. Not even in the southern counties where blacks heavily outnumbered whites was there any explosion of the bloodshed that Jefferson had dreaded and John Brown envisioned in his tormented soul.

The second clause was even more important for the future self-respect of the freed slaves. *And I further declare and make known, that such persons of suitable condition, will be received into the armed services of the United States to garrison forts, stations and other places, and to man vessels of all sorts in said service.*

Here Lincoln was reaching back to that early emancipator, George Washington, and his decision to give black Americans the right to fight for the independence of the United States from 1775 to 1783. Thanks to this clause in the proclamation, 200,000 black Americans served in the Union army, displaying heroic courage on some of the war's bloodiest battlefields.[15]

.   .   .

On December 13, another battle cast the darkest shadow yet over the proclamation. Big-bellied Ambrose Burnside of Rhode Island, arguably the worst general of the war, was now in command of the Union army. He attacked Robert E. Lee's army of 78,500 men, entrenched on the south side of the Rappahannock River at Fredericksburg, Virginia. Burnside ordered his 106,000 men to cross the icy stream and hurl themselves at Lee's men in a series of suicidal frontal assaults that piled Union dead in heaps at various points along the ten-thousand-yard front. The Union army finally retreated with 12,700 men killed or wounded. In an explosion of frustration they looted and wrecked most of the town of Fredericksburg. It was the most humiliating defeat of the war. Burnside had attacked because the abolitionists in Congress had warned him that he would be hauled before the Committee on the Conduct of the War if he did not become more aggressive.[16]

.   .   .

Some people wondered if Lincoln might abandon the Emancipation Proclamation after this catastrophe. Wouldn't it now seem to be what Secretary of State Seward had warned against—the last cry of a collapsing federal government? If Lincoln confronted this possibility, he mentioned it to no one. He went ahead with the January 1, 1863, announcement, as planned.

On December 31, Lincoln revised the proclamation's text one more time, working far into the night. The next morning, he sent his handwritten copy over to the State Department for "engrossing" in the heavy type of an official document. A servant brought him his usual light breakfast. As he ate, his wife Mary appeared in the doorway. Three of her Kentucky brothers were fighting for the Confederacy. She had repeatedly tried to convince him not to issue the proclamation. "Well," she said. "What do you intend doing?"

"I am a man under orders," the president said. "I cannot do otherwise."

At 11:15 Mary joined him, and they descended the wide White House staircase to spend the next three hours smiling and shaking hands in the traditional New Year's Day White House reception for the diplomatic corps, the army's generals and the navy's admirals, the judges of the Supreme Court, and other government officials. At noon, the doors were opened to admit a huge crowd of average citizens. Noah Brooks told his newspaper that the president seemed "in fine spirits and cracked an occasional joke with intimate friends."

That afternoon, Secretary of State Seward and his son Fred arrived with the engraved copy of the proclamation. Lincoln read it carefully one more time and picked up a pen. As he leaned forward to sign it, his hand and then his whole forearm started trembling violently. He put down the pen, rubbed the arm and hand and tried again. The same thing happened. Fearing he would splatter ink on the document, he pushed back his chair.

A wave of dread swept Lincoln's mind and body. Was this a terrible mistake, as Mary had been telling him? Were these tremors a warning that he was about to perpetrate a disaster? Would the proclamation, coming on the heels of the bloody defeat at Fredericksburg, destroy order and harmony in the North as well as sow additional rage and fear in the South?

As the tremors slowed, Lincoln decided they had been caused by the three hours of handshaking at the White House reception. These sessions always left his hand bruised and his arm muscles stretched to the snapping point. He glanced at the two Sewards, who were staring at him with puzzlement and apprehension on their earnest faces. "I never in my life was more certain that I was doing right than I do in signing this paper," he said.

These were the words of a man who had achieved this certainty on his knees, in communion with his God. Later Lincoln told a friend that as January 1 approached, he had asked God "to let this cup pass from me." Clearly he knew he was risking his own life, and he feared until these very last moments that he was risking the survival of the Union. But he had decided that the Union was in equal danger if he did not issue it. The abolitionists in Congress were threatening to throw the country into chaos by refusing further funds for the war. Those final resolute words were spoken not only to the Sewards but to himself, affirming his conviction that this document was God's intention far more than his own.

The Sewards nodded encouragingly. Lincoln said he hoped his signature would not waver. "They will say I had some compunctions."

He gazed at the proclamation and said, again more to himself than to his witnesses, "Anyway it is going to be done." Slowly, carefully, he signed his full name: *Abraham Lincoln.*

Then he sat back in his chair and laughed briefly—again mostly to himself, banishing the last fragments of fear. "That will do," he said.

The war had become a struggle for the Union—and a new birth of freedom. Lincoln had rescued the noble side of the abolitionists' crusade, their hatred of slavery, and separated it from its ruinous side, their hatred of southern white men. That left him free to deal with the defeated South on his terms.[17]

CHAPTER 25

The Hunt After the Captain

By this time the war was changing many minds and hearts in ways that the abolitionists would never understand or approve. More and more, it became apparent that the chief motivation of most of the men in the armies of the North was the preservation of the Union. One of the best historians of the Civil War has recently devoted a book to this phenomenon.[1]

Early in the war, the shrewd politician William Seward wrote a memorandum to President Lincoln urging, "we must change the question before the public from one upon slavery or about slavery for a question upon Union or Disunion." By the fourth year of the war, the wisdom of this observation had become apparent. Lincoln did not run for reelection as a Republican. He ran with a Democrat—Andrew Johnson of Tennessee—on a "Union" ticket.

Again and again, in diaries and letters, soldiers revealed that the Union was the chief reason for their decision to join the war and endure its appalling bloodshed. William Bluffton Miller, a sergeant in the Seventy-Fifth Indiana Infantry, was typical. In his diary he noted mournfully, "There are thousands now sleeping in unknown graves, and many more will have to die yet to perpetuate the best government in the world." In the perspective of this book, all these men were paying tribute to the power of George Washington's central message in his Farewell Address: the crucial importance of the Union to America's hopes for prosperity and peace.[2]

Along with this positive motivation, there was a tendency as the war dragged on to divide the blame for the conflict between slave-owning "southern oligarchs" and abolitionists. There was a saying in the army General William Tecumseh Sherman led through Georgia that most men were more inclined to shoot an abolitionist than a rebel. They learned on that march that only a small minority of Southerners owned slaves. For the rest of the Confederate soldiers, it was "a rich man's war and a poor man's fight." But very few understood why the southern poor men were fighting so ferociously: their fear that black emancipation would be a prelude to a race war.

One of the first evidences of this phenomenon was an article in *The Atlantic Monthly*, "My Hunt After the Captain," written by one of New England's most popular authors, Dr. Oliver Wendell Holmes.

Dr. Holmes was famous for his witty, often sardonic essays, issued by the so-called Autocrat of the Breakfast Table in books with variations on that original title. He had never been an abolitionist, and when his handsome Harvard-educated son, Oliver Jr., declared his intention to join the Union army, the father had urged him not to do so.[3]

The son had disagreed with his famous parent and had become a captain in the Twentieth Massachusetts regiment. At the Battle of Ball's Bluff, another Union rout several months after Bull Run, Oliver Jr. had received a wound above his heart. As soon as he recovered, he had gone back to his regiment. A day after the battle of Antietam, Dr. Holmes received a telegram informing him that the captain had been wounded again. Holmes immediately set out by train and wagon for Antietam. His journey across the battlefield, less than a week after the dying had ended, was told with the careful eye for detail of the trained physician.

Antietam had replaced Shiloh as the bloodiest battle ever fought on American soil up to that time. Most of the thousands of dead bodies had been buried by the time Dr. Holmes arrived, but everywhere he saw patches of caked blood and bullet-torn hats and fragments of bloody uniforms. A crude sign announced that a rebel general and eighty of his men were all buried in "this hole." Tens of thousands of wounded writhed in makeshift hospitals in churches and private houses, overwhelming the Union army's exhausted doctors. No one Holmes spoke to knew anything about his son.

A friendly fellow physician took Holmes through one church hospital, constructed of boards laid over the tops of pews. The wounded lay on bundles of straw on this improvised floor. The escort held a lantern over each man, but none was Captain Holmes. The process was repeated far into the night at other crude hospitals. One sufferer was a captured Confederate officer from North Carolina. Holmes found him "educated, pleasant, gentle, intelligent." It only took a few minutes of conversation with such an enemy to wipe away "all personal bitterness toward those with whom we or our children have been but a few hours before in deadly strife."

At another point in his search, Dr. Holmes found himself in a camp for rebel prisoners. He asked them why they were fighting. "For our homes," several said. The doctor turned to a Mississippi officer, "about twenty, with a smooth boyish cheek." He told Holmes he "liked the excitement of it" and added he had read many of the doctor's books. Soon Holmes was in "magnetic relation" with him. Although he had become a public denouncer of the rebellion, Holmes had not let opposition diminish his "human sympathy" for all the young men trapped in the carnage.[4]

Finally, the wandering doctor caught up to his wounded son. He had been shot in the neck this time. A single expert glance told Dr. Holmes he would survive the wound. "How are you, Boy?" he said.

"How are you, Dad?" the Captain coolly replied.

Holmes realized he was speaking to a son who would never again be a boy. Oliver Jr. had become a man in his own right.

Captain Holmes soon returned to the war. He rejected an offer to be a major in a black regiment. Back in the Twentieth Regiment, he was greeted by his best friend and fellow captain, Henry Abbott, who told Holmes how pleased he was that he had decided to remain a captain and stay with them. Abbott and most of the Twentieth regiment were totally disillusioned with the war. Only their sense of honor as soldiers kept them in uniform. Above all else they detested the abolitionists, who had gotten them into this murderous nightmare.[5]

Holmes's letters from the front explain this angry disillusionment. "It is singular with what indifference one gets to look at dead bodies," he wrote. "As you go through the woods you stumble constantly and if after dark, as last night on picket, perhaps tread on the swollen bodies already fly blown and decaying, of men shot in the head, back or bowels—many of the wounds are terrible to look at—Well, we licked 'em." In 1863, in a slide into total discouragement, he thought he and his fellow soldiers were "working to effect what never happens—the subjugation (for that is it) of a great civilized nation."[6]

Abbott was killed leading his company in the chaotic Battle of the Wilderness in 1864. A heartbroken Captain Holmes anonymously published a poem to his memory in the *Boston Evening Transcript*. Its last two lines summed up his admiration:

> *Noble heart, full soon we follow thee*
> *Lit by the deeds that flamed along thy track.*

After the war, Oliver Wendell Holmes Jr. rose in the legal profession to become an Associate Justice of the U.S. Supreme Court. For seventy years, he repeatedly condemned the abolitionists and others who claimed they had a message from some higher power that everyone had to obey. Above all he voiced his contempt for people whose claim to certitude often persuaded other men to kill each other.

In a letter to the British radical Harold Laski, Holmes wrote, "You put your ideals or prophecies with the slight superior smile of a man who is sure he has the future (I have seen it before in the past from the abolitionists . . .)." In another letter, he said, "Communists show in the most extreme form what I came to loathe in the abolitionists—the conviction that anyone who did not agree with them was either a knave or a fool."[7]

Perhaps his most devastating postwar comment was one that cut through a hundred years of mythical American history to one of the central truths about the war. Holmes said he now realized he had been fighting for the United States—the Union. He thought he had been fighting for Boston.[8]

Lincoln's Visitor

On April 9, 1865, General Robert E. Lee's 27,000 gaunt, exhausted soldiers trudged into the village of Appomattox Court House in southern Virginia to find the road ahead of them blocked by thousands of Union cavalrymen. Almost simultaneously, a courier arrived with a message from fleeing President Jefferson Davis, declaring he hoped to fight on. "Tell the President that the war is ending just as I have expected it would from the first," Lee replied. The words add retrospective depth to Robert E. Lee's inner anguish when he refused command of the Union army in 1861.

Pursuing Lee's men was a 120,000-man Union army led by stumpy General Ulysses S. Grant. "Sam" Grant had recovered from his near defeat at Shiloh to win crucial victories in the western theater. President Lincoln had made him the Union army's commander in chief in March 1864. Like Lee he was a West Point graduate, but his career in the Union army before the war had been undistinguished.

What would the country think if he surrendered, Lee asked his staff officers? One tear-choked young aide replied, "There has been no country, General, for a year or more. You are the country to these men."

Lee's thirty-year-old artillery commander, General Edward Porter Alexander, spoke for the younger officers. "Why not disband the army, order the men to scatter like rabbits and partridges in the bushes?"

Here was a moment when a word of assent from Lee would have launched a guerilla war that might have lasted for decades. "The men would have no rations," Lee said. "They'd have to rob and plunder."

"A little more blood or less now makes no difference," Alexander persisted. "Spare the men who have fought under you for four years the mortification of having to ask Grant for terms and have him say unconditional surrender . . . General—spare us the mortification of that reply!"

Unconditional surrender was the merciless terms that the abolitionists in Congress were recommending. Although it was sometimes invoked when demanding the surrender of a fort or a city—Grant had used it twice in his victories over Confederate armies in the West—it had not been invoked in negotiating peace between warring nations since Rome had demanded it of Carthage in 126 BC.

"General Grant will not demand unconditional surrender," Lee assured Alexander. "He will give us as honorable terms as we have a right to expect."

West Point's spirit of brotherhood played a part in Lee's response. Far more influential were words that President Abraham Lincoln had spoken on March 4, 1865, when he was inaugurated for a second term:

> With malice toward none; with charity for all; with firmness in the right, as God gives us to see the right, let us strive on to finish the work we are in; to bind up the nation's wounds, to care for him who shall have borne the battle, and for his widow and his orphan—to do all which may achieve a just and lasting peace among ourselves, and with all nations.

Whether General Lee had read these words, or heard only fragments of them, we do not know. But we can be sure that even fragments would have stirred a profound response in a man who, more than any other soldier, personified the divisions of heart and mind that had begun the war. We know that General Grant had heard the words. In addition, he had conferred with President Lincoln on April 3, when the president visited Richmond after Lee's army had retreated from the wrecked Confederate capital.

Grant and Lee met in the Appomattox home of man named McLean. After they chatted briefly, Lee asked if Grant was ready to discuss surrender terms. Grant's reply was succinct and simple. The surrendered men would be paroled and "disqualified from taking up arms again." Once they gave up their weapons and ammunition, they would be free to return to their homes. They would not be "disturbed by the United States authority" as long as they observed their paroles.

Lee replied with a request. Could the cavalrymen and artillerymen keep their horses? They all owned them privately. Grant instantly agreed. Anyone who claimed a horse or mule would be allowed to take it home "to work their little farms."

"This will have the best possible effect upon my men," Lee said. "It will be very gratifying and it will do much toward conciliating our people."

Next Lee confessed his men were close to starvation. Grant turned to his commissary general, who was sitting nearby. Within hours, fresh beef, salt, hard bread, coffee, and sugar were flowing into the Confederate lines. As the food arrived, Union army bands began playing and artillery batteries fired victory salutes. General Grant ordered an immediate halt to these celebrations. "The rebels are our countrymen again," he said.[1]

. . .

On the evening of April 11, 1865, two days after General Lee surrendered, a jubilant crowd gathered in front of the White House and began calling for President Lincoln. Noah Brooks, the reporter for the *Sacramento Daily Union* who was visiting the president, described the throng as "a vast sea of faces, illuminated by the lights that burned in the festal array of the White House, and stretching far out into the misty darkness."

Lincoln appeared at the window over the mansion's main entrance, a place from which he and other presidents often spoke. The crowd fell silent. Instead of a few random remarks, Lincoln had a prepared speech. It swiftly became apparent that he was using this opportunity to begin discussing his postwar policy toward the defeated South.

Brooks held an oil lamp so Lincoln could read the speech, while the president's young son, Tad, grasped the pages as they were read and fluttered to the floor. Lincoln began by expressing his hope for a "righteous and speedy peace." Then he turned to what he called "the re-inauguration of national authority" in the South. He warned his listeners that this might be a difficult task. "We, the loyal people, differ among ourselves" about how to reconstruct the shattered Union.

Lincoln was aware that a number of abolitionist Republican politicians in Congress did not agree with the policy of forgiveness he had enunciated in his second inaugural speech. Senators Ben Wade of Ohio and Zachariah Chandler of Michigan and their allies wanted to prosecute Robert E. Lee, Jefferson Davis, and other Confederate leaders for treason, and hang them. Then they planned to rule the South as a captured province, divided into military districts. Senator Wade had made it clear that he had no hesitation about forcing Lincoln to accept this policy. Senators were not the president's "mere servants, obeying everything that we may ascertain to be his wish and will," Wade had snarled.

Lincoln was now in even stronger disagreement with Wade and his circle. The president's visit to ravaged Richmond had appalled him. Southern civilization had been all but eradicated. There were no courts, no banks, no police. Union army officers told the president that other southern cities were not in much better condition.

Along with restoring the government of the Southern states as swiftly as possible, Lincoln told his listeners that he wanted to give African Americans the right to vote. He planned to begin by conferring the privilege "on the very intelligent and those who had served our cause as soldiers."

Those words showed how far Abraham Lincoln had travelled from the politician who had assured Illinois voters in 1858 that he did not think blacks and whites could live together, and that colonization was the only solution to racial peace. Now he was saying he favored black participation in the electorate, and by implication full citizenship for all the ex-slaves when education made them ready for its privileges and duties.[2]

Among the listeners in the crowd was the mustachioed actor John Wilkes Booth and burly Lewis Paine, his partner in an already simmering plot against Lincoln's life. When the president said he wanted to give the vote to blacks, Booth turned to Paine and muttered: "That's the last speech he'll ever make."[3]

·   ·   ·

Listening to Lincoln's words at a nearby White House window was a visitor who was a link to George Washington. Adolphe, the Marquis de Chambrun, was a grandson of the Marquis de Lafayette through his daughter Virginie. Chambrun had come to Washington, DC, in February 1865 as an informal representative of the French government. Relations between America and France had been strained by Emperor Louis Napoleon's decision to set up a puppet government in unstable Mexico, headed by Archduke Maximilian of Austria. The venture was a foolish fragment of the dream of a New World empire that had led Napoleon Bonaparte to his ruinous invasion of Saint-Domingue (Haiti).[4]

Chambrun had charmed Mrs. Lincoln and become part of the White House's inner circle. Mary Lincoln had invited the Frenchman to accompany them when she and the president visited ruined Richmond. Chambrun had seen the liberated slaves of that city singing joyous hymns in the street and falling on their knees with cries of gratitude to the president. It was a remarkable fulfillment of Lafayette's dream of joining George Washington in eliminating slavery from the republic they had fought to create.[5]

In early 1862, Lincoln had testified to another link to Washington when he warmly approved a proposal to read the founder's Farewell Address aloud in Congress. It was a perfect way to underscore the president's decision to make the primacy of the Union the central reason for his decision to resist southern secession. His 1863 proclamation, emancipating the slaves of the seceded states, was intimately linked in Lincoln's mind with the war powers Washington and his collaborator James Madison had made sure that the Constitution gave the president.

After his reelection in 1864 made it clear that the war was almost won, Lincoln took a step that confirmed his deep personal commitment to freedom for all Americans. He backed and even encouraged abolitionists in Congress who called for an amendment to the Constitution banning slavery from all the states of the American Union. Lincoln welcomed its passage, because it removed once and for all the possibility that sometime in the future a hostile Supreme Court might declare the Emancipation Proclamation unconstitutional. The amendment, Lincoln said, was "a King's cure for all the evils" of slavery.

·   ·   ·

As Lincoln ended his speech, people in the audience called out for a song. An army band had serenaded them for a half hour before the president appeared at the White House window. Many if not most of the listeners expected the president to choose one of the war's hymns to vengeance: "John Brown's Body" or "The Battle Hymn of the Republic."

"Dixie," Lincoln said. He was telling the crowd that the South's favorite song (and one of his favorites) belonged to everyone now. It was another way of saying America was one country again.

·   ·   ·

On April 12, Lincoln met with his cabinet and discovered several of them disapproved of his policy of forgiveness toward the South. Ohio-born Secretary of War Edwin Stanton, who shared many abolitionist views, was especially vehement. "It would surely bring trouble with Congress and the people would not sustain you," he growled. The president assured him and the other doubters that he would do his best to meet their objections.[6]

Two days later, Lincoln convened another cabinet meeting and resumed discussing his policy. This time everyone, even the short-tempered Stanton, agreed with his approach. Frederick Seward, the son of the secretary of state, who sat in on the meeting for his ailing father, reported that there was "a unanimously kindly feeling toward the vanquished Confederates and a hearty desire to restore the peace and safety of the South with as little harm as possible to the feelings and property of the inhabitants."

General Ulysses Grant was at this cabinet meeting. Lincoln nodded with approval as the general told how he had advised Robert E. Lee's soldiers to go back to their homes and families, and promised they would not be harassed or prosecuted if they did no more fighting.

This change of mood, if not of mind, suggests Lincoln the politician had been at work, reassuring the cabinet critics that he would listen to their advice in the months to come. The president ended the discussion by noting that Congress was not in session. If he and the cabinet were "wise and discreet," they could get the governments of the southern states in successful operation before the legislators returned in December. "We can accomplish more without them," he said. There were too many men among them who had "good motives" but were full of "hate and vindictiveness." There was no doubt that he was talking about Senator Wade and his fellow abolitionists.[7]

·   ·   ·

In Charleston, South Carolina, on that same day, April 14, 1865, abolitionists celebrated raising the American flag over Fort Sumter. The city had been in Union hands since General William Tecumseh Sherman's army had occupied it after their destructive march through Georgia. The chief speaker was the Reverend Henry Ward Beecher, brother of Harriet Beecher Stowe, the author of *Uncle Tom's Cabin.* Beside him on the platform sat William Lloyd Garrison, the man who had launched the abolitionist movement.

Beecher had been a strong supporter of the Union cause throughout the war. Garrison too, while not always able to restrain his sharp tongue, had backed the president after Lincoln issued the Emancipation Proclamation. A grateful Lincoln had yielded to their desire to go to Charleston for the symbolic flag raising.

Henry Ward Beecher paid no attention whatsoever to Lincoln's inaugural plea for malice toward none and charity towards all. "I charge the whole guilt of this war upon the ambitious, educated, plotting political leaders of the South," he roared. There could be no lasting reunion without the kind of retribution that the God of the Old Testament so often visited upon the enemies of ancient Israel. "God shall say: Thus shall it be to all who betray their country!"[8]

Nothing illustrates the psychological and spiritual limitations of the abolitionists more than this heartless speech, flung in the face of a defeated South. The seeds of a hundred years of future sectional and racial antagonism were in those words. One of their first by-products was an indictment for treason against Robert E. Lee, issued by a Federal grand jury three months later. General Grant threatened to resign as the Union army's commander in chief and the charge was dropped.[9]

Late on the night of April 14, the telegraph in the Union army's Charleston headquarters clicked words that changed the history of the nation and the world: "The President was shot in a theater tonight and perhaps mortally wounded."

·   ·   ·

If Lincoln had lived to serve out his term, could he have overcome the abolitionist haters and maintained a policy of forgiveness that healed the wounds of the war? Would he have been able to win acceptance and equality for black Americans in both the North and the South? No one can or should minimize the hugeness of both these tasks. But one of the most important things to remember about Lincoln was the nickname his White House aides gave him: The Tycoon.[10]

Four years of wielding the presidency's war powers had made him a political leader in every sense of the word: a man who was ready to master every challenge that confronted him, from winning the most terrible war in America's history to surmounting the difficulties of peace. He had become a master at rallying a divided people at war. Now he was ready to master the even more difficult art of modifying the public mind for the politics of peace. During the war his aides placed dozens of anonymous articles in key newspapers, backing his policies. The Associated Press, coming into its own as a news source for papers everywhere, seldom published anything that opposed his views. Reporters like Noah Brooks became virtual disciples, committed to his ideals.

At least as important for meaningful reconciliation were numerous southerners who were ready to cooperate with Lincoln. None was more central to this hope than Robert E. Lee. Even before the last Confederate armies surrendered, Lee had given an interview to a northern reporter. He told the man that he was prepared "to make any sacrifice or perform any honorable act that would lead to the restoration of peace."[11]

. . .

Let us close with a recollection of the potential Lincoln, the Tycoon with this southern ally, in the words of a senator who visited him on the last day of his life. The senator was used to seeing a haggard, sleepless president enduring a seemingly interminable war. On April 14, the visitor could scarcely believe his eyes. Lincoln's "whole appearance, poise and bearing had marvelously changed," the senator said. "He seemed the very personification of supreme satisfaction. His conversation was exhilarating."[12]

The senator was looking at a triumphant Tycoon. It is heartbreaking— but also somehow inspiring—to imagine what this extraordinary man might have accomplished if he had lived. Remembering this Lincoln may persuade the Americans of the twenty-first century to achieve the central message of his legacy—and the reason for writing this book—genuine brotherhood between North and South, and between blacks and whites. An understanding of the diseases of the public mind that caused the war's cataclysm of blood and fury is now possible, thanks to the work of generations of historians. The truth, as Lincoln once remarked, is often "the daughter of time."

. . .

When the Marquis de Chambrun heard the news of Lincoln's assassination, the stricken Frenchman remembered the day he and the president and Mrs. Lincoln were returning from their visit to Richmond. As they approached Washington, DC, the capitol's looming dome reminded Mary Lincoln of her husband's congressional critics. "This place is full of enemies," she said.

"Enemies?" Lincoln said. He shook his head, thinking of the devastated South. "We must never use that word again."[13]

ACKNOWLEDGMENTS

My favorite metaphor for writing a history book is the image of an author standing on the shoulders of dozens of previous scholars. This image is especially true for this book. My debt to various writers, some of them friends, is large and humbling. At the top of my friend list is Harold Holzer, Lincoln scholar extraordinaire, whose books have helped me see Father Abraham's greatness and his complexity. In the same category is Charles Bracelen Flood, whose riveting narrative, *1864: Lincoln at the Gates of History*, prompted Mr. Holzer to say, "No one can comprehend Lincoln without reading this essential book."

A similar thank you must ascend to Elysium for the late James Thomas Flexner, who stirred similar realizations for George Washington. Allied with him in my mind is a biographer of Washington whose insights into various aspects of his personality, especially his relationship to his slaves, is unparalleled—Peter Henriques. Although I have met him only briefly, letters and emails have more than justified the word friendship.

If there is one book that awoke my desire to understand more about American slavery, it is *Time on the Cross: The Economics of Negro Slavery*, by Robert William Fogel and Stanley L. Engerman. This controversial attempt to find a new, more positive view of the black American experience in bondage resonated with me for a special reason, aside from its original point of view. It stirred comparisons to the Irish/Irish-American experience of the long dark night of three hundred years of semi-slavery in Great Britain's oppressive grip, and the impact of freedom for those who emigrated to America's shores, like my four grandparents. I am equally indebted to Mr. Fogel's later books, *Without Consent or Contract, The Rise and Fall of American Slavery,* and *The Slavery Debates.* The latter is an essential tool for anyone writing about the complex, ever-evolving scholarship on this sensitive subject.

Closely allied in my psychological historical map is Stephen Hahn, whose groundbreaking books on black achievements as slaves and as a pseudo-free (a.k.a. segregated) minority I have read with special interest. I have known Steve since I played a part in bringing his Yale Ph.D. thesis to the attention of the Society of American Historians, which awarded him the Allen Nevins prize. Later published as *The Roots of Southern Populism,* the book won the Frederick Jackson Turner award of the Organization of American Historians, launching Steve's notable career. His 2004 book, *A Nation Under Our Feet: Black Political Struggles in the Rural South from Slavery to the Great Migration,* won three major prizes and has deeply influenced my understanding of the slave experience.

Next on my gratitude list comes my wife, Alice Fleming, author of more than thirty superb history books for young readers. She devoted two of these books to the very different lives of Frederick Douglass and Martin Luther King Jr. They are full of insights into the black struggle for freedom that have put me in her debt in a new way. For years beyond counting, she has been my in-house editor, and more recently, thanks to her proficiency on the computer, my researcher-in-chief in the exploding world of internet sources. Even a casual glance through my endnotes will make this apparent.

Two friendships that I have valued were with Ralph Ellison, author of *The Invisible Man,* and with John A. Williams, author of *The Man Who Cried I Am.* I praised the latter book in the *New York Times Book Review.* This led to a visit to my apartment, during which we talked with memorable frankness about black-white relationships in America. Thanks to these two men, I glimpsed the wound that slavery and segregation inflicted on even the most gifted and generous-spirited black Americans, who were ready to reach across the barrier to extended white hands.

Linked to these black friends in memory is the late Benjamin Quarles, the gifted black historian whose book *The Negro in the American Revolution* was a revelation to me—and to many others. I invited him to speak at a dinner meeting of the American Revolution Round Table of New York. Talking with him for several hours made me realize we were soul brothers—an extravagance that I hasten to add neither of us uttered aloud.

Next comes a debt that anyone and everyone writing about slavery must acknowledge: to David Brion Davis. His magisterial books on the history of slavery, most notably that remarkable summation of his life's work, *Inhuman Bondage: The Rise and Fall of Slavery in the New World,* are in a class unto themselves. I owe a special debt to his brief but oh-so-pungent volume, *The Slave Power Conspiracy and the Paranoid Style.* During the same period of study, I discovered David Blight's *Race and Reunion: The Civil War in American Memory,* a searing exploration of the abolition-driven hatred of the South in a post–Civil War nation shorn of Lincoln's healing power.

Among other books I should mention as contributors in a large way to this book's point of view are *The Comparative Histories of Slavery in Brazil, Cuba, and the United States* by Laird Bergad and *Written in Blood: the Story of the Haitian People, 1492–1971* by Robert Debs Heinl and Nancy Gordon Heinl. The latter was recommended to me by my close friend Robert Cowley, who was the editor. The book brings alive in awful detail the source of the South's primary disease in their public mind, the dread of a race war. Equally important is Henry Mayer's *All on Fire,* a definitive biography of the founder of abolitionism, William Lloyd Garrison. Again and again we see Garrison's inability to summon an iota of sympathy for or understanding of the Southerners' anxiety as the number of slaves swelled to four million and fear of an insurrection clotted the good intentions of men like Thomas Jefferson and his grandson, Thomas Jefferson Randolph.

Perhaps most influential to my overall view of the war as a gigantic tragedy is Drew Gilpin Faust's *The Republic of Suffering: Death and the American*

Civil War. With sympathy and clarity and not a trace of sentimentality, Faust has rediscovered the tidal wave of pain and grief and loss that the war flung over both the North and the South.

I must also thank the many librarians who have been helpful in my toils. Mark Bartlett and his staff at the New York Society Library have again been indispensable. Also valuable have been Gregory S. Gallagher, librarian of the Century Association in New York City, and Lewis Daniels, director of the Westbrook (Connecticut) Public Library. Lew's readiness to hunt down obscure and out-of-print books in the Steady Habits state's libraries made my summer months as productive as my winter ones in New York City. At least as helpful in exploring the Library of Congress and other Washington, DC, collections, as well as trolling years of microfilms of southern newspapers, was Steven Bernstein, a talented researcher I have called on for several books. Steve has recently published a superb Civil War history of his own, *The Confederacy's Last Northern Offensive*, about Jubal Early's 1864 raid on Washington, DC. My son, Richard Fleming, a graduate of the Columbia University School of Library Science, used his access to his alma mater's great collections with equally helpful results.

A very large thank you goes to my literary agent, Deborah Grosvenor, and my editor at Da Capo Press, Robert Pigeon. I have wanted to write this book for two decades. Thanks to their openness to new ideas, it has come to life. Bob's steady encouragement and his suggestions for improving the manuscript were equally invaluable.

Finally, I must thank my favorite West Pointer, Colonel Charles M. Adams, who helped me realize Robert E. Lee's central role in understanding the history of the Civil War. Charlie was my escort on the day in 1964 that I began researching my history of the U.S. Military Academy. Over the next four years, as I pondered the lives of the men who made that fateful commitment to Duty, Honor, and Country, Charlie and I became close friends. After the book was published, he invited me and my wife to spend a weekend with him and his wife, Cindy, at the Army War College in Carlisle, Pennsylvania. The visit ended with a tour of the nearby Gettysburg battlefield under his tutelage. When we reached Cemetery Hill, we paused, gazing up that harrowing slope in the deepening twilight. Charlie turned to me and said, with just a hint of his native Texas in his voice, "I was brought up to believe Robert E. Lee was the greatest man that ever lived. I believed it until I came here, and saw what he asked Pickett's men to do."

THOMAS FLEMING

NOTES

PREFACE

1. J. David Hacker, "Recounting the Dead," Opinionator, Exclusive Online Commentary from the Times, *New York Times*, September 20, 2011. Mr. Hacker is an associate professor of history at Binghamton University in New York. I have found further evidence for the probability of Mr. Hacker's figures in the research I did for World War I casualties for my book *The Illusion of Victory: America in World War I* (New York: 2003). At the end of the war, the total number of reported deaths was 120,139. In 1930, the Veterans Bureau estimated that war-related diseases, wounds, and other kinds of trauma inflicted on the Western Front had raised the total to 460,000.

2. Laird W. Bergad, *The Comparative Histories of Slavery in Brazil, Cuba and the United States* (New York: 2007).

3. Thomas Fleming, *1776: Year of Illusions* (New York: 1975) and *The Illusion of Victory: America in World War I* (New York: 2003).

4. Thomas Jefferson to George Washington, "The Writings of Thomas Jefferson," May 23, 1792, Modern History Sourcebook, Fordham University. Abraham Lincoln, Special Session Message [to Congress], July 4, 1861, Presidential Speech Archive, Miller Center, University of Virginia, http://millercenter.org/president/speeches/detail/3508. Adlai Stevenson, speech given in Albuquerque, NM, *New York Times*, September 12, 1952.

5. A good example is the recent book *The American Public Mind*, by William E. Claggett and Byron E. Shafer (New York: 2010). It is a study of what Americans think about politics and public policy in four key areas: social welfare, international relations, civil rights, and cultural values.

6. Nathaniel Hawthorne, *The House of the Seven Gables* (Columbus, OH: Centenary Edition, 1965), 7–8.

PROLOGUE: JOHN BROWN'S RAID

1. Merrill D. Peterson, *John Brown: The Legend Revisited* (Charlottesville, VA: 2002), 92. James M. McPherson, *Ordeal By Fire* (New York: 1991), 117.

2. David S. Reynolds, *John Brown: Abolitionist* (New York: 2005), 240–241.

3. Edward J. Renehan, *The Secret Six: The True Tale of the Men Who Conspired with John Brown* (New York: 1995), 1–8.

4. Oswald Garrison Villard, *John Brown, 1800–1859: A Biography Fifty Years After*, reprint (Gloucester, MA: 1965), 426–427.

5. Peggy A. Russo and Paul Finkelman, eds., *Terrible Swift Sword: The Legacy of John Brown* (Akron, OH: 2005), 119–137. Kenneth A. Carroll, the psychologist who diagnosed Brown, noted, "The manic's enthusiasm for his project does not issue from careful logical thought but is a product of his emotional illness that intoxicates the subject with a grandiose and unshakable faith in the supreme importance of himself." Carroll cites affidavits from Brown's neighbors in Ohio, where he grew up, full of recollections of Brown's manic behavior. "The evidence that he was mentally ill is clear and abundant."

6. Villard, *John Brown*, 430.

7. Renehan, *The Secret Six*, 197.

8. Villard, *John Brown*, 433.

9. Reynolds, *John Brown*, 319–320.

10. Villard, *John Brown*, 439–440.

11. Reynolds, *John Brown*, 322–323.

12. Douglas Southall Freeman, *R. E. Lee: A Biography*, vol. 1 (New York: 1934), 394–396.

13. Villard, *John Brown*, 448–449.

14. Freeman, *R. E. Lee*, 399.

15. Villard, *John Brown*, 451–455.

16. Reynolds, *John Brown*, 329–333.

CHAPTER 1: SLAVERY COMES TO AMERICA

1. Genesis 9:18–27 (Revised Standard Edition).

2. David Brion Davis, *Inhuman Bondage: The Rise and Fall of Slavery in the New World* (New York: 2006), 62.

3. T. F. Earle and K. J. P. Lowe, *Black Africans in Renaissance Europe* (New York: 2005), 281. Innocent VIII reportedly had sixteen illegitimate children, which won him the title "Padre della Patria" (Father of the Fatherland). Thomas More, *Utopia*, edited by George M. Logan and Robert M. Adams (Cambridge, England: 1989), 77–78.

4. Robert W. Fogel, *Without Consent or Contract: The Rise and Fall of American Slavery* (New York: 1989), 18–19.

5. Davis, *Inhuman Bondage*, 80.

6. Edgar J. McManus, *Black Bondage in the North* (Syracuse, NY: 1973), 65–66. Unfortunately, Judge Sewall also believed that "Ethiopians" could "never embody with us and

grow up into orderly families, to the Peopling of the Land." Both Sewall's pamphlet and Saffin's reply are available online, as part of the PBS documentary "Africans in America," at www.PBS.org/wgbh/aia/part1//. Also see *Amazing Grace: An Anthology of Poems About Slavery, 1660–1810*, edited by James G. Basker (New Haven, CT: 2002), 37.

7. Thomas P. Slaughter, *The Beautiful Soul of John Woolman, Apostle of Abolition* (New York: 2008), 103–104.

8. John Woolman, *Journal of John Woolman, and A Plea for the Poor*, John Greenleaf Whittier edition text (Gloucester, MA: 1971), 15.

9. Slaughter, *Beautiful Soul*, 232–233. Woolman, *Journal*, 113.

10. This story is based on an oral tradition. It may be a dramatization of the overall reaction of the Meeting to Woolman's testimony. One man later said his "simplicity, solidity and clearness" made doubt and opposition "vanish as mists at the sun's rising" (Slaughter, *Beautiful Soul*, 344).

11. Harvey Wish, "American Slave Insurrections Before 1861," *Journal of Negro History* 22, no. 3 (July 1937): 302–303. Wish cites several stories of slave suicides.

12. The British slave ship *Zong* is a good example of this horrific practice. The captain threw 132 men overboard in 1781. Over the protests of a British antislavery advocate, the court awarded him the insurance money. See PBS, "Africans in America," part 1. Also see Wish, *Insurrections*, 303; and Adam Hochschild, *Bury the Chains: Prophets and Rebels in the Fight to Free an Empire's Slaves* (New York: 2005), 79–83.

13. Peter C. Hoffer, *Cry Liberty: The Great Stono River Slave Rebellion of 1739* (New York: 2010), 103ff.

14. Peter C. Hoffer, *The Great New York Conspiracy of 1741: Slavery, Crime and Colonial Law* (Lawrence, KS: 2003). Some historians have dismissed the plot as the product of wartime hysteria. A majority believe that a genuine conspiracy existed. The author spent a year studying it for his novel, *Remember the Morning* (New York: 1998), and is convinced the majority are correct. The conspiracy was real—and lethal. Like John Brown's foray, it had no hope of succeeding.

15. George Washington, letter of July 20, 1774, Writings of George Washington, vol. 3, 232–234, http://etext.virginia.edu/toc/modeng/public/WasFi03.html.

16. James Otis, *The Rights of the British Colonies Asserted and Proved* (Boston: 1763), http://oll.libertyfund.org/index.php?option=com_content&task=view&id=1069&Itemid=264.

17. Robert Olwell, "'Domestick Enemies': Slavery and Political Independence in South Carolina, May 1775–March 1776," *Journal of Southern History* 55, no. 1 (February 1989): 21–48.

18. Michael Lee Lanning, *African Americans in the Revolutionary War* (New York: 2005), chap. 5, "Liberty to Slaves: Lord Dunmore's Ethiopian Regiment," 51ff.

CHAPTER 2: SLAVERY'S GREAT FOE—AND UNINTENDED FRIEND

1. Dumas Malone, *Jefferson the Virginian* (Boston: 1948), 121–122.

2. Papers of Thomas Jefferson, edited by Julian P. Boyd, vol. 1 (Princeton, NJ: 1950), 423–428. Also see Julian P. Boyd, *The Declaration of Independence* (New York: 1945), for illustrations of this "Original Rough Draft."

3. Carl Lotus Becker, *The Declaration of Independence: A Study in the History of Ideas* (New York: 1922), "The Rough Draft," Online Library of Liberty, http://oll.libertyfund .org/title/1177.

4. James Boswell, *The Life of Samuel Johnson* (New York: 1930), 747–748.

5. Henry Wiencek, *An Imperfect God: George Washington, His Slaves, and the Creation of America* (New York: 2003), 203–204.

6. Ibid., 208–214. Washington later permitted his aide, Joseph Reed, to have the poem published in *Pennsylvania Magazine*.

7. Ibid., 261.

8. Fritz Hirschfeld, *George Washington and Slavery: A Documentary Portrayal* (Columbia, MO: 1997), 148–150.

9. Thomas Jefferson, *Notes on the State of Virginia*, Writings, vol. 2. Also see Malone, *Jefferson the Virginian*, 264–268.

CHAPTER 3: THE FIRST EMANCIPATION PROCLAMATION

1. Gregory D. Massey, *John Laurens and the American Revolution* (Columbia, NC: 2000), 63.

2. Washington feared that freeing some slaves to serve in the army would "make slavery more irksome to those who remain in it." Hirschfeld, *George Washington and Slavery*, 150–151.

3. Papers of Alexander Hamilton, edited by Harold C. Syrett, vol. 2, 17–19.

4. Massey, *John Laurens*, 132–133.

5. Ibid., 137.

6. Ibid., 141–143. Dr. David Ramsay, one of Laurens's supporters, said the proposal was "received with horror" by the legislature.

7. Laurens received invaluable aid and advice from America's ambassador, Benjamin Franklin, in this venture. See Thomas Fleming, *The Perils of Peace* (New York: 2007), 72–74.

8. Massey, *John Laurens*, 207–208. A crucial opposition speech accused Laurens of fostering racial intermarriage, a fear that disturbed southerners almost as much as a slave insurrection.

9. Washington, Writings, vol. 24, 421.

10. Massey, *John Laurens*, 224–225.

11. Ibid., 225–227.

12. Papers of Alexander Hamilton, vol. 3, 183–184.

CHAPTER 4: ONE HEAD TURNING INTO THIRTEEN

1. Thomas Fleming, *Liberty! The American Revolution* (New York: 1997), 366.

2. George Washington to Joseph Jones, May 21, 1780, Writings, vol. 18. Nathanael Greene lamented that "a rage for the sovereign independence of each state" was destroying all hope of national unity "and national revenue." Papers of Nathanael Greene, vol. 2 (Chapel Hill, NC: 1980), 656.

3. Robert C. Alberts, *Benjamin West: A Biography* (New York: 1978), 123.

4. Papers of Alexander Hamilton, vol. 3, 255–256.

5. Jefferson to Madison, April 25, 1784, *The Republic of Letters: Correspondence Between Thomas Jefferson and James Madison, 1776–1826,* vol. 1, edited by James Morton Smith (New York: 1995), 308–309.

6. William W. Crosskey, *Politics and the Constitution in the History of the United States,* vol. 3 (Chicago: 1980), 395.

7. Samuel Eliot Morrison, *The Oxford History of the American People* (New York: 1965), 39. The first printing press in the New World began operating in Mexico City in 1539.

8. Stuart Leibiger, *Founding Friendship: George Washington, James Madison, and the Creation of the American Republic* (Charlottesville, VA: 1999).

9. Letter from George Washington to Henry Lee, October 31,1786, Writings, vol. 29, 34.

10. Clinton Rossiter, *The Grand Convention* (New York: 1966), 226. In a final vote on the subject, Washington held out for a three-fourths majority to override a veto, but he was outvoted.

11. Ibid., 266–268. Rossiter underscores his conviction that "the decisions and non-decisions of 1787 about slavery were . . . decisions for the Union."

12. Ibid., 217, 250. Ellsworth was convinced slavery would gradually disappear. Rossiter called him "the halfway man" of the century, a genius at the art of compromise.

13. Leibiger, *Founding Friendship,* 85.

14. Junius P. Rodrigue, ed., *Slavery in the United States, A Social, Political and Historical Encyclopedia* (Santa Barbara, CA: 2007), vol. 2, 515–516. Also see "The Man Who Made Cotton King," by Stephen Yafa, *American Heritage of Invention and Technology* (Winter 2005).

15. Letter from Washington to Mercer, Writings, vol. 29, 5; letter to Morris, vol. 28, 408.

16. Peter R. Henriques, *Realistic Visionary: A Portrait of George Washington* (Charlottesville, VA: 2006), 153.

17. Ibid., 158. Mr. Henriques's chapter on Washington and slavery, "The Only Unavoidable Subject of Regret," is a remarkably thoughtful treatment of Washington's changing view of blacks' abilities and their essential humanity.

CHAPTER 5: THE FORGOTTEN EMANCIPATOR

1. Thomas Jefferson to Philip Mazzei, April 24, 1796, *The Works of Thomas Jefferson,* vol. 8, edited by Paul Leicester Ford, Online Library of Liberty, http://oll.libertyfund

.org/title/805/87066. For Callender quotation see John A. Carroll and Mary W. Ashworth, *George Washington, Volume 7: First in Peace*, completing the biography by Douglas Southall Freeman (New York: 1957), 231.

2. Richard Norton Smith, *Patriarch: George Washington and the New American Nation* (Boston: 1993), 213–218. Smith notes that Washington first sent a peace commission to negotiate with the rebels. By the time he acted, the rebellion had spread to twenty counties in four states.

3. Wiencek, *An Imperfect God*, 273–274.

4. Carroll and Ashworth, *First in Peace*, 403–407.

5. Ibid., 541.

6. Hirschfeld, *George Washington and Slavery*, 127. Hirschfeld finds grave fault with Washington for his failure to act in concert with Lafayette. He has no awareness of the political difficulties Washington encountered, and his concern for the Union as a first and foremost necessity.

7. The Papers of Benjamin Franklin, March 23, 1790. Yale University has a draft of the essay that was published in the *Federal Gazette*.

8. Hirschfeld, *George Washington and Slavery*, 72–73. The visitor was a popular British actor, John Bernard. He left a vivid account of his conversation with Washington.

9. Ibid., 209–223. Hirschfeld reports that Washington's heirs spent $10,080 in cash and provided food and shelter for those slaves who were too old or ill to leave Mount Vernon. The last payment was made in 1833 for the burial of a slave named Judy.

10. Stewart Mitchell, ed., *New Letters of Abigail Adams, 1788–1802* (Boston: 1947), 13.

11. Patricia Brady, *Martha Washington: An American Life* (New York: 2005), 234. In her will, Martha gave her grandson, George Washington Parke Custis, "my mulatto man, Elijah," but he was already a dower slave and she was merely transferring ownership within the family. See "The Will of Martha Washington," in *Worthy Partner: The Papers of Martha Washington*, edited by Joseph E. Fields, with an introduction by Ellen McCallister Clark (Westport, CT: 1994), 406–410.

CHAPTER 6: THOMAS JEFFERSON'S NIGHTMARE

1. Robert Debs Heinl and Nancy Gordon Heinl, *Written in Blood: The Story of the Haitian People, 1492–1971* (Boston: 1978), 26–27.

2. Winthrop Jordan, *White Over Black: American Attitudes Toward the Negro, 1550–1812* (Chapel Hill, NC: 1968), 376–377.

3. Robert Hendrickson, *Hamilton*, vol. 2 (New York: 1976), 460–462.

4. Merrill D. Peterson, *Thomas Jefferson and the New Nation* (New York: 1970), 748–749.

5. Jordan, *White Over Black*, 280–282.

6. Harlow Giles Unger, *The Last Founding Father: James Monroe and a Nation's Call to Greatness* (New York: 2009), 140–142.

7. Dumas Malone, *Jefferson and the Ordeal of Liberty*, vol. 3 (Charlottesville, VA: 2006), 480.

8. Heinl and Heinl, *Written in Blood*, 100–108.

9. Petersen, *Thomas Jefferson*, 748–750.

10. Dennis A. Castillo, *The Maltese Cross: A Strategic History of Malta* (Westport, CT: 2005), 126. Disagreement over the French acquisition of Malta was the chief cause of the rupture of the peace of Amiens. The British balked at handing it over because of aggressive French moves elsewhere in the Mediterranean, and Napoleon threatened "Malta or war."

11. Dumas Malone, *Jefferson the President: First Term*, vol. 4 (Boston: 1970), 284–310.

12. Heinl and Heinl, *Written in Blood*, 123–130.

13. Annals of Congress, House of Representatives, Eighth Congress, First Session, 813. "Some gentleman would declare St. Domingo free," Eppes said. "If any gentleman harbors such sentiments, let him come forward boldly and declare it. In such case he would cover himself with detestation" (Annals, 996).

CHAPTER 7: NEW ENGLAND PREACHES—AND ALMOST
PRACTICES—SECESSION

1. Malone, *Jefferson the President*, 297.

2. James K. Hosmer, *History of the Louisiana Purchase* (New York: 1902), 157–158. Annals of Congress, House of Representatives, Eighth Congress, First Session, 463–464.

3. Peterson, *Thomas Jefferson*, 793–794.

4. Gerald H. Clarfield, *Timothy Pickering and the American Republic* (Pittsburgh, PA: 1980). This is a seminal book for those seeking to understand how passionately New England regarded its right to lead America. See 219–225, in which many other New England leaders besides Pickering are cited, declaring that the Louisiana Purchase was part of a "deliberate plan" to diminish New England's influence.

5. Richard Buel Jr., *America on the Brink* (New York: 2005), 54ff. This is a superb account of New England's resistance to the embargo.

6. Ibid., 156–160.

7. Freeman, *R. E. Lee*, 14–17.

8. Buel, *America on the Brink*, 165–166.

9. Ibid., 190–191.

10. Samuel Eliot Morrison, *Harrison Grey Otis: The Urbane Federalist* (Boston: 1969), 356–357.

11. Ralph Ketcham, *James Madison: A Biography*, rev. ed. (Newtown, CT: 2003), 592–593. A Virginia friend reported that Madison's mind was "full of New England sedition."

12. Robert A. Rutland, *James Madison: The Founding Father* (New York: 1987), 230–231.

13. Leon Litwack, *North of Slavery: The Negro in the Free States, 1790–1860* (Chicago: 1961), 20–24.

14. Julie Winch, *A Gentleman of Color: The Life of James Forten* (New York: 2002), 189ff.

15. Davis, *Inhuman Bondage*, 274–279; Fogel, *Without Consent or Contract*, 290–293.

16. Peterson, *Thomas Jefferson*, 995–998.

17. Antislavery Northerners were skeptical about diffusion. One said it was "as effectual a remedy for slavery as it would be for smallpox or the plague." Davis, *Inhuman Bondage*, 277.

18. David M. Robertson, *Denmark Vesey: The Buried History of America's Largest Slave Rebellion and the Man Who Led It* (New York: 1999). Historians have disagreed about the size and scope of Vesey's revolt, some claiming he was a victim of white hysteria. This is a well-researched, solid account of the tragic episode.

CHAPTER 8: HOW NOT TO ABOLISH SLAVERY

1. Henry Mayer, *All on Fire: William Lloyd Garrison and the Abolition of Slavery* (New York: 1998), 110–124.

2. Ibid., 125.

3. *The Historical Encyclopedia of World Slavery*, vol. 2 (Santa Barbara, CA: 1997), 568–569.

4. Mark Arkin, "The Federalist Trope: Power and Passion in Abolitionist Rhetoric," *Journal of American History* (June 2001). This article brilliantly connects Garrison to New England's grievances against the South for the three fifths clause in the Constitutional Convention, the Louisiana Purchase, and other supposedly evil maneuvers to give Southerners national power and humiliate New England.

5. Mayer, *All on Fire*, 116–117.

6. Thomas C. Parramore, "Covenant in Jerusalem," in Kenneth S. Greenberg, ed., *Nat Turner: A Slave Rebellion in History and Memory* (New York: 2003), 58–76. Also see Matthew J. Clavin, *Toussaind Louverture and the American Civil War* (Philadelphia: 2010), 14–15.

7. Freeman, *R. E. Lee*, 111–112.

8. Mayer, *All on Fire*, 120–123.

9. Winch, *A Gentleman of Color*, 239–249. James Forten wrote for *The Liberator* and donated considerable amounts of cash. He also supplied Garrison with much negative information about the ACS and Liberia.

10. John L. Thomas, *The Liberator: William Lloyd Garrison* (Boston: 1963), 158–162. Also see Hochschild, *Bury the Chains*, 346–347.

11. "George Thompson," American National Biography Online, http://www.anb.org/articles/15/15-01311.html. When MP Thomas Buxton asked Garrison how the British could assist him, Garrison replied, "By giving us George Thompson."

12. Mayer, *All on Fire*, 160–161.

13. Thomas, *The Liberator*, 167–170.

14. Mayer, *All on Fire*, 166–167.

CHAPTER 9: NEW ENGLAND REDISCOVERS THE SACRED UNION

1. James Haw, "The Problem of South Carolina Reexamined: A Review Essay," *South Carolina Historical Magazine*, vol. 107, no. 1 (January 2006), 9–10.

2. James Roark et al., *The American Promise: A Compact History*, vol. 1 (New York: 2000), chap. 11.

3. Ketcham, *James Madison*, 640–643.

4. "A Century of Lawmaking for the New Nation: U.S. Congressional Debates, 1774–1875," Register of Debates, Twenty-first Congress, First Session, January 26–27, 1830.

5. John Robert Irlean, *The Republic: A History of the United States Administrations, from the Monarchic Early Days to the Present* (Charleston, SC: 2010), 252.

6. James Madison to Nicholas Trist, December 23, 1832, *Writings of James Madison*, edited by Gaillard Hunt (New York: 1900), Online Library of Liberty, http://oll.liberty fund.org/?option=com_staticxt&staticfile=show.php%3Ftitle=1940&chapter=119243 &layout=html&Itemid=27. Jackson Proclamation, December 10, 1832, Avalon Project, Lillian Goldman Law Library, Yale University.

CHAPTER 10: ANOTHER THOMAS JEFFERSON
URGES VIRGINIA TO ABOLISH SLAVERY

1. Louis P. Mazur, *1831: Year of the Eclipse* (New York: 2001), 51.

2. Ibid., 50–52.

3. Ibid., 60.

4. Avery Craven, *The Coming of the Civil War* (Chicago: 1942), 52–55. Also see John W. Cromwell, "The Aftermath of Nat Turner's Insurrection," *Journal of Negro History*, vol. 5, no. 2 (April 1920): 223–224.

5. Craven, *The Coming of the Civil War*, 57.

6. Cromwell, "The Aftermath," 225.

7. The bill to remove free Negroes was indefinitely postponed in the Virginia State Senate and eventually abandoned (Cromwell, "The Aftermath," 230).

8. *Richmond Enquirer*, January 28, 1832.

9. Report on Thomas Jefferson and Sally Hemings, University of Virginia Library, accession no. 8937.

CHAPTER 11: THE ABOLITIONIST WHO LOST HIS FAITH

1. Robert H. Abzug, *Passionate Liberator: Theodore Dwight Weld and the Dilemma of Reform* (New York: 1980), 1–5.

2. Gilbert Hobbs Barnes, *The Anti-Slavery Impulse, 1830–1844*, with a new introduction by William C. McLoughlin (New York: 1964), 64–73.

3. James Brewer Stewart, *Holy Warriors: the Abolitionists and American Slavery* (New York: 1976), 56–58.

4. Barnes, *The Anti-Slavery Impulse*, chap. 8, "Weld's Agency," 79–87.

5. Thomas, *The Liberator*, 130–133.

6. Stewart, *Holy Warriors*, 72–73. Mobs were active elsewhere, attacking other abolitionists with often lethal fury.

7. Barnes, *The Anti-Slavery Impulse*, 86–87.

8. Abzug, *Passionate Liberator*, 150–152.

9. Ibid., 210–214.

10. Ibid., 240–241.

CHAPTER 12: ABOLITIONISM DIVIDES AND CONQUERS ITSELF

1. Barnes, *The Anti-Slavery Impulse*, chap. 9, "Garrisonism," 88–99. His "hateful self portrait . . . could not have been more ruinous to the abolitionist cause." Stewart, *Holy Warriors*, 95. Theodore Weld "rejected all factions as self serving and morally bankrupt."

2. Whitney Cross, *The Burned Over District: A Social and Intellectual History of Enthusiastic Religion in Western New York* (Ithaca: 1950), 300–308. Theodore Weld's wife, Angelina Grimke, was a convert to Millerism. Abzug, *Passionate Liberator*, 228–229.

3. Mayer, *All on Fire*, 358 (Rogers dispute). Morrison, *Harrison Gray Otis*, 474–475.

4. Thomas, *The Liberator*, 203–205.

5. Ibid., 206–207. James Stewart contends that Phillips did not become a committed abolitionist until Elijah Lovejoy was murdered. James Brewer Stewart, *Holy Warriors: The Abolitionists and American Slavery* (New York: 1976), 76.

6. David S. Reynolds, *Waking Giant: America in the Age of Jackson* (New York: 2008), 193–194.

7. Mayer, *All on Fire*, 227–229.

CHAPTER 13: ENTER OLD MAN ELOQUENT

1. Samuel Flagg Bemis, *John Quincy Adams and the Union* (New York: 1956), 334–335.

2. John Greenleaf Whittier, "Massachusetts to Virginia," Bartleby.com, *English Poetry III: From Tennyson to Whitman*, The Harvard Classics, http://www.bartleby.com/42/794.html.

3. Bemis, *John Quincy Adams*, 336–340.

4. Memoirs of John Quincy Adams, vol. 5, p. 210, Google e-book.

5. George Wilson Pierson, *Tocqueville and Beaumont in America* (New York: 1938), 418–420.

6. Letters from John Quincy Adams to Charles Francis Adams, in Bemis, *John Quincy Adams*, 332. For Calhoun's declaration of "slavery as a positive good," see "A Century of Lawmaking for a New Nation," U.S. Congressional Debates, 1774–1875, Register of Debates, Twenty-fourth Congress, Second Session, 709–710.

7. Jack Shepherd, *Cannibals of the Heart: A Personal Biography of Louisa Catherine and John Quincy Adams* (New York: 1980), 345–347.

8. Lynn H. Parsons, *John Quincy Adams* (Madison, WI: 1998), 39. Worthington Chauncey Ford and Charles Francis Adams, *John Quincy Adams* (Cambridge: 1902), 110. Also see Joseph Wheelan, *Mr. Adams's Last Crusade* (New York: 2008), 110.

9. James Buchanan, *The Works of James Buchanan*, vol. 1 (Philadelphia: 1908), 202.

10. "A Century of Lawmaking," 1313–1314.

11. Ibid., 1587–1588.

12. Davis, *Inhuman Bondage*, 16–26.

13. John Dryden, *Absalom and Achitophel*.

14. Bemis, *John Quincy Adams*, 427–439.

15. Gilbert Barnes and Dwight Dumond, eds., *Letters of Theodore Dwight Weld, Angelina Grimke and Sarah Grimke, 1822–1844*, vol. 2 (New York: 1934), 905.

16. Martin Duberman, *Charles Francis Adams* (Palo Alto, CA: 1960), 84.

17. Memoirs of John Quincy Adams, vol. 12, p. 116.

CHAPTER 14: THE SLAVE PATROLS

1. Sally E. Hadden, *Slave Patrols: Law and Violence in Virginia and the Carolinas* (Cambridge, MA: 2001), 41–70. This superb book is the first time slave patrols have received the detailed attention necessary for an understanding of how southern slavery affected daily life.

2. Ibid., 78.

3. Ibid., 138.

CHAPTER 15: THE TROUBLE WITH TEXAS

1. Reynolds, *Waking Giant*, 356–357.

2. Bemis, *John Quincy Adams*, 354.

3. Reynolds, *Waking Giant*, 116–118.

4. Bemis, *John Quincy Adams*, 353–354.

5. David Brion Davis, *The Slave Power Conspiracy and the Paranoid Style* (Baton Rouge: 1969), 16–18.

6. Bemis, *John Quincy Adams*, 356–357.

7. Ibid., 369–370.

8. Ibid., 465.

9. Robert Seager, *And Tyler Too* (New York: 1963), 209–242.

10. Bemis, *John Quincy Adams*, 466–468.

11. Ibid., 471–472.

12. Edward P. Crapol, *John Tyler: The Accidental President* (Chapel Hill, NC: 2006), 220.

13. Bemis, *John Quincy Adams* , 473, 478.

14. Matthew F. Steele, *American Campaigns*, vol. 1 (Washington, DC: 1922), 81.

15. Kevin Dougherty, *Civil War Leadership and Mexican War Experience* (Jackson, MS: 2007), 15.

16. Robert Johanssen, *To the Halls of the Montezumas: The Mexican War in the American Imagination* (New York: 1988), 217–218.

17. Freeman, *R. E. Lee*, 237–248.

18. Ibid., 272.

19. Ibid., 294.

20. John C. Morone, *Hellfire Nation: The Politics of Sin in American History* (New Haven, CT: 2003), 203.

21. Allen C. Guelzo, *Lincoln's Emancipation Proclamation: The End of Slavery in America* (New York: 2004), 24. Also see Eric Foner, *The Fiery Trial: Abraham Lincoln and American Slavery* (New York: 2010), 57–59.

CHAPTER 16: SLAVE POWER PARANOIA

1. Morone, *Hellfire Nation*, 145ff (the slaveholders's sins). Davis, *The Slave Power Conspiracy*, 30–31.

2. Arkin, "The Federalist Trope," 94.

3. Davis, *The Slave Power Conspiracy*, 53.

4. Charles Sumner, *The Works of Charles Sumner* (Boston: 1875), 64.

5. Davis, *The Slave Power Conspiracy*, 62.

6. Joel Williamson, *New People: Miscegenation and Mulattoes in the United States* (New York: 1984), 24–26.

7. Drew Gilpin Faust, *James Henry Hammond and the Old South: A Design for Mastery* (Baton Rouge, LA: 1982), 86–87, 311–317.

8. Robert E. May, *The South's Dream of a Caribbean Empire* (Baton Rouge, LA: 1973). May recounts how widespread this idea was in the 1850s. Even some northern newspapers backed the proposal. There were several failed attempts to conquer Cuba and parts of Central America by military adventurers financed by Southerners.

9. David M. Potter, *The Impending Crisis, 1848–1861*, completed and edited by Don E. Fehrenbacher (New York: 1976), 90–95.

10. Ibid., 105–120. The chapter on this subject is aptly titled: "The Armistice of 1850"—what it soon turned out to be.

11. Craven, *The Coming of the Civil War*, 303–308. In Alabama, the Union party won a two-to-one majority in the legislature.

12. Renehan, *The Secret Six*, 65–72. Mayer, *All on Fire*, 440–442.

CHAPTER 17: FROM UNCLE TOM TO JOHN BROWN

1. Thomas F. Gossett, *Uncle Tom's Cabin and American Culture* (Dallas, TX: 1985), 100–106.

2. Ibid., 106–107.

3. Ibid., 95.

4. Harriet Beecher Stowe, *Uncle Tom's Cabin* (New York: 1986), 613–617.

5. Gossett, *Uncle Tom's Cabin*, 167.

6. Louis Menand, *The Metaphysical Club* (New York: 2001), 97–101.

7. Ibid., 102–105.

8. Ibid., 129.

9. "The Southern System of Labor," *Charleston Mercury*, January 17, 1856, 2, reprinted from the New Orleans *Delta*.

10. Davis, *Inhuman Bondage*, 283–284.

11. Ibid., 227, 285–286.

12. *Charleston Mercury*, February 16, 1856, 2, reprinted from the New Orleans *Picayune*.

13. Davis, *Inhuman Bondage*, 285.

14. Craven, *The Coming of the Civil War*, 325–344.

15. Villard, *John Brown*, chap. 1, "The Moulding of the Man."

16. Ibid., 78. This myth was still alive in 1909 when Villard published this biography. The "wastefulness and short-sightedness" of the South's methods of cotton culture and the "uneconomic and shiftless character of slave labor itself" made "the appetite for virgin lands insatiable."

17. Ibid., 92.

18. Reynolds, *John Brown*, 156–157.

19. Villard, *John Brown*, 151–167.

CHAPTER 18: THE REAL UNCLE TOM AND THE UNKNOWN SOUTH HE HELPED CREATE

1. Gossett, *Uncle Tom's Cabin*, 107–109.

2. Josiah Henson, *Father Henson's Story of His Life, with an Introduction by Mrs. H. B. Stowe* (Boston: 1858), 1–24.

3. Ibid., 25–54.

4. Ibid., 197. For the interview with the archbishop, see 135ff.

5. Robert Willliam Fogel and Stanley L. Engerman, *Time on the Cross: The Economics of American Negro Slavery* (Boston, MA: 1974), 200–201.

6. Ibid., 77.

7. Ibid., 38–39, 152.

8. Charles B. Dew, "David Ross and the Oxford Iron Works: A Study of Industrial Slavery in the Early 19th Century South," *William and Mary Quarterly* 31 (April 1974): 189–224. Mr. Dew has published a lengthier treatment of this important subject in a book of the same title in 1995.

9. Fogel and Engerman, *Time on the Cross*, 241.

10. Ibid., 213.

11. Ibid., 149.

12. Ibid., 247–249.

13. Ibid., 244.

14. James L. Huston, *Calculating the Value of the Union: Slavery, Property Rights and the Economic Origins of the Civil War* (Chapel Hill, NC: 2003), 26–31.

15. Fogel, *Without Consent or Contract*, 352–353.

CHAPTER 19: FREE SOIL FOR FREE (WHITE) MEN

1. Foner, *The Fiery Trial*, 67. Abraham Lincoln, *Speeches, Letters, and Miscellaneous Writings, 1832–1858*, Library of America, vol. 1 (New York: 1989), 315–317.

2. Richard H. Thornton, with Louise Hanley, *An American Glossary*, vol. 1 (Philadelphia: 1912), 67. Thornton cites among many examples a Democratic Tennessee congressman who used the term twenty-two times in a short letter to his constituents, denouncing a Pennsylvania town for naming a "Black Republican" as their postmaster.

3. Craven, *The Coming of the Civil War*, 367–368, 374–377.

4. Ibid., 341–343.

5. Potter, *The Impending Crisis*, 262–264. On October 24, 1856, the *Richmond Enquirer* ran a front-page article attempting to convince readers that revolts of labor against capitol in the free states were more likely than a slave insurrection in the South. On October 17, 1856, another article declared that if the slaves were emancipated, "the loss of the cotton, sugar and rice crops now produced by Negro slavery would . . . break up commerce and starve one half the laboring whites" in Europe and America.

6. Franklin Pierce, Fourth Annual Message, December 2, 1856, The American Presidency Project, http://millercenter.org/president/speeches/detail/3731.

7. Michael Fellman, *The Making of Robert E. Lee* (New York: 2000), 79–81. Also see Elizabeth Brown Pryor, *Reading the Man: A Portrait of Robert E. Lee Through His Private Letters* (New York: 2008), 269.

8. Villard, *John Brown*, 367–371, 383–390.

9. For a graphic picture of the murder and mayhem that the vigilantes wreaked in California, see Charles Royster, *The Destructive War* (New York: 1991), 134–136.

10. Reynolds, *John Brown*, 208–238.

11. Ibid., 239–240.

CHAPTER 20: THE WHOLE WORLD IS WATCHING

1. Potter, *The Impending Crisis*, 320–322.

2. Craven, *The Coming of the Civil War*, 381–384.

3. Foner, *The Fiery Trial*, 99–103. Also see Lincoln, *Speeches*, vol. 1, 426–427.

4. Guelzo, *Lincoln's Emancipation Proclamation*, 27.

5. Potter, *The Impending Crisis*, 340–342.

6. Orville Vernon Burton, *The Age of Lincoln* (New York: 2007), 113–114.

7. Craven, *The Coming of the Civil War*, 393.

8. Pryor, *Reading the Man*, 271–272.

9. Fellman, *The Making of Robert E. Lee*, 70–71.

10. Pryor, *Reading the Man*, 270–272.

11. Fellman, *The Making of Robert E. Lee*, 67.

12. Freeman, *R. E. Lee*, 400–402.

13. Lawrence S. Barmann, S. J., "John Brown at Harpers Ferry: A Contemporary Analysis," *West Virginia History Journal* 22, no. 2 (April 1961): 5.

14. Ibid., 6. Also see Reynolds, *John Brown*, 416.

15. *Richmond Enquirer*, December 2, 1859.

16. Pryor, *Reading the Man*, 283.

17. Reynolds, *John Brown*, 412–413.

18. Mayer, *All on Fire*, 494–498. Mayer, Garrison's best biographer, describes his eulogy of Brown as a veritable epic of spiritual "dishevelment," 502.

19. Oliver Carlson, *The Man Who Made News: James Gordon Bennett* (New York: 1952), 275. Bennett predicted that Brown's raid was "the first act of a terrible drama."

20. Brian McGinty, *John Brown's Trial* (Cambridge, MA: 2009), 224–226.

21. Villard, *John Brown*, 164.

22. McGinty, *John Brown's Trial*, 252–253.

23. Villard, *John Brown*, 563–564. Poet Henry Wadsworth Longfellow wrote that the day of Brown's execution would be "the date of a new Revolution—quite as much needed as the old one."

24. James Redpath, *The Public Life of Captain John Brown: With an Autobiography of his Childhood and Youth* (Boston: 1860), dedication. Phillips declared that George Washington "would be proud to welcome Brown" beside him in his grave.

25. Renehan, *The Secret Six*, 222–224.

26. Ibid., 227–228.

27. Reynolds, *John Brown*, 342.

28. Pryor, *Reading the Man*, 281–282.

29. Reynolds, *John Brown*, 405–406.

30. McGinty, *John Brown's Trial*, 256–257. Brown kissed the two-year-old son of his kindhearted jailer, John Avis, as he left the prison.

31. Renehan, *The Secret Six*, 246–251.

CHAPTER 21: AN EX-PRESIDENT TRIES TO SAVE THE UNION

1. New York Democratic Vigilant Association, *Rise and Progress of the Bloody Outbreak at Harpers Ferry*, vol. 63, p. 16, Google e-book. Reynolds, *John Brown*, 359. Walter Stahr, *Seward: Lincoln's Indispensable Man* (New York: 2012), 180. The accomplice was a British soldier of fortune, Hugh Forbes, who withdrew from Brown's scheme and predicted it would end in disaster.

2. William B. Hesseltine, ed., *Three Against Lincoln: Murat Halstead Reports the Caucuses of 1860* (Baton Rouge, LA: 1960). Allen Johnson, *Stephen A. Douglas: A Study in American Politics* (New York: 1908), 415–428.

3. Proceedings of the Conventions at Charleston and Baltimore, Published by Order of the National Democratic Convention (Maryland Institute, Baltimore), 120–129, 139–147, 151–155, http://books.google.com/books/about/Proceedings_of_the_conventions_at _Charle.html?id=qhZQAAAAYAAJ. Also see Philip S. Klein, *President James Buchanan: A Biography* (University Park, PA: 1962), 340–344, titled "Democracy Dividing." Newspaperman Murat Halstead wrote: "Douglas was the pivotal figure. Every delegate was for him or against him."

4. Proceedings of the Conventions at Charleston and Baltimore, 231–235.

5. "Astounding Triumph of Republicanism," *New York Times*, November 7, 1860.

6. Clavin, *Toussaint Louverture*, 62–64.

7. *Charleston Mercury*, December 21, 1860.

8. B. P. Gallaway, *Texas: The Dark Corner of the Confederacy* (Lincoln, NE: 1972), 10. James M. McPherson, *Battle Cry of Freedom* (New York: 1988), 237.

9. Constitution of the Confederate States, March 11, 1861, Avalon Project, Yale Law School.

10. Freeman, *R. E. Lee*, 412. Pryor, *Reading the Man*, 284.

11. Fellman, *The Making of Robert E. Lee*, 84.

12. Pryor, *Reading the Man*, 285.

13. Freeman, *R. E. Lee*, 425.

14. Ibid., 417. Pryor, *Reading the Man*, 287.

15. William B. Hesseltine, *Lincoln and the War Governors* (New York: 1948), 110.

16. Seager, *And Tyler Too*, 444–445. Also see Roark et al., *The American Promise: A Compact History*, vol. 1 (New York: 2000), 310. Blacks outnumbered whites in South Carolina and Mississippi (U.S. Census Office, 1860, Population [Washington, DC: 1864]).

17. Seager, *And Tyler Too*, 446.

18. Ibid., 447–451.

19. Crapol, *John Tyler*, 261–262.

20. Seager, *And Tyler Too*, 456.

21. Crapol, *John Tyler*, 262.

22. Ibid., 264. Seager, *And Tyler Too*, 450–451.

23. Ibid., 470–471.

CHAPTER 22: THE ANGUISH OF ROBERT E. LEE

1. Charles Francis Adams Jr., "The Reign of King Cotton," *The Atlantic* (1861), http:// www.theatlantic.com/magazine/print/1861/04/the-reign-of-king-cotton/8740.

2. A. R. Boteler, "Mr. Lincoln and the Force Bill," in *The Annals of the War Written by Leading Participants North and South*, edited by Alexander Kelly McClure (Philadelphia: 1879), 220–227.

3. Abraham Lincoln, *Speeches, Letters, and Miscellaneous Writings, 1859–1865*, Library of America, vol. 2 (New York: 1989), 215–224. Also see Stahr, *Seward*, 240–241.

4. Seager, *And Tyler Too*, 461.

5. Pryor, *Reading the Man*, 288.

6. Freeman, *R. E. Lee*, 432–433.

7. Shelby Foote, *The Civil War: A Narrative*, vol. 1 (New York: 1986), 47.

8. Lincoln, *Speeches*, vol. 2, 232–233.

9. Hesseltine, *Lincoln and the War Governors*, 148–149.

10. Pryor, *Reading the Man*, 285–291.

11. Freeman, *R. E. Lee*, 440–441.

12. Pryor, *Reading the Man*, 289–291.

CHAPTER 23: THE END OF ILLUSIONS

1. Pryor, *Reading the Man*, 294.

2. *Alexandria Gazette*, April 20, 1861. Freeman, *R. E. Lee*, 445–449, 450.

3. Emory M. Thomas, *Robert E. Lee: A Biography* (New York: 1995), 189.

4. Scott Sumpter Sheads and Daniel Carroll Toomey, *Baltimore During the Civil War* (Linthicum: 1997), Maryland Room, Enoch Pratt Library, Baltimore, MD. John Lockwood and Charles Lockwood, *The Siege of Washington: The Untold Story of the Twelve Days That Shook the Union* (New York: 2011), 89.

5. Ibid., 111–125. Also see "Museum Stands Near Attack Site," *Washington Times*, December 15, 2001.

6. "John Brown's Body, Battle Hymn of the Republic," Library of Congress, http://www.loc.gov/teachers/lyrical/songs/john_brown.html.

7. Daniel W. Barefoot, *Let Us Die Like Brave Men: Behind the Dying Words of Confederate Warriors* (Winston-Salem, NC: 2005), 6.

8. *New York Tribune*, June 26, 1861.

9. Lincoln, Special Session Message, July 4, 1861.

10. Edward S. Ellis, *Camp-Fires of General Lee: Reminiscences of the March, the Camp, the Bivouac and of Personal Adventure*, chap. 5 (Philadelphia: 1886), http://leearchive.wlu.edu/reference/books/ellis/05.html. Also see Carl Sandburg, *The Prairie Years and The War Years* (New York: 2002), 302.

11. Craven, *The Coming of the Civil War*, 411–412.

12. Edward Porter Alexander, *Fighting For the Confederacy: The Personal Recollections of General Edward Porter Alexander*, edited by Gary Gallagher (Chapel Hill, NC: 1989), 57. William Davis, *First Blood: Fort Sumter to Bull Run* (Alexandria, VA: 1983), 143.

13. Davis, *First Blood*, 138–139.

14. Ibid., 148–150. Alexander, *Fighting for the Confederacy*, 58. Alexander thought the Confederates should have pursued the Federals.

15. James Ford Rhodes, *History of the Civil War, 1861–1865* (New York: 1917), 43.

16. Mr. Lincoln & Friends, http://mrlincolnandfriends.org/inside.asp?pageID 54&subjectD=4. Also see Robert C. Williams, *Horace Greeley: Champion of American*

Freedom (New York: 2006), 222. After Bull Run, Greeley admitted to himself and others that he was "done as a politician."

CHAPTER 24: THE THIRD EMANCIPATION PROCLAMATION

1. Gary Joiner, *Shiloh and the Western Campaign of 1862* (New York: 2007), 427. For the letter in full see L. U. Reavis, *A Representative Life of Horace Greeley* (New York: 1872), 253–258.

2. Letter from Abraham Lincoln to Horace Greeley, August 22, 1962, in *Speeches*, vol. 2, 357–358.

3. Guelzo, *Lincoln's Emancipation Proclamation*, 92–97.

4. Ibid., 29–31.

5. Ibid., 44–51, 74.

6. J. Michael Moore, *The Peninsula Campaign of 1862: A Military Analysis* (Jackson, MS: 2005), 16. "A History of Notable Senate Investigations," Joint Committee on the Conduct of the War, U.S. Senate Historical Office, http://www.senate.gov/artandhistory /history/common/investigations/pdf/JCCW_Fullcitations.pdf. For an excellent balanced history of this committee, see Bruce Tap, *Over Lincoln's Shoulder* (Lawrence, KS: 1998), Introduction.

7. Essay by Howard Jones, in *Presidents, Diplomats and Other Mortals: Essays Honoring Robert Ferrell*, John Gary Clifford et al. (Columbia, MO: 2007), 22.

8. Brian McGinty, *The Body of John Merryman: Abraham Lincoln and the Suspension of Habeus Corpus* (Cambridge, MA: 2011), 96. Also see Benjamin Quarles, *Lincoln and the Negro* (New York: 1991), 86; and Michael Burlingame, *Abraham Lincoln: A Life* (Baltimore, MD: 2008), 397.

9. Michael Burlingame, ed., *Lincoln Observed: Civil War Dispatches of Noah Brooks* (Baltimore, MD: 2002), 210. William Jackson Johnstone, *Abraham Lincoln: The Christian* (New York: 1913), 88.

10. Robert Striner, *Lincoln's Relentless Struggle to End Slavery* (New York: 2008), 152–154.

11. Letter from Abraham Lincoln to Hannibal Hamlin, Sept 28, 1862, *Speeches*, vol. 2, 375.

12. Larry Tagg, *The Unpopular Mr. Lincoln: The Story of America's Most Reviled President* (New York: 2009), 317.

13. J. M. Blackett, *Divided Hearts: Britain and the American Civil War* (Baton Rouge, LA: 2001), 175.

14. Abraham Lincoln, Annual Message to Congress, December 1, 1863, *Speeches*, vol. 2, 393–415. Tagg, *The Unpopular Mr. Lincoln*, 334. Burlingame, *Abraham Lincoln*, 397.

15. Guelzo, *Lincoln's Emancipation Proclamation*, 260.

16. Tap, *Over Lincoln's Shoulder*, 142–148.

17. Guelzo, *Lincoln's Emancipation Proclamation*, 181–185. Also see James C. Welling, editor of the *National Intelligencer*, on the abolitionists' threats in *Reminiscences of*

Abraham Lincoln by Distinguished Men of His Time by Allen Thorndike Rice (New York: 1909), 533.

CHAPTER 25: THE HUNT AFTER THE CAPTAIN

1. Gary W. Gallagher, *The Union War* (Cambridge, MA: 2011). Anyone who seeks to understand the Civil War should read this book.

2. Ibid., 52 (Seward memorandum), 63 (Miller diary).

3. "My Hunt After the Captain," *The Atlantic*, http://theatlantic.com/magazine/print/1862/12/my-hunt-after-the-captain/308750.

4. The reference to fighting to defend their homes is further evidence of the persistence of Thomas Jefferson's nightmare in the southern public mind.

5. Albert W. Altschuler, *Law Without Values: The Life, Work, and Legacy of Justice Holmes* (Chicago: 2000), 39–40. The Twentieth Regiment was known as the "Copperhead Regiment."

6. Ibid., 43–44.

7. Ibid., 46.

8. Menand, *The Metaphysical Club*, 67.

EPILOGUE: LINCOLN'S VISITOR

1. Freeman, *R. E. Lee*, 113–148.

2. David Herbert Donald, *Lincoln* (New York: 1995), 581–585.

3. Ibid., 588.

4. Marquis Adolphe de Chambrun, *Impressions of Lincoln and the Civil War: A Foreigner's Account*, translated from the French by General Adelbert de Chambrun (New York: 1952), preface, v–x.

5. Ibid., 72–82.

6. Donald, *Lincoln*, 589–590.

7. Ibid., 591–592.

8. John Raymond Howard, ed., *Patriotic Addresses in America and England from 1850–1865* (New York: 1891), 688–689. Also see David Blight, *Race and Reunion: The Civil War in American Memory* (Cambridge, MA: 2001), 67–68: "The Reverend Henry Ward Beecher, orator of the day, condemned South Carolina's secessionists to eternal damnation: the South's "remorseless traitors" were held fully responsible for the war."

9. Freeman, *R. E. Lee*, 206–207.

10. John Hay, *Inside Lincoln's White House: The Complete War Diary of John Hay*, edited by Michael Burlinghame and John R. Turner Ettinger (Carbondale, IL: 1997), 67, 69, 70. Hay used the word so often that he sometimes shortened it and called Lincoln "The T" (68, 76).

11. Charles Bracelen Flood, *Lee, The Last Years* (Boston: 1981), 51.

12. Donald, *Lincoln*, 593. The visitor was Senator James Harlan of Iowa.

13. Chambrun, *Impressions of Lincoln*, 84.

INDEX